Brookside 1
Changing Lives

BARRY WOODWARD

Brookside 1
Changing Lives

Methuen

A Methuen Paperback

CHANGING LIVES

First published in Great Britain 1986
by Methuen London Ltd
11 New Fetter Lane, London EC4P 4EE
Copyright © in television format and novel Phil Redmond Enterprises 1986

British Library Cataloguing in Publication Data

Woodward, Barry
  Changing lives. — (Brookside; 1)
  I. Title   II. Series
  823'.914[F]   PR6073.O63/

ISBN 0-413-41420-5

Printed and bound in Great Britain
by Richard Clay (The Chaucer Press) Ltd,
Bungay, Suffolk

This book is sold subject to the condition
that it shall not, by way of trade or otherwise,
be lent, resold, hired out, or otherwise circulated
without the Publisher's prior consent in any form
of binding or cover other than that in which it is
published and without a similar condition
including this condition being imposed
on the subsequent purchaser.

Chapter One

'Tara, Mam.'

Doreen Corkhill closed the front door of her mother's house and quickened her step. The nights were beginning to draw in rapidly and these days she never felt safe on the streets and footpaths where once she played games like The Ally-o and Hopscotch. These days the newspapers called her home area of sprawling council houses 'Smack City'. And each night the columns of the *Echo* seemed to be full of stories about teenage lads and girls ready to mug anyone for the price of a little bag of brown heroin. Doreen had never heard of anyone she knew being mugged. She certainly didn't know any heroin addicts. But she was glad to be off the estate.

As she turned on to the better lit main road, she thought about the new house just half a mile away at Brookside Close. She and Billy had worked hard to get a deposit together for the three-bedroom semi. Billy had done as much overtime as he could get, not to mention the foreigners – rewiring shops and houses, once even a chicken farm – and never going out for a drink for months at a time. Slowly, the cash in the savings bank had added up. Doreen had done her share, too. Her wage as a part-time receptionist at a dental practice didn't add up to much, but she'd made a genuine effort to save at least five pounds a week. With two teenage kids and their expensive demands, it wasn't easy. But they'd finally made it.

Standing at the bus stop, trying to ignore the four-letter words and unruly behaviour of two other teenagers, she was glad they had succeeded in making the move from the council house they shared with Doreen's mother, Julia. Doreen hated the thought that Rod and Tracy might behave like the two yobs busy kicking at each other in the corner of the graffiti-covered bus shelter. Billy laughed at her ideas sometimes, but she was convinced that the kids would have a better chance of getting through those difficult teenage years if they lived in a decent neighbourhood, well away from the council estate. The way Doreen saw it, if there wasn't the temptation to go out and hang around the chippy or the off-licence, her kids might spend a bit more time on their studying. Rod had already started his A Level course and Tracy's O Levels were coming up. Neither she nor Billy had ever got that far. She wanted her children to do well. When they got married they'd never consider a council place, not if they'd had the opportunity of living on a private estate.

The bus arrived. Doreen had to stand back as the two teenagers jostled in front of her, not even giving other passengers the opportunity to alight. She took her seat on the lower deck and looked out of the window. If Billy hadn't been on lates he'd have picked her up from her mother's in the Renault. That was the only problem with living at Brookside. It wasn't as handy for the buses. Still it was a small price to pay for having a place of your own. Maybe one day she'd be able to take driving lessons and get a little car of her own. Why not? Three out of her five women neighbours in the Close had their own cars. Why not?

Four miles away, Heather Haversham eased the nose of her black Scirocco into the side courtyard of Blackwood Court. The first time Tom Curzon had mentioned his address, Heather said it sounded like a gentleman's country residence. In fact, it was a recently built, small block of service flats in a leafier part of South Liverpool.

Heather locked the car and glanced up at Tom's flat on the second floor. The light was on. No doubt he was busy scrabbling round the kitchen trying to concoct dinner for two from a collection of Marks and Sparks boil-in-the-bags. The last dinner for two at Tom's flat had been just that, his idea of a change from the endless restaurant meals that had become a way of life for a busy company chairman. Heather laughed to herself as she entered the flats, nodding to the caretaker watching the local news on a portable TV. How long would his enthusiasm for dinners at home last? Not long, she imagined. Tom was a man of crazes. As a boy he'd been involved in activities as diverse as astronomy and weight lifting. None of them had lasted, until he developed an interest in radio and then electronics.

The passion had lasted right through his childhood, right through University. He'd worked as a postgraduate with a couple of big multinationals in research and development, then taken a big step — at least in the view of his father — by setting up his own small enterprise. Now at the age of thirty-five, Tom Curzon was a wealthy man. Curzon Communications had gone public and the lad who once cannibalized car radios in the back bedroom of a council house was a millionaire.

Heather unlocked the door with the key Tom had given her. Immediately, the fruits of his industry — and its eccentricities — were apparent. Who else would leave the innards of a radio-controlled model Porsche strewn across a five thousand-pound oriental carpet? Or hang an expensive original watercolour opposite a cheap poster of the Golden Gate Bridge?

Although the lights were on, the flat was silent. Heather dumped her coat and bag on a sofa and moved through the lounge and dining room to the kitchen. No Tom.

'Tom?' No answer.

She retraced her steps through the quiet rooms and entered the big bedroom. Still no Tom. When he'd phoned Hamilton Devereux that lunchtime with the invitation to come for dinner, Heather had told him she was seeing a client until after six. He said he was taking the afternoon off and would be home by five at the latest. Well ... that was typical of Tom. Was it a deliberate ploy to ensure she made the dinner? She grinned to herself. She wasn't falling for that one. She started to undress. When the errant Mr Curzon turned up for his Seafood Mornay, or whatever he'd sent his secretary out to buy, she would be having a leisurely shower.

Heather walked into the en suite bathroom and turned on the shower. She was just about to step inside when she remembered the ansaphone. Tom was obsessed with gadgets. No doubt the lights in the flat had been switched on with a light-sensitive (or was it dark-sensitive?) timer. And he spent his life, it seemed sometimes, leaving messages on telephone answering machines. Hadn't he even installed one in Heather's house? She went to the machine at the side of the big double bed and flicked it on. The first message was from a journalist in the trade press, apparently an old friend of Tom's. The next was from a plummy-voiced young man, whom Heather gathered was an investment consultant. He seemed to talk for ever. Heather let the noise of the shower drown out his voice and enjoyed getting clean. Then she recognised Tom's voice.

She stepped quickly out of the shower and wrapped a towel about her. By the time she'd reached the bedroom, the message had ended. With water running on to the carpet, she perched on the edge of the bed and rewound the tape. The message was brief. Tom was sorry but something had cropped up. She was welcome to stay at the flat overnight, but he had had to fly out to Dusseldorf that afternoon. If she wanted to eat out alone, his secretary had booked a table at a small restaurant near Blackwood Court. It ended on the suggestion that if she wanted to eat *à deux* at the flat tomorrow evening she should call round after work.

Heather sighed. She pulled the towel round her and started to dry herself. How many times had she told him in the previous week? Three times at least. Heather might be involved personally with a millionaire businessman, but she still had her own work to do. And tomorrow night she was due to meet a client.

Bobby Grant hated meetings.

He was dawdling down the middle lane of the M57 in his union-issue Montego and for a moment he wondered how many of the other home-going men and women in their company cars had spent that day in meetings. Probably ninety per cent, he decided.

In the old days, before he became district secretary of the union, going to a meeting had meant either the monthly branch and a few pints afterwards, or a mass meeting outside the factory gates. Ever since he was issued with his first union card, he'd always looked forward to the branch. Up in the club room at the Pacific Star was where he'd cut his teeth in the sometimes rough world of branch union politics. Old timers like Albert Stratton and Luke Heaney had given him the benefit of their wisdom. In a way they had been Bobby's heroes when other young men looked to Elvis Presley or Stanley Matthews. He was twenty-three and when the older men had sunk enough pints they would hint at times to come; times when young men like Bobby would have to carry on the daily struggle to improve the lot of their members. Bobby laughed aloud at the memory and accelerated into the fast lane to overtake a tanker.

Then there were the mass meetings. Grey winter mornings, collars turned up against the cold. They *had* been exciting. Mentally urging his colleagues to put their hands up for the correct motion after the stirring rhetoric and earnest recommendations of men like Heaney and Stratton. He remembered the night before his first mass meeting. He'd been convenor for a month and he hadn't slept for a minute. The issue had been a simple pay claim. Issues always were simple, it seemed, in those days. He was shaking with nervousness as he made his way to the meeting. But once he'd mounted the makeshift rostrum, the nervousness disappeared. He'd recommended strike action and was rewarded with a massive show of hands. Within a week the management had capitulated. Everyone was delighted with a pre-Christmas wage packet full of backdated pay rise. But Bobby was more elated by winning and seeing his members fairly rewarded.

These days, however, he never felt like he was winning anything. More often than not the members of the ETWU he met were strange faces at plants and premises he'd never even heard of until that morning. The area he had to cover was large and the meetings which dominated his days were not branch meetings and very rarely mass meetings. While factories closed and multi-nationals rationalized away the livelihoods of thousands, Bobby seemed to spend more and more time on internal meetings. Sometimes he felt his union was trying to change the whole world. Yes, he cared about Chile, about ethnic minorities – even homosexuals – but only in the sense that anyone with a conscience should. How many conferences had he sat through in run-down seaside towns while young men and women who had never seen a factory floor in their lives harangued him and people like him with motions against fox hunting and other issues of major concern to members of the ETWU?

Bobby ran the car on to the driveway of Number 10, Brookside, and got out. At least there were no more meetings to attend that day. He looked forward to an evening in front of the telly with Sheila. Then he remembered. Tonight was one of the two evenings a week Sheila attended tutorials for her course on the Return and Learn scheme. Bobby swore quietly to himself as he opened the front door.

Sitting in someone else's front room in such a small group of comparative strangers made Sheila feel a little awkward. There was just herself, Sally Dinsdale, the owner of the house, a younger woman called Barbara, and their tutor, Alun Jones, a patient man with just a hint of a Welsh accent. She might have felt easier if Matty had been there. But he'd phoned earlier to say he was joining a group jog for charity at one of the city's bigger parks. Sheila hoped Matty wasn't considering dropping out of the course, as he was the reason for her being there in the first place.

Matty had found the leaflets in the library and when he mentioned them to Bobby, Bobby had been keen for him to enrol. Sheila knew Bobby felt guilty over the fact that Matty had been made redundant with a pittance from Brocklebank's, the factory where they had both worked for more than twenty years. Bobby had hung on longer, right through the abortive fight to save the plant, only to be made redundant himself. But he had been fortunate enough to leave with a £5,000 pay-off. While Bobby worked as a union official, Matty spent his days jogging. Bobby's eagerness for Matty to do something more positive had as its root the guilt that over the past few years, as Bobby's star had gradually risen, Matty's had sunk inexorably below the horizon. Matty, though, his confidence eroded by dozens of unanswered applications for jobs and a recent disastrous interview, had been loth to take such a step. Sheila had joined Bobby in twisting his arm and before she knew it she'd been delegated to make sure Matty turned up on enrolment night. The upshot of their outing was that Sheila had enrolled too. And she loved it.

Within weeks she felt a new confidence in herself. Why hadn't lessons at her old elementary school in Anfield been as interesting as this course? Sheila and the others were involved in exploring the social and economic history of Liverpool. With the exception of holidays, Sheila's whole life had been spent in the city. How little she knew about it. Its rise to the second most important city in the British Empire, its pioneering in the fields of art, science and health care; the factors which years ago had foretold its economic decline. Apart from the acquisition of knowledge, the course also made her feel a more interesting person. Much to her delight recently she'd found herself engaged in real conversations. With Alun Jones, with Sally, but more importantly to her, with her own daughter, Karen. In the past their conversations had tended to relate to ordinary domestic matters, family problems, not to mention a fair number of rows. The first time that they slipped into a debate on multinational companies and their sins they had been talking for ten minutes before Sheila realised what was happening.

'Eh, just a minute!' Sheila said. 'Is this me talking, or someone else?'

Karen had laughed. 'I felt the same way, Mum. Those first few weeks at university. It suddenly hits you – "I'm as good as anyone else."'

Despite her initial shyness at the classes, Sheila had gradually begun to understand Karen's point. But it was the more intimate environment of the tutorial that still gave her difficulties. She found it hard to express her opinions under the gaze of her companions. Especially in somebody else's front room.

'What do you think, Sheila?' Her thoughts were interrupted by Alun Jones.

Sheila dithered. Alun repeated the question. His patient smile certainly helped. This was a long way from Mr Mahoney's sadistic glare when she was a grubby-kneed kid in Anfield and failure to answer could mean a painful tap with a long ruler. If only Bobby could understand what she was gaining from this course – from spreading her wings a little for the first time in her married life, from softly-spoken Alun Jones.

Sheila took a deep breath and waded into her opinions on what had gone wrong in Liverpool before she had even been born.

Matty Nolan breathed steadily as he jogged along the tree-lined street of older council houses. He wasn't in company. He wasn't running for charity. Nor was his route a purposeless circle. He knew exactly where he was going. But why?

He'd asked himself the question a million times since he had met Mo Francis that high-spirited evening when he and Sheila had walked arm in arm, old friends, into the school hall at Northside Comprehensive to enrol for Return and Learn. He'd noticed her talking to some other women who were signing up for a course in car maintenance, cookery, or something. Matty hadn't been able to take his eyes off her and Mo knew it. He could tell she'd noticed him, too.

'You keep your eyes to yourself, or I'll tell on you to Teresa,' Sheila said, nudging him in the ribs.

'What?!' He'd tinged red with embarrassment.

'I can see you blimping that girl in the leather trousers.'

'Her! She'd eat the likes of me for breakfast,' he'd said lightly.

But Sheila was wrong. Mo Francis wasn't wearing leather trousers. She'd mistaken the target of his attention.

As he and Sheila waited to be enrolled, the woman with Mo gradually moved away. When she walked over and joined their line, Matty felt strangely excited. He knew she was only a few places behind him and Sheila, but after Sheila's earlier accusation he daren't look over his shoulder.

After they'd signed on the dotted line and Matty had fished out his UB40, which meant he didn't have to pay for the course, he and Sheila had lingered for a cup of coffee. Sheila, delighted with herself for joining the course, was avidly reading all the posters on the big noticeboard when Mo moved slowly over to join her. She made a remark or two about the course and Sheila got talking to her.

'No, I've never been on any kind of course,' Sheila replied to another question from Mo.

Matty was sipping coffee from a paper cup, pretending to read the noticeboard. But every few moments he would steal a glance at the pretty profile presented by Mo Francis.

'How about your husband over there? Has he?'

Sheila laughed. 'He's not my husband, just a friend.'

'Oh,' Mo said, flatly.

'And I don't mean we're just good friends, either,' Sheila said. She explained how she and Bobby had undertaken to get Matty signed up for the course. And how she'd taken the plunge, too.

Matty had laughed at Mo's confusion and shortly they'd said goodbye. Now, some weeks into the course, Matty and Mo were paired for a project and what was perceived by the rest of the class as an academic relationship was much more than that.

His breathing coming out in clouds against the orange street lamps, Matty slowed to a walk and walked up the front path of an end-of-terrace house. As usual, he didn't go to the front door. He unlatched the back gate and made his way round to the back yard. He tapped twice on the glass panel of the door.

What was he doing here? Teresa was at home watching telly, thinking he was jogging round a park to help research into heart disease. Why had he lied?

As soon as the kitchen light clicked on through the frosted glass, Mo Francis's trim body swirled into view. He knew why.

'Where's our Tracy?' Billy Corkhill's speech was just a little slurred as he came into the living room from upstairs. ''Ere, shove up,' he added, as he squeezed on to the sofa beside his son, Rod, who was engaged in reading a soccer magazine – and watching television.

Doreen was in the kitchen end of the room, making three mugs of coffee. 'She's at Julie Mitchell's. Playing her records.'

'At this time?' said Billy, his eyes on the TV screen.

Doreen presented them with mugs and sat in the armchair, putting her mug carefully on the feature stone fireplace she'd built herself. 'She'll be home soon.'

'I'd better pick her up,' Billy said.

'She's getting a lift.'

'You're sure about that?' Billy asked.

'The girl's dad's bringing her,' she said.

Rod looked at his parents.

'Anyway, you're in no fit state to drive her back, are you?' said Doreen.

'I've had two pints, that's all,' said Billy.

'With your Jimmy, don't make me laugh.'

'He had to go. We only had time for a quick one.' Billy turned his attention back to the screen.

'Another girlfriend?'

'I suppose so.'

'I hope she's a bit older this time. It's disgusting sometimes. Me mam said he brought someone round on Saturday. Couldn't have been older than eighteen.'

'He's me brother, not me son,' Billy said, sharply.

'It upsets me mam. Can't you have a word with him?'

'Get off!' said Billy. 'What do you think I am?'

Rod and his father stared unseeing at a commercial for washing powder.

That day, Rod had been the recipient of jeered abuse in the toilets at Brookside Comprehensive. He'd merely glared at the two lads and said nothing. But he'd been concerned at what they'd said. He hoped their Tracy really was at Julie Mitchell's house playing records.

Cigarette ash hissed as it dropped into the dregs of a cup of tea and Terry Sullivan winced. He looked up from his Woolworth's account book and across at Pat and Sandra. It was all right for some. He was trying to tidy up the book-keeping for the van hire business and his partner was busy snogging and wrestling on the sofa with Sandra.

'Do you have to do that?' he said.

Pat broke away from Sandra. 'Eh?'

'Does she have to drop fag ash in the cups?'

Sandra sat up.

'Do you have to drop fag ash in the cups?' Terry repeated.

Sandra stood up abruptly. 'So sorry,' she said, and waltzed out into the kitchen with the offending crockery. She rinsed it under the tap and Terry heard the ring as she slammed it down on the draining board.

Sandra came back in. 'So sorry,' she said again in the Scots accent which could be so devastatingly sarcastic. Terry didn't reply. He turned back to his accounts. He was trying to come up with a calculation for a new hourly charge for his and Pat's services as a two-man, one-van outfit. Sod it, it's too late, he thought. He was much better at humping fridges up staircases than keeping accounts.

Behind him Sandra had been provoked into giggles by Pat tickling her. Thank God, for that, Terry thought. At least she won't be sulking for twenty-four hours. His feet weren't far enough under the table in the house the three of them rented from Harry Cross for him to risk upsetting Sandra too much. But he did like tidyness, which using cups as ashtrays certainly did not constitute in his mind. And he certainly hated smoking.

Terry's mother, Agnes, died of lung cancer at the age of forty-two. Ever since he could remember, she'd always had a Senior Service or a Woodbine between her lips. Even when she was confined to her bed in that cold upstairs room, when she'd lost stones in weight and the will to carry on, the incessant smoking had continued.

Over the years since his mother's death, the nearest Terry Sullivan had ever got to living with a family was his occasional invitations for Sunday tea at his friend Barry Grant's house. In a way, as a teenager, Sheila Grant was his mother. She'd mended his clothes, even bought them for him on occasion. The Grants had been good to him. His next surrogate family had been the Jacksons. He'd let them down by introducing George Jackson to local gangster, Tommy McArdle. Terry had suffered a bad beating from McArdle's thugs, but at least he hadn't gone to prison like poor George.

When Marie Jackson had moved to Leeds to be closer

to George, Terry had pinned his hopes on marriage to Marie's sister Michelle. He'd been content with the life. Then Michelle had betrayed him by sleeping with a one-time bricklayer called Albert Duff. They parted, and Marie's house, in which they'd been living, had been sold from under his feet.

In a way, the siege at the house occupied by Pat, Sandra and Kate was a godsend. He hated himself for thinking so. He liked Kate, they'd had some good times together. He'd been shaken to the core when she was killed by that nutter John Clarke. But life goes on and Pat and Sandra needed someone else to help meet the monthly rent. Terry had been on the verge of desperation when Pat and Sandra had asked him to share.

Before the siege Terry had never pictured Pat and Sandra having a sexual relationship. He knew they'd shared flats together in the past, but it was a surprise, a month after Kate's death, when they'd returned from Glasgow as lovers. He hoped they'd stay that way. He and Pat had a £2,000 loan out for the van. He didn't want anything to change.

Terry stared blankly at the account book. Pat tapped him on the shoulder. He and Sandra were going to bed.

Like babes in the wood, Pat and Sandra lay in bed with their arms around each other. The position was excruciatingly uncomfortable. But each night, no matter what the circumstances of the day had been, disagreement or harmony, whenever they went to bed together they immediately adopted that position. It was their comfort, their talisman against the bad dreams, against what did happen – and what could have happened to them both – that dreadful week in August.

Pat and Sandra had known each other as colleagues and flatmates for more than three years. But their real relationship had its beginnings in the siege. Their nightmares stemmed from the hot afternoon when they had left Kate inside the house with that madman. A little later had come those heart-stopping gunshots. Then there was the interrogation by the police. Official word that Kate was dead. And the constant pestering of the press and broadcast media.

Under the threat of John Clarke's gun they had lain together for hours, hands and feet bound, their bodies stinking of sweat and fear. Then, on the night of freedom, they had bathed and, both exhausted but clean, had squeezed into a single bed together in Marie Jackson's house. Without cords at their hands and feet they'd clung to each other in relief that they had survived and a sick guilt that Kate had died. Weeks later, neither of them could sleep without that babes in the wood ritual being repeated. Perhaps not the grief now, nor the guilt, but the need to hold each other persisted. They needed to reassure themselves.

Pat lay awake and wondered what might have happened between him and Sandra without the intervention of Clarke and his gun. He recalled that afternoon, two weeks after the siege, at Sandra's friend's flat in Glasgow. It had been totally fulfilling. But would it have happened anyway? Pat had been to bed with plenty of girls, but that afternoon in Scotland was the first time it had ever meant anything. He hated the idea that their relationship as lovers had come about only because of that bloody siege.

Alongside him, Sandra felt Pat's breathing alter in rhythm. She hoped he wasn't going to have another nightmare. Hers had been less frequent lately. She thought she was getting over it all. All Sandra wanted to do now was to forget; to get on with her work and make something of herself. But what about Pat?

She felt deeply for him. It wasn't love, perhaps, but a bond formed by a fairly long friendship and a week of intense mutual suffering at the hands of John Clarke. She was concerned that his experiences had had a far worse effect on him than herself. He still harboured feelings of guilt that he could have overpowered Clarke and saved

Kate. This sometimes manifested itself in an increased need to act on the spur of the moment.

What would Pat do with himself? Sandra wondered. Currently he was messing around with Terry in this van business. It was ridiculous. He had a degree in food technology which could easily be applied to finding a worthwhile job. If only he'd been more settled when Clarke walked into their lives. If he'd been trying to build a career, was generally more positive towards life, then perhaps he might not have taken things so badly. Perhaps the nightmares would stop.

Sandra held him towards her more closely. They were safe. At least they were safe. Slowly, she became aware of his hand moving down her hip. Gently, she stopped its progress. There was no protest, no insistence from Pat. His hand moved back to its former position. Sandra's arms were beginning to hurt, but she would hold him like that for as long as necessary. Until they both surrendered to sleep.

Chapter Two

As the first rays of morning light from the east flicked out over the English Channel, Annabelle Collins turned away from the aircraft window and looked at her husband Paul. Slumped in his seat he was gently snoring, sleeping off the wine – and the elation – of last night's farewell supper with their children Lucy and Gordon.

Annabelle turned back to the window. Far below, beyond the shifting grey sea, she could just make out the roads and still lit street lamps of Brighton and Hove. She was still elated. Their ten-day trip to France had been perfect.

Since Gordon had left Brookside abruptly and fled to join Lucy in France, not a day had passed without Annabelle worrying about him. The revelation from Joanna

Duncan, a schoolfriend's mother, that Gordon had been having a homosexual relationship with head boy Peter Duncan had been a massive shock for her and Paul.

Gordon had been loth to discuss his sexuality. Annabelle had flown out to France immediately after her visit from Joanna Duncan. But Gordon had refused to discuss the matter. He insisted in staying in France and would neither confirm nor deny his alleged relationship with the Duncan boy.

'He must have offered some explanation,' Paul said, as he carried her cases to the car park at Liverpool Airport when she had returned.

But the fact was that Gordon hadn't. 'He's happy, Paul, that's all that matters to me,' Anna replied.

Paul was far from happy, but after long talks with Anna he accepted that his son could be a homosexual. He preferred thereafter not to talk about the matter. But he found himself growing more tolerant daily of what he had formerly considered to be mere sexual perversion. Gradually he became resigned to the idea and distance helped. So much easier to say, 'My boy lives in France now. He thought he might loaf around for a while before university,' than to take the risk of friends, business associates and neighbours perhaps witnessing Gordon's 'coming out'.

As he dozed on the early morning flight from Charles De Gaulle to Liverpool, Paul thanked God for the generosity of Gerard Dubois and his wife Monique. If ever an old army friend had come up trumps it was Gerard. Since Lucy had 'flunked' her O Levels, after months of acrimony following the family's move from Heswall to Brookside, Gerard and Monique had provided her with a home at their flat in Paris and the family's castellated mansion near Fontainebleau. That they should now take in Gordon, too, was unbelievably kind. He could never repay a favour like that, ever.

The Dubois were involved in the manufacture of agricultural machinery as well as providing a hire service for most of Northern France. In addition, they owned farm land, racing stables and had interests in a chain of restaurants situated in and around the outlying districts of Paris. It was in one of these restaurants last evening that Gerard and Monique, Paul and Anna and Lucy and Gordon had gathered for their farewell dinner. It was a double celebration, for that morning Gerard had found a job for Gordon — as a trainee in an auction house for paintings and objets d'art. Gordon's delight at his new job overcame Paul's immediate reaction, which was the urge to inquire what had become of his son's interest in electronics and computers. He stifled the urge and raised his glass of Bordeaux in Gerard's toast to Gordon's future happiness.

Throughout the dinner, he had glanced at Anna. He'd not seen her happier in a long time. She missed Gordon and Lucy even more than he did. At least he had his work, which was fairly demanding. All Annabelle had was her catering business, which although fairly busy these days, was not profitable enough to justify the time expended upon it. Paul had grown to tolerate the catering, seeing it as a necessary distraction, something to take Anna's mind off the enforced loss of her children.

During the holiday, at which the Fontainebleau house had been at the Collins' family's disposal, Gordon had been lively, outgoing and energetic company. Privately Paul and Anna had each tried to ascertain if he had formed any relationships, with girls or boys. They didn't question Gordon direct. But it seemed he had not. In the main, the people he moved around with were friends Lucy had cultivated during her three years with the Dubois — the sons and daughters of neighbours, colleagues from the large agricultural estate agency where Lucy did what seemed to Paul and Anna a highly overpaid, but part-time job, and one or two nieces and nephews of Gerard and Monique. He seemed to have no single attachment among this group and had, in fact, tended to usurp Lucy as the natural leader of the group.

It was Lucy who worried Paul. She had always been a difficult child, especially after his redundancy from Petrochem when her private education was scrapped while Gordon's – the family could afford only one set of fees – had been continued. She had been sent to stay with the Dubois for just six months, but she had enjoyed the life and Gerard had been willing to continue to provide her with a home.

Now, these past few days, her moods had seemed erratic. One minute she would offer to join them on some jaunt or other, the next she would opt out. One day on a picnic in the forest near Villefranche she had burst into tears for no apparent reason. Anna, then Paul, had tried to find out what was wrong, but she could offer no explanation. Anna seemed to think that it was an emotional response to the family being reunited, but Paul wasn't so sure. He suspected a man's involvement, but even a quiet word with the Dubois failed to confirm that theory. They had noticed no change and certainly knew of no man friend, though there had been short romances in the past.

Perhaps Annabelle was right about the emotional reaction to the family being reunited. At last night's dinner, tears had come to her eyes when Gerard had made a short, rather pompous speech about his friendship with the Collins and his devotion to Lucy and Gordon. In fact, she had had to leave earlier than the others and she declined a lift home, saying she didn't want to break up the party. She had left at ten o'clock by taxi, kissing her mother and father, and adding that she hated airport farewells.

As Anna was so happy, Paul decided not to worry any more about Lucy. She would be all right. And so, hopefully, would Gordon. He shifted in his seat and leaned across Anna to look out of the window. They were losing height. He could see clearly the patchwork of harvested fields and now golden woodland.

Anna smiled at him. 'Happy?' she asked.

Paul leaned back, closed his eyes and grinned. 'Very,' he said.

Fifty miles away, Damon Grant yawned and scratched.

'Damon!' His mother's voice could penetrate concrete walls when it came to waking the family.

Damon crawled out of bed and started to pull on his jeans and socks. A glance at the clock told him he should have been up ten minutes ago. With a bit of luck, he could bum a lift off his dad or one of the neighbours. This week he and three other painters were working in a sports hall in Prescot. They had started the job the previous day and there were plans today for a game of five-a-side football during the dinner break. Damon remembered his boast to run rings round his mates and groped under the bed for his best pair of trainers.

Damon had been working for Halligan's, a small painting contractor, for almost twelve months. He wasn't an official apprentice, just one of the thousands of young people up and down the country earning twenty-five pounds a week from the Government on the Youth Training Scheme. Deep down, Damon knew that the primary purpose of the scheme was to disguise the number of young people out of work in Britain, but at least it was some sort of a job and preferable to lying in bed half the day, struggling to find enough money to sit in hamburger places and pubs. Moreover, he felt lucky because he was doing work he actually enjoyed.

Damon had always enjoyed decorating. He'd done the living room and hall and stairs for his mother after little Claire was born last Christmas. He'd also done the living room at Pat and Sandra's before the siege. One of his first thoughts at the time he was evacuated from the house by police marksmen was to hope that any resultant activity at the house wouldn't spoil his work. Two weeks ago he had earned forty pounds by decorating a bedroom at his friend Neil's parents' house. Obviously, he wasn't supposed to do other work while on the YTS, but everyone else seemed to do it. Why not him? He was sure his elder brother Barry would approve.

But what Damon needed was a proper job. With bonuses a painter could get over a hundred quid a week. If he could earn that much Neil's mam could paint her own bedroom.

Since his first interview with his boss Derek Halligan, Damon had been hopeful of being taken on full-time at the end of the year-long attachment to the YTS. His foreman Ted Cook, a laconic Liverpudlian with a lifetime's experience of weeding out the deadbeats from the reliable workers, had made a few vague hints that Damon might be suitable material for an apprenticeship. As a result, Damon had been enthusiastic. Sometimes he worked voluntary overtime if it helped to get a job finished on time and Ted was ever ready to praise his keenness and the standard of his work. The only time he told Damon where to get off was the Bank Holiday morning when Damon had turned up on the dot of eight o'clock to join colleagues pressganged into working for double time!

Yes, being a painter on the YTS was much better than school and a lot better than being on the dole. Damon whistled and clumped down the stairs to his waiting cornflakes.

His heavy footsteps woke his sister Karen from a troubled sleep. As she turned, her head banged with pain. She shouldn't have drunk that last bottle of lager in the Cambridge last night. But Richard was buying and she couldn't say no to the offer of a drink from the editor of the student newspaper.

Since joining the media and communications studies course at the University of Liverpool, Karen had been immediately attracted to the idea of working on the university newspaper. Traditionally, it was a good way of getting freebie tickets for concerts and films, as well as review copies of books and records. But in Karen's case she felt her contributions might be better than some of those she had seen published. Most of the reviews were quite good, but the editorial content concerned with what was going on in her own city, she thought, was pretty poor. Maybe it was because so many of the students came from other parts of Britain and even further afield? But she believed she could do better. Based on her own experience, she wrote a short article advising new students of the best and cheapest places to eat, buy clothes and see live music. At first she was embarrassed and not a little hurt when the article was returned. But with it was a note asking her to meet Richard Paling in the Students' Union. Richard, a third-year reading English, had explained that a similar piece had been written before the summer holidays and was due to appear in the next edition. But he went on to praise what she had written.

Karen felt good about that and even better when Richard asked her to give him five hundred words on the kind of piece she herself would like to see in the paper. He'd asked her what she had in mind. As she had nothing in mind she waffled and bluffed a little and eventually presented him with a five hundred and fifty-word article, researched by herself at the cost of skipping several lectures, on the subject of health and women students. Richard was impressed. He'd published the piece as a page top with Karen's by-line and sent her out with the photographer to get some suitable accompanying pics.

Karen was the only first year at the university to get really involved with the paper. Since starting her course, her opinions on what university life entailed had changed. She was now swimming with the mainstream of undergraduates who were more intent on a good time than sitting night after night writing essays. Three years seemed such a long time. There was always plenty of opportunity to work later on.

Though she had adopted this attitude it wasn't completely without guilt. Right through school she had worked hard and her parents had always encouraged her. Bobby and Sheila were both proud that she was the first child in both families ever to enter a university. Her elder brother, Barry, was proud of her too and so was Damon, but with perhaps a hint of jealousy for what he considered a 'dead cushy life'. She had had a great deal of support and encouragement, but she hated the idea of letting down her family.

The previous evening she was about to leave the campus for tea with the family, determined to spend the evening completing an essay. But she had been waylaid by Richard and invited to join him and his editorial colleagues for a drink at the Cambridge.

'We're having a brainstorming session,' Richard said. 'I want some ideas. It's not going to be a formal meeting. Everyone can just throw in what they like.'

Karen was flattered to be invited. But conscious of the overdue essay she pointed out that she had work to do.

'Like what?' Richard asked.

'An essay.'

He laughed. 'You can do that anytime, I'd like you to get involved.'

'Okay.'

Yet again she phoned her mother to cancel tea and joined the writers of the paper. Despite the fact she drank more than she was used to in such sophisticated second and third-year company, she had found a receptive audience for some of her ideas.

She groaned at the memory that she had promised to develop some of them and show them to Richard. Her head ached. And she still hadn't finished that lousy essay.

Karen turned over carefully and went back to sleep.

Billy Corkhill was woken by the front door slamming as Doreen left the house for the dentists' surgery. Sleeping in the day had always been difficult for him, but he had to admit he slept much better since moving to Brookside.

When they had lived with Doreen's mother, it had been virtually impossible to sleep during daylight hours. If it wasn't barking dogs and screaming kids at the houses on each side of the mid-terrace, it was Julia laughing downstairs with her neighbour Mrs Kerfoot. Or banging round doing the washing and housework. So when the chance of the house in a quiet, tree-surrounded cul-de-sac – with no apparent sign of young kids – had turned up in the newsletter from Menskip-Pearce, the estate agents, Doreen had been quick to add the silence factor to her sales pitch when she showed the polaroid snap of Marie Jackson's old house to Billy. 'Just think, love,' she said, 'you won't be going out to work shattered 'cause of the likes of them next door. I bet nearly everyone there is out at work all day. It'll be dead peaceful.'

'How much?' was Billy's only answer.

The house had been a little more than they could afford. But when Doreen had phoned Menskip's the next morning she had been delighted to hear Mrs Jackson had reduced the price by £1,500. The house was now £27,500 and Doreen couldn't wait to phone the building society. Then she nipped out to the bank to check their savings. She was confident they could manage.

Together that evening they had filled in the mortgage application form. Or rather Doreen had. Billy was uncertain. It was a big step. 'You can't put that!' Billy had practically shrieked, as Doreen had written in Billy's average monthly earnings. 'It's nowhere near that for Christ's sake!'

'Yeah, but it says ovies and other earnings.'

'I know, but we can't rely on them.'

'It's over twenty-five years, love, you're bound to get some in that time.' She grinned at his concerned face. 'And there's the foreigners. . . .'

'I'm not going to live another twenty-five years if I'm working, doing overtime *and* foreigners,' Billy said, flatly.

'We'll manage, love, I know we will. . . .'

'It's a lot of money to borrow,' said Billy.

'Lots of other people manage, I don't see why we can't. And they haven't got the sort of money you earn. Look at McCoomb's eldest, she got married to that layabout from –'

'All right, all right,' said Billy, 'as long as you think we can do it. . . .'

Doreen was confident they could. After all, they'd saved the deposit money, nearly two thousand pounds now. 'And think of the privacy, too,' she said. 'We won't have me mam round our necks all the time.'

Billy appreciated the point. Nearly all their married life they had shared with Julia. The house was pretty big for a corpy house, but they still lived in each other's pockets. The house at Brookside might be smaller, but at least they'd be on their own, just him and Doe and the kids.

Now, as he lay back staring at the ceiling, he realised he had enjoyed the privacy since they moved in. But the cost of the place frightened him. Nearly half his wages each month went to pay the mortgage. Then there were the rates, they cost a bomb and he couldn't pay them on the drip till next year. They'd spent quite a bit on new curtains and some bits of furniture, too, all on HP. That fireplace kit for Doreen had been over a hundred on its own. It looked good, mind. Then there was the gas, the lecky and –

'Christ!' Billy sat up in bed abruptly. He'd forgotten to take the by-pass lead off the electricity meter at Julia's. How long ago had they moved out? His brain raced. Then he relaxed. They had a bill just before leaving, the meter reader wouldn't be round for a while yet. But he reminded himself to nip round one day after work to take off the illegal wiring which had reduced their former electric bills to less than half the amount they should have been.

Billy sat on the side of the bed and reached for his trousers. Just time to get some breakfast and read the paper before he clocked on for lates. No sign of any overtime this week.

Tracy Corkhill rubbed at the pencilled lines on the page of her geography exercise book. The diagram in the text book showed the major grain-producing regions of the world. But Tracy couldn't get her version right.

She looked up and surveyed the rest of the class. Apart from the gigglers and the yobs, busy whispering and messing around on the back row of Class Five, everyone was intent on the diagram. The more they did now, the less there would be for homework.

Tracy chewed her pencil and looked at Peter Montague. He was slightly younger than most of the teachers at Brookside Comprehensive and a hell of a lot dishier. 'Dishy' was the nickname the girls gave him when he joined the school at the start of the previous year. Tracy hadn't taken much notice. She thought the other girls were idiots, fawning over him, making suggestive remarks in his presence and trying to outdo each other as they showed off to him on every available opportunity. Mr Montague took it all in his stride and laughed off their behaviour. One or two of them now positively hated him for his reaction to their more extreme attentions. He had sent one girl to the headmaster and several had found themselves in detention.

No, Tracy had not taken much notice of Peter Montague, until the night she had to serve a detention for being found chewing gum in Miss Forshaw's maths lesson. Peter Montague had been the teacher on detention duty and, unusually for Brookside Comprehensive, Tracy had been the only pupil in detention that evening. Tracy had thought she was in the wrong place until Mr Montague had turned up with the detention book.

'This is a bit embarrassing, don't you think,' he said.

'What?' she said quietly.

'It's just you and me. No other sinners tonight.'

'Nobody else is in?'

'No.' He sat at the desk with his arms folded. The atmosphere was awkward. 'Well I'm not going to ask you to write a pointless essay. I'm probably just as anxious to get home as you are,' he said, eventually.

Tracy smiled sheepishly.

'But the rule is one hour and I suppose we'd better go along with that, eh?'

Tracy nodded and smiled. She really was an attractive girl, Peter Montague thought. At first sight she looked like so many of the other girls in the school, with a sullen expression and attitude which invariably covered a basic shyness and lack of confidence. But when she smiled, her whole appearance changed.

Montague realised he was staring at her. Tracy's face coloured. Montague snapped out of his reverie.

'Well,' he said, now embarrassed himself, 'what shall we do to fill in an hour?'

Tracy shrugged.

'No suggestions?' He smiled at her now.

'You could let me off. . . .' Tracy said.

'Yes, I could.' He consulted the detention book. 'But what would Miss Forshaw say about that?' Tracy was looking downwards, fiddling with her hair, twirling it round and round her index finger. 'I'd imagine,' Montague continued, 'she might be tempted to put me in detention too.'

Tracy grinned at him.

'I'm afraid we don't get on very well, Miss Forshaw and me. The generation gap, they used to call it.'

Tracy looked up. 'Don't you?'

Montague shook his head and grinned to himself at the memory. 'I upset her the first day by sitting in her staff-room chair. And she's for ever accusing me of pinching her tea bags. . . .'

Tracy smiled again. Yes, she was a very attractive girl. Peter Montague had a mad urge to keep her smiling.

'We call her Agatha Christie in the staffroom. She accuses everyone of interfering with her belongings. If it's not tea bags, it's something else. Her slippers, or something.'

Tracy laughed. 'What?'

'Didn't you know she wore slippers in the staffroom?'

'You're kidding.'

'I'm not. It's true.'

Montague didn't know why he was doing this. But he

enjoyed the feeling that he could amuse this shy young girl. She was more relaxed now. And that smile.

'Still, I don't suppose I should be telling you this. . . . Let's talk about something else, shall we?'

They'd talked for almost an hour. Montague made the running, asking about her family, where she lived, what she wanted to do. Tracy enjoyed herself. She forgot she was in detention for a punishment. She enjoyed talking to an adult on what seemed to her equal terms. It was different at home. Other girls seemed to get away with murder. Unlike Billy, their fathers didn't rant and rave if they came home a few minutes late from a disco. And they didn't seem to bother about their daughters wearing make-up. Tracy felt hard done by because she had to put hers on in the girls' toilets, or on the school bus. Her mum wasn't so bad, but her dad treated her like a kid.

Peter Montague, however, didn't. And hadn't done for some months now. After detention that night, Peter, or Pete as she now called him when they were alone, had given her a lift in his car. On the way he'd offered to lend her some books and said she could call round at his flat one evening, or perhaps on Saturday. Tracy wasn't all that interested in the books, but she was suddenly interested in Peter Montague. She said she would call round.

It was a fortnight before she did drop round one Saturday – in her lunch break from Kane's Mini Mart, where she worked as a Saturday girl for six pounds a day. She didn't go without prompting, however, as Peter Montague had approached her on the corridor and asked why she hadn't visited.

Saturday calls had become a regular pattern and sometimes Tracy could also manage to drop round during the evenings. The flat was only a bus ride from Brookside. Peter was very careful that they weren't seen together and they spent a lot of time out in his car, just driving to places like Chester and Preston and Southport.

Tracy lived for these evenings and Saturdays. In between times, she would write to him. Great long, over-written letters on how she enjoyed last Saturday, how she looked forward to next Saturday. Peter never replied, but she knew he kept them. She'd seen them in the sideboard at his flat.

In all these weeks there had been no physical contact between them, except for long sessions of kissing. Tracy had experimented with boys from school at parties and in other less salubrious places, but for her it had been unsatisfying, something done out of curiosity. She would willingly have gone to bed with Peter, but it was always him who cut short the physical contact when they both became heated.

'When you're older,' he had said dozens of times, 'it'll be all right then.'

Looking across the classroom at him now, she caught his eyes. He smiled and she returned it. Involuntarily, she shivered as a thrill of pleasure ran up her spine. She wished she was older. How she wished she was older.

'I love you,' she mouthed silently across the bent backs of her fellow geography pupils.

Peter Montague coloured slightly and bent his head to his marking.

Chapter Three

'Leave it, I'll do it!' snapped Harry Cross.

But Ralph snatched the kettle away from his hands. 'You're all right, Harry, leave it to me.'

Harry left him to making their tenth cup of tea that day and wandered through to the small bungalow living room. Beyond the patio doors, the little garden had now surrendered to the weeds which strayed in from the belt of woodland which surrounded Brookside Close. How many months ago had he, Ralph and Edna finally straightened out the garden after that idiot Alan Partridge had turned it into a Manchurian showpiece? It wasn't long ago. But now there was no Edna. While they should have been enjoying the summer, keeping the garden neat and tidy, Edna had been lying in the North Liverpool Infirmary dying from a stroke.

Harry had always expected to die first. With angina as bad as his it was only to be expected. Edna had always seemed so healthy. That was the cruellest blow to Harry that night that Edna had finally died. All his planning had been to leave her comfortably off. He knew he was an awkward old sod to live with. Edna had told him often enough. What he had wanted, really wanted, was for Edna to outlive him, to spend some time on her own, perhaps going to stay with Kevin and Sally and Kevin's adopted child Jessica, whom Edna had accepted as her real grandchild right from the day the youngster and her new 'gran' had met.

Kevin had hardly bothered to contact him since Edna died. Harry had seen him once since the funeral and had talked to him on the phone perhaps three or four times. If it hadn't been for Ralph, Harry might never have bothered getting out of bed in the morning. He saw this time, this endless time, as a waste. It should have been Edna enjoying it. She wouldn't have let Kevin get away with such scant contact. She'd have been on that train to Marlow once a month at the least. Harry grinned to himself at the thought of Edna the lone traveller. She'd always said he held her up with his moaning and his fussiness.

Still, Edna would be glad that Ralph Hardwick now lived with him. Good old straightforward Ralph, ever eager to help anyone who needed a hand. Ralph had been a friend of Edna since they lived next door to each other and both men worked on the railways. There'd been times often in the past when Harry had been jealous of Ralph's relationship with Edna. Especially when they were younger. But when Harry and Edna had left Liverpool in the early fifties for Harry to take up a new driving post at King's Cross Station, the two couples, Harry and Edna and Ralph and Grace, had drifted apart. The relationship was sustained only by the odd letter and Christmas cards.

When Harry retired and he and Edna sold the house in North London to move to Brookside, Harry didn't give a thought to Ralph and Grace. It was Edna that brought them together again, much to Harry's annoyance. Grace had died within months. The poor woman had suffered years of pain, condemned to a wheelchair with severe arthritis. Ralph had been destroyed at first. But through the renewed friendship with Edna, she had given him something to live for.

Harry moved to his usual armchair and sat down. And giving him something to live for meant betting. Ralph had reawakened Edna's old passion for gambling, particularly on the gee-gees. There'd been times in their marriage that Harry had had to go into debt to pay off Edna's gambling debts. When Ralph took the plunge and moved in with the Crosses, he had recklessly encouraged Edna to start a telephone credit account with a local bookie. The adventure had been disastrous. Edna even pawned her wedding ring to try to escape her debts. Fortunately Harry had found out about it before matters had got any worse. Ralph had felt the sharpest edge of Harry's tongue and for several months the relationship between the two men had been strained.

All that was in the past now, though. In the bad days and weeks after Edna's death, Ralph had talked of returning home to his own bungalow. But Harry would have none of it. He needed the companionship. On top of that, too, he'd bought a second-hand Ford Fiesta and he couldn't drive. Ralph was the driver and what would Harry do without a car?

You couldn't find a better mate than Ralph, Harry mused.

Ralph came in from the kitchen carrying two cups of tea. 'Here you are, Harry. Tea up.'

'I don't want tea.'

'It was you that got up to make it.'

'Yes, well I've changed me mind, haven't I?' said Harry, picking up his newspaper.

Ralph exhaled. Why did he put up with it? But, of course, he knew the answer. He needed the company.

Rod Corkhill never felt quite right with his mates in the lower sixth at Brookside Comprehensive. In fact, they weren't mates as such, they were class mates. His real mates tended to come from the fifth form, a group of lads just a little younger than him who mainly lived on the estate.

The only reason he was in the sixth form was because his mother had made up her mind that Rod should go to university. The pressure had been even greater when she found out that their one-time neighbours from the estate, the Grants, had got their girl into university.

If it had been up to Rod he'd have left last year and taken his chance. He might even have left Merseyside to find a job. He just didn't have the commitment that the other lads in his class had. Now they were lower sixth they carried on as if they were some sort of club. They did things like bringing umbrellas to school and reading *The Guardian*. It was as if they'd changed overnight. Rod thought most of them were prats.

No, he was happier with the lads from the fifth form. There the talk was of girls, cars, but most of all football. Rod was the doyen of the Everton supporters at Brookside Comprehensive and had been known to stick one on anybody who disagreed with his views on Howard Kendall's heroes.

He was also beginning to find the work harder. Right through school he'd not had to stretch himself. He got the marks in the end of year examinations and he got just enough O Levels to move on to the lower sixth. Doreen and Billy considered him a genius, but whenever he tried to tell them otherwise, he was told off by Doreen for not believing in himself. That was the trouble. He did believe in himself. He knew exactly how far he was capable of going. And most of the time he didn't think it was university.

Now, sitting on the low wall between the two main blocks of the school with Brian Moloney, Dave Haggerty and Kevin Wilson, Rod was busy taking the piss out of passing pupils.

'Eh, Wocko, where's your brolly, then?'

Stephen Watkinson hurried away nervously, hugging his shiny attaché case to him as though it contained Cabinet papers. Haggerty made to run after him and Wocko put a spurt on to reach the doors of the science block. Haggerty came back laughing.

'Have you seen his shoes? I bet his mam polishes them for him.'

Just then, Tracy Corkhill came out of the science block and past Rod and company.

'Eh, don't crack on, will you?' called Kevin Wilson.

Tracy gave him a withering look and carried on. 'Prefer the fourth years, then, do you?' Wilson taunted her.

Tracy didn't look back, but Rod was immediately at Wilson. 'What's that meant to mean? Eh?'

'Nothing,' Wilson replied.

'Don't tell him Kev, for Christ's sake,' said Moloney, moving nearer to watch the fun.

'Don't tell me bloody what? Eh, Wilson?' He took hold of Kevin Wilson's collar and shook him.

'Nothing, nothing!'

'Ah, leave him, will you? He's only joking,' Haggerty said. 'Someone was saying your Tracy's been having it off with the fourth years, that's all. It's just a joke.'

'Some joke!' said Rod. Turning back to Wilson he pushed him away. 'I don't care if it is a joke, don't you go repeating it. Right!' Rod addressed all of them. 'If anyone says anything about our Tracy they're in trouble. Okay?'

The tension passed. The cat-calling resumed. But Rod was uneasy. Three girls in the fifth form had got pregnant last year and had to leave the school. He didn't want that happening to his sister.

Joyce and Heather crossed the car park from the rear entrance of Hamilton Devereux, on their way to lunch at the Corn Exchange. Joyce was revealing to her subordinate in the firm of chartered accountants the latest chapter in her disastrous marriage to a disturbed advertising account executive.

'Thank God it was one of his things and not one of the partners' dinners,' she was saying. 'But I had to leave. It was so embarrassing. I don't know why he hasn't had the sack.'

'What was it? This party?' Heather asked.

Joyce never usually gave away details about her marriage. It was generally understood, though, that she had a hard time at home. And it often seemed to her colleagues that she would sooner stay on in the office than make the journey back to the marital home in Wallasey.

'A promotional thing for a wine shipper. A wine shipper! I should have known better! He was knocking the stuff back like Lucozade from the minute we arrived. He didn't bother to introduce me until he was well into his cups, then he had to do it in that horrible sarcastic way he has, you know.' Joyce looked sideways at Heather. 'Then you don't know, do you?'

'No.'

Joyce laughed. 'Take it from me. He has. It's one of the reasons he never sets foot in H and D and I come to the Christmas junkets on my own.'

Heather was about to ask how long they'd been unhappy when they were interrupted by three toots of a car horn. Tom Curzon swept up to them, braking hard, in his Audi Quattro. The window rolled down. 'Hi,' said Tom.

'I thought you were in Dusseldorf!'

'I was. Before breakfast,' Tom replied. He got out of the Audi. 'And how's Joyce, then?'

'Mustn't complain,' Joyce said. She felt a little uncomfortable with Curzon. She wasn't used to talking on such a familiar level with the company's clients, particularly those as important as the chairman of newly-floated Curzon Communications.

'Sorry about last night,' Tom said. 'You *did* get the message?'

Heather looked at Joyce. 'Yes.'

Tom continued. 'So I thought I'd take you out to lunch to make up. Any suggestions where? I have booked a table at the Oriel.'

Heather's face showed her irritation. 'Tom, I'm going to lunch with Joyce. She invited me.'

Joyce butted in quickly. 'Oh, it's all right, Heather. I can do some shopping. I have to get a few things. . . .'

'But . . .' Heather began. But Tom stood there smiling, as if to say, 'This is what we're doing, no arguments.'

'Honestly, it's all right, Heather. You go,' Joyce insisted.

'That's what I call an understanding boss. Thanks Joyce,' Tom said. Then hamming it up as the gentleman, he moved round to the passenger door of the Quattro and opened it.

Heather turned to Joyce. She was quite embarrassed. Joyce had walked into her office earlier that morning and asked Heather to join her at the Corn Exchange. 'I didn't expect this, Joyce. I'm sorry.'

Joyce nodded and smiled. 'It's okay. Be thankful you've got someone who'll take you out to lunch.' She laughed, but Heather could see there was genuine regret in Joyce's eyes. She must have had hell with that husband of hers.

Joyce left and Heather got in the car with Tom Curzon. Tom kissed her. 'Glad to see me?'

'Yes, but . . .' She hesitated, then pressed on, 'Well it's always on your terms, Tom.'

But he wasn't listening. He put the car into gear and drove off. After a moment, he said, 'Fancy the bowls tonight?'

'I'm working,' Heather said, a touch sharply. 'Anyway, I thought you wanted us to eat at the flat. If you're not going to Dusseldorf this afternoon.'

'I think we'll have to scrub it. I've let me dad down a couple of times lately. He expects me there tonight.'

There was a close bond between Tom and his father Jim Curzon. Jim, a big, grey-haired man, was exceptionally proud of his son, and the relationship had blossomed since the death of Tom's mother, Margaret, when the boy was a teenager. Jim had seen his lad go from success to success. Now, all he wanted was for Tom to marry, settle down a little and produce a couple of grandchildren.

Heather liked Jim and her feeling was reciprocated. She knew that if they came close to marriage, the plan would have Jim's total support. In fact, on the previous occasion Heather had joined father and son for one of their traditional summer evening bowling sessions behind a suburban pub, Jim had made some heavy hints. Heather had been a little taken aback, but pleased.

Heather insisted she had to meet a client. Tom interrogated her on the business they had to discuss and, as usual, had the last word. 'Well ... Get that over and come round to the bowling green. You're not going to be all night, are you?'

As Tom manoeuvred the car into a tight parking space in a side street at the heart of the city's business quarter, Heather reflected on Tom's attitude to their relationship. If he was busy, any arrangements went by the board. But if she had commitments ... well, it was another story.

As they walked into the Oriel, Tom's carphone started to bleep.

James Fleming didn't have a telephone in his hired Peugeot. For the first time in his working life he felt as free as a bird. He worked for an import export business in Liverpool, but for the past three and a half months he had been on a business trip in France.

James had been found a hotel in Fontainebleau and been given the job of finding suitable premises. It wasn't his kind of work really, but a promotion was in the offing and James thought this might be some kind of trial. It had been a wrench to leave Liverpool and his wife and two daughters, but he had determined to make the best of it. From the first day of his arrival in France he had worked long days trying to locate the perfect site for a new warehouse. That was how he met Lucy Collins.

One morning he had called in at the agricultural estate agency where she worked part-time. Nearly two weeks doing the rounds had given him a short list of four suitable sites, but he wanted to explore all avenues. He decided there would be no harm in checking the agricultural estate agency, so he parked outside and walked in. The well-dressed young woman with the curly, dark brown hair had looked very French, but James's imperfect grasp of the language quickly led to Lucy addressing him in English and soon they were swapping information on their respective home areas. James was originally from London, but had moved to Liverpool for work. Lucy was quick to point out the irony, saying that all she seemed to read about in the French press was Liverpool's unemployment problems. After the Brussels soccer riots, the continental media had stopped treating Merseyside objectively and didn't miss a chance to put the boot in.

Forty-five minutes later, after James had gone off to discuss his needs with one of the agents, Lucy handed over the job to the married woman with whom she split the work and went out to her green Citroen CV, a gift from Gerard and Monique. As she opened the door, she was hailed from the doorway.

'Hello again.' James crossed to her, 'Sorry to bother you, but do you know a picture gallery called Aquarelle? A chap I met yesterday told me about it. I'd like to have a look.'

'Aquarelle, yes,' said Lucy. 'If you don't mind following me, I'll show you.'

'It's no bother?' James said, diffidently.

Lucy shook her head. 'Not at all.'

Lucy drove a little more slowly than usual, keeping an

eye on James at the wheel of the following Peugeot. She thought he was rather nice. Polite, good-looking. Much as she liked France and the French, it was a change to meet someone from home.

When they reached the gallery, she got out and looked in the window with James. The gallery sold inexpensive oils and contemporary watercolours. 'There's lots more inside,' Lucy said. And she found herself accompanying him round the gallery's interior.

James liked this bright, rather witty girl. Out on the road, living in a hotel in a foreign country, he had had little conversation with any woman since he left home.

He glanced at his watch. It was twelve-fifteen and the shops were beginning to close for their long lunch break. 'You've been very kind,' he said, 'I wonder ... could I buy you lunch, or perhaps just a drink, if you're in a hurry ...?' He expected a brush-off. A girl like that would surely have other plans for the afternoon.

Indeed, Lucy did have plans, but nothing that couldn't be cancelled in the interests of meeting somebody new. 'I'd love to,' she said, 'I haven't seen anyone from England – apart from my brother – in weeks.'

That first meeting with James had been two months ago. They'd enjoyed a few glasses of wine and a simple meal of ham and bread. The conversation had been easy and James was flattered at Lucy's appreciative laughter as he described the humorous aspects of his stay in France.

They met again next day. James had almost settled on one of the four sites and he deliberately began to spin out the work involved, so much had he begun to enjoy his time with Lucy. From the start he made no secret of the fact he was married. Not that he spoke much of his marriage and Lucy was careful never to mention it first.

As their relationship moved inexorably towards the physical, James voiced his fears. He had never been unfaithful to Penny. By this time matters had gone too far for Lucy. To her shame, she had come up with the old line that 'What the eye doesn't see, the heart ... etc.' Eventually, she had succeeded in breaking down James' reserve, not that it took much breaking-down. Her shame at encouraging a married man into infidelity occasionally surfaced, but in the main it was overcome by the pure joy of her first serious affair. For the past eight weeks she had been extremely happy.

Apprehension at the situation in which James had allowed himself to become involved was present in his every waking hour, except when he was with Lucy. Long lunch hours together, evenings spent exploring the countryside and making love at his hotel – and once or twice at hotels on weekend jaunts – added up to a delirious adventure for him. He had never known anything like it before.

The bombshell had come a week ago. In a message from his firm, he was told to report back to the Liverpool office on the following Monday. Since the message arrived, Lucy had ended each of their meetings with tears.

Now, as they sat at the rusting table in the courtyard of a bar-café, Lucy was shaking with emotion. James had only three more days left. In a way he wanted to get home, back to his wife and children. He had to face reality again. But what had he done to Lucy? How could he face saying goodbye?

James Fleming picked up his glass of wine and wished he'd never met her.

Chapter Four

The bonnet on Billy Corkhill's battered old Renault was propped up. As he filled the screen washer reservoir with a lemonade bottle full of tap water, he cast an envious glance at Bobby Grant's A-reg Montego. These union officials did themselves okay, he thought. I'm paying me subs week in, week out for the likes of him to swan round in smart cars, and what do they do to earn them? Not a lot, he decided.

He wasn't anti-union by any means. In all the jobs he'd had, Billy had joined the union whether or not he'd had to. But he didn't think their priorities fitted in with the way modern industry worked. Too much time in his opinion was spent trying to hold on to former manning levels. He'd seen it happen several times in places where he'd worked. No, Billy thought, the unions should be more concerned with trying to get more retraining and more reallocation.

Five years ago he'd been a machine minder. Two hundred others in the food processing factory had been 'rationalised' out of the factory gates after a long struggle by unions to preserve the status quo. Billy had survived temporarily, but had then opted for a Government retraining scheme at the skill centre, where he'd gained the qualification of electrician. He didn't expect to be a hardwire electrician for the rest of his working life. He prided himself on having more foresight than the leadership of the unions. If he'd been retrained from machine minder to electrician, why couldn't he be retrained for something else in years to come? He thought it all made sense. Why the hell couldn't the union bosses see it?

He laughed to himself. The train of thought had been brought on by a brief meeting with Bobby Grant a few minutes earlier. He was under the impression Bobby was a sales rep, but Bobby had revealed his position with ETWU. As Billy, now a maintenance electrician at Pollocks, was a member of AETU, he had no reservations in giving Bobby his views. Bobby had not pursued the argument.

He'd have to be careful who he did foreigners for with a union official living just across the Close.

At that moment, however, Bobby was more concerned with a confrontation of a different kind – with Sheila.

'I said I'd be home for dinner. I'm working late.'

'Do you think I've nothing else to do?' Sheila replied.

He'd walked in to find her sitting with Claire on her knee at the kitchen table. With her free hand, she was writing up notes from the Return and Learn class.

'I know, but I did say!'

'When?'

'You were changing the baby. Before you did breakfast.'

Sheila exhaled and pushed away her notepad. 'Yeah, when I was up to my eyes and run off my feet. I never heard you.' She handed Claire to Bobby. 'Here, you have a turn. . . . What do you want?'

'Anything.'

'It'll have to be anything,' Sheila replied. 'I haven't been to the shops yet.'

Bobby was about to remark that if she'd left the course work, she would have had time to go shopping, but he held back. There'd been enough minor friction over that just recently. He didn't want any serious problems to arise between them. It had not been an easy year. The birth of Claire had been followed by an unusually long period of post-natal depression and he had brought the marriage close to ruin by sneaking off to have a vasectomy operation without talking Sheila through her Roman Catholic objections.

'Will egg on toast do?' asked Sheila.

'Yeah, fine.'

Bobby rubbed his forehead against little Claire's nose. It made her giggle. He repeated the exercise. She giggled again. With Barry working away, Karen and Damon out most of the time, it was good to come home to a family. Even if his wife was out more and more these days.

Karen was trying to write, but it was difficult. She still hadn't got over her boozy, late night and Pam never stopped talking. Now she was busy name dropping and talking about Liverpool as though she'd lived in the city all her life.

They were in the Students' Union common room. Karen was attempting to write down some of the ideas for articles she'd promised the university newspaper crowd. But Pam's non-stop chatter obliged her to put it aside. Pam would – and could – talk to anyone. Karen admired her facility for socialising. With her good looks and the 'posh' Surrey accent, she seemed to be able to cope with any situation.

'Oh, you've got to come,' she was saying. 'Going to one little party isn't going to screw up your degree.'

'I know that,' Karen replied pointedly. She'd had some ribbing from other students she'd met about her guilt over not working and she didn't want any more. She'd also had some comments on her sanity for staying at home. Most of the others she knew, including Pam, lived at the Halls of Residence, a few miles from the campus. To them the greatest part of university life was being away from home.

'I don't know any of them, do I?' Karen continued.

'What does that matter?' said Pam, 'They've got their own house, four of them sharing. It'll be much better than the usual junket in halls.'

'I'll think about it,' Karen said.

'It's nothing to do with him, is it?' Pam said suddenly. Karen followed her eye-line. David Hargreaves was on his way over.

'Why should it be?' Karen said.

'Well . . .' Pam said, 'he goes home to mummy and daddy every night, doesn't he?'

'If I want to go to a party I decide for myself,' Karen said in a low voice.

'Hi . . . Hi, Pam.' David sat down next to Karen. 'Busy, are we?'

'I was,' Karen said.

'Oh.' He looked a little put out.

'I'm talking about her,' Karen said. She looked at Pam. 'She's trying to corrupt me away from work, inviting me to wild parties.'

'I think anything after eight o'clock's a wild party to

45

you scousers,' Pam said. 'So do you want to come, or not?'

'I'll think about it, I said.'

'Suit yourself,' said Pam, getting up. 'You know where to find me. . . .' She left David and Karen alone.

'What was all that about?' David asked.

'She says I'm too concerned about working and not enough about going out and that.'

'She might think a bit differently in three years when she's suicidal about Finals.'

Karen watched Pam disappear through the double doors. 'I don't think she will be. Not Pam.'

'I wouldn't bet on it,' he replied. They were both silent for a moment. Then David added, 'Do you fancy a coffee?'

'No thanks.'

David went over to the coffee machine to fetch his own. Karen watched him. Their relationship had cooled since the flattering days during A level study when they'd met at the Picton Library. They had been so much more involved then – he persuading her to go to Liverpool University, she forcing him to stop seeing his other girlfriend. Once she set foot on the campus, things had begun to change. There'd been so much to do and so many new people that she hadn't really noticed until recently. Their meetings had become fewer and fewer. These days they went for an occasional drink. Sometimes they caught the same bus in or out of the City.

Just recently, Karen was a little suspicious of David. She hadn't asked him, but she felt sure he had renewed the relationship with his former girlfriend. That would explain his refusal to attend the parties she was invited to. As she watched him chatting to a second-year girl at the coffee machine, Karen was pleased to find that she didn't really care. Perhaps Pam was right and David wasn't using his chance at university to best advantage. But that was his business. She had more than enough to do without worrying about a boyfriend. So far, all her romances had been disastrous – and nowhere near as exciting as college life was proving to be.

Karen gathered up her papers, stuck them in her bag and slipped quietly out of the common room.

Even pressing the clutch pedal made Pat's leg ache. They'd been fetching and carrying all day. The easiest job had been moving rolls of wire netting from a DIY store to the back garden of an intense young man who was building a huge pen for keeping foreign birds. But the other jobs had got progressively heavier. First a washing machine, then a washing machine and freezer and, finally, a gigantic, mahogany chiffonier which unfortunately had to be lugged up to the first floor of a big house in Aigburth.

'Talk about portering, I thought that was hard labour till we started this,' Pat said. He glanced at Terry. He was counting a handful of notes and coins. 'How much?'

'Hang on....'

'I've put ten quid's worth of juice in already. You want to have a look at the engine. We can't have done in a tenner's worth.'

'Thirty-four quid!' Terry announced triumphantly, and stuffed the cash into a tobacco tin and put it under the van's floor mat.

Pat turned off the main road towards Brookside. 'Thirty-four quid, minus ten for juice, minus two bacon butties at 60p each, minus two pints of bitter at 72p, minus two cups of tea at 20p, equals ...'

'Twenty-one pounds, ninety-six pence,' said Terry, pleased.

'Equals ten pound, ninety-eight poxy pence, each,' said Pat. 'Blimey, is that all? I feel like I've moved half of Merseyside. If we'd been bricklaying or something, with the energy we've used we'd have been rolling in it!'

'What're you moaning for?' said Terry. 'It's better than yesterday. I'm gonna put an advert in the paper this week. That'll get the work.'

Pat pulled up outside the house. 'Mind you, mate, at least we've got the dole.'

'Just shut up about that,' said Terry. His dad had once been done for working while he was signing on. And they were much hotter on it these days. He didn't want to end up in court – or worse.

Pat jumped down from the van. 'If we weren't signing on we wouldn't survive, would we?'

But Terry had noticed a tall, grey-haired man loitering at the bottom of Heather's front path. 'Eh, eh! Keep your voice down, will you?' He looked at Pat and nodded towards the man, 'I don't like the look of him.'

Pat pulled a face. 'Gerroff, he's no dole snooper!'

'Keep it down!' Terry said. He lowered his voice to a hiss. 'How do you know what they look like?'

But Pat was already moving over to the man. 'Hiya, mate. You look lost. Anything I can do?'

Terry cringed. Thank God he hadn't got their names stuck up on the side of the van yet. That would be a real give-away. He opened the passenger door of the van and retrieved the tin of takings, pushing it up the elasticated sleeve of his bomber jacket. He wondered whether Social Security spies had the power to search. He sidled suspiciously over to Pat and the stranger.

'Nah, haven't seen her since first thing,' Pat was saying. 'But she does come home late a lot. Sorry, mate.'

Terry caught Pat's eye and nodded towards the stranger. 'He's not, you know . . .?'

'He's Tom Curzon's dad. He thought he might be here.'

Terry breathed a sigh of relief. 'Sorry, I haven't seen him for a few days. That's a smart car he's got, that Quattro.'

But Jim Curzon was distracted. Tom never let him down when he'd promised him a game of bowls. Hadn't he been on the phone just before dinner time to confirm the date? Jim had waited over an hour at the pub before phoning Curzon Communication's office in town. A receptionist said Tom had been called away.

Terry had just offered to let Jim use their telephone when Heather turned her car into the Close. Jim moved quickly along the pavement towards her, almost stepping in the path of the car. Terry and Pat exchanged mystified glances and went inside. Heather parked and got out, fishing in her bag for the door key.

'This is a surprise. I thought you and Tom were playing bowls. I was just going to get changed and nip down to join you.' She unlocked the door, moving to the burglar alarm, a legacy of her ex-husband Roger's security consciousness.

Jim was right behind her. 'I thought we were playing too. He rang to say he'd be there definite this morning.'

Heather had moved through into the kitchen and put the kettle on to boil. She really would have to have a word with Tom about this. She knew the regular bowls games were very important to Jim. It was so irritating the way he went through life these days just breaking appointments willy-nilly. He might pride himself on being a successful company chairman, but he had well-paid staff to whom he could delegate work. There was no need to rush off every five minutes, no need at all.

'I'm afraid he's done this to me once or twice lately,' Heather said, moving back to the living room.

'Well he's never done it to me,' Jim said, sourly. 'I don't mind missing if he lets me know, but ... I could have invited Archie. It could've been embarrassing.'

Jim sat down. 'If I know him he'll be sat in the works buggering about with some computer thingymagig or other. . . .'

Heather smiled. She could see a little of Tom in him. The way he moved, some of his mannerisms. She regretted that Tom had been living a lie with his father for seventeen years and she – just a girlfriend – knew something he had never ever told Jim. Tom could never tell him now. It had been enough of a shock to Heather, as until one afternoon in the summer, Tom had never mentioned his daughter Rowena. Heather had called at

Curzon Communications 'on spec' to see Tom. As she drew up outside, Tom had come down the steps arm in arm with an attractive young girl. Heather's heart had skipped a beat. After a weekend in Portugal during which she had slept with Tom, her first sexual activity since the day she booted Roger out, she felt committed to the relationship. To see him with another woman, or so it seemed, within a few days was shattering. She'd sat in the car and waited for them to go.

It took twenty-four hours before she could bring herself to ask him. At first he'd laughed, then, seriously, had told her about his illegitimate daughter Rowena, the product of a casual affair when he was only a lad. She now lived with her mother in Colwyn Bay, but they saw each other infrequently. Tom, however, supported Rowena and her mother, Janet, financially. On the day Heather had seen them arm in arm, Rowena had been visiting her father to mark her seventeenth birthday. When Janet had become pregnant, Tom had hidden the whole affair from his father. At the time he was working hard and he felt that he might have been forced into an unsuitable marriage, or accused by his father of throwing away all he had worked to achieve.

Heather looked at Jim. If only Tom had told his father all those years ago. Jim was a decent man. Heather felt sure he would have coped with his son's accidental fatherhood. Better to have faced the trouble at the time than have to live a lie.

Jim's insistent question brought her back from her thoughts. 'He definitely didn't mention anything to you, love?'

Heather shook her head. 'No, Jim, he didn't.' Then she had an idea. She switched on the ansaphone, installed in her house mainly for Tom's convenience. 'He leaves messages for me on this. He might have phoned.'

She moved towards the kitchen. 'Tea or coffee?'

'Oh, tea, please, love.'

Before she reached the kettle and tea bags, Tom's voice

crackled into the air from the answering machine. He said he was phoning from Colwyn Bay. He was sorry, but Rowena had been rushed to hospital with appendicitis. As her mother was away, he had no option but to go there immediately.

Heather listened with a sort of paralysed fascination. Then she reacted. Dropping a cup on the kitchen floor, where it shattered, she raced into the living room and hit the ansaphone's off button.

Jim whipped round and stared at her. Heather was stunned. She could feel the heat moving to her face.

That damned answering machine. What could she say? Why should she have to? This was all Tom's problem. Not hers.

Damon Grant and Rod Corkhill were practically the same age. They had both grown up on the estate. They both liked football. But there the similarities ended – for Rod was an Evertonian and Damon, by long tribal tradition, was a fan of Liverpool F.C.

Walking down towards Brookside from the main road, the two lads flung insult after insult at each other's heroes. Each tried to outdo the other with obscure facts and figures dredged up from boxfuls of match programmes and a fanatical readership of the sports pages. The argument, of course, was futile. For years Liverpudlians have argued the merits of the two teams. Nobody ever wins. Each season brings new arguments and never any solutions. Damon and Rod were no exception.

When they reached the Close, Damon had worked himself up into enough of a pitch to accuse Rod of being a new Evertonian. Rod was furious. He'd been an Evertonian since he was a kid, his uncle Jimmy had started taking him to matches before he was ten. He bet Damon he'd never started at matches that young. Damon had to concede he hadn't.

'So don't say I've just started following them, all right?' Rod said, pointing an accusing finger.

'Well I'd like to see how many fans there are next season!' Damon retorted. And he'd sauntered across the Close chanting. 'Man United ... Man United ...,' a taunt about Everton's F.A. defeat.

'Piss off!' Rod shouted after him.

But Damon merely grinned over his shoulder and chanted it again ... 'Man United, Man United ...'

Rod opened the door and went inside, immediately to be confronted by Doreen.

'What did you say?' She was right up against him, her index finger jammed into his throat.

Rod stepped back in surprise. 'What?'

'You heard! What did you just say out there?'

'Nothing!' He moved sideways, out of Doreen's way. But she followed him. 'I know what you said and I'm not having it! Right!'

But Rod insisted he didn't know what Doreen was talking about.

Then Tracy butted in. She was sitting at the kitchen table reading, a paperback copy of *The Far Pavilions*. 'I heard you,' she said.

'The whole flamin' street probably heard him!' Doreen peeped out of the front window, as if looking for a mob of protesting neighbours.

'Creep!' Rod snarled at Tracy.

Doreen waved a finger at her son. 'If I hear anything like that again there'll be trouble. I mean it! We've not been here that long and I don't want us getting a bad name!'

Rod slumped on to the settee, ignoring his mother. She seemed to be obsessed with what the neighbours thought since they'd moved to the Close.

Doreen turned her attention to Tracy. 'And that goes for you too, madam. Do you hear?'

Tracy stuck her head back in her book. Rod looked at her and she looked up for a moment. A look passed between them. Tracy's face coloured slightly. Immediately, she got up and went upstairs.

*

Jim Curzon walked out of the Close carrying his 'woods' in a leather bowling bag. He was upset about missing a night's bowling with his son, but, he supposed, that was one of the penalties of being father to such a successful businessman. Still, it was a nuisance. And why on earth did he have to go to North Wales just because some secretary was ill? At one time he thought Tom was soft, too soft to make it in business. He'd been proved wrong on that, but he still thought there was a soft streak in him. He couldn't run round after ex-staff for evermore. It was a ridiculous notion for a man in Tom's position. And he still didn't know when Tom would be back in Liverpool. He tutted to himself and walked towards the main road.

From the living room window of her house, Heather watched until Jim walked out of sight. She felt a great sense of sadness on his behalf. He obviously worshipped Tom. How much more he might have worshipped a pretty granddaughter like Rowena. But Tom's refusal to face the music all those years ago, it seemed, had robbed him forever of seventeen years of observing a child grow into an adult.

Jim disappeared from view and Heather moved to the settee. She sat down, suddenly hating herself for being forced into lying to Jim, a man who obviously liked her a great deal. That single fact made the lies so hard to bear.

Immediately, she had switched off the ansaphone, airily stating that the mystery was solved and they now knew where Tom had got to, Jim had logically pointed out that the message had not been finished. They still didn't know when he was coming back.

Jim had attempted to switch the device on again, but Heather had stopped him. She coyly explained that Tom was in the habit of making more intimate remarks at the end of his recorded messages to her.

Jim had been a little embarrassed. Then he'd offered to go upstairs, or something. He felt he was intruding and said so, but Heather then started to waffle about him

53

always being welcome. She disappeared to the kitchen and quickly made the tea, only to return to all manner of questions on the subject of this person Rowena.

Heather, thinking on her feet, had eventually persuaded him that Rowena was an ex-secretary of Tom's. Jim, of course, thought it odd that Tom should chase across to North Wales because of an ex-employee's illness, but Heather magnanimously complimented Tom on his concern for others. Eventually, she thought, she had got Jim off the subject. She was thankful when he finished his tea and decided to go home, refusing a lift.

Sitting alone, she felt drained. Skipping his dates with her was one thing, but forcing her to live his lies too... Whenever she wanted to talk to Tom he was never there. If it had been anyone else she would have ended the relationship from that moment. But it was Tom...

Damon was sitting on his bedroom floor rooting through a cardboard box full of soccer magazines. Beside him were scissors and a roll of sticky tape. When he'd gone upstairs after tea and glanced out of the window, he'd seen Rod Corkhill at the smaller front bedroom window across the Close. He had sellotaped an Everton poster on to the window pane. Rod had caught sight of Damon glaring and he responded with an 'under the arm' gesture of scorn for Damon – and more precisely his team. Damon had set to immediately. After ten minutes he had found the pictures and folded posters he needed. Carefully, he sellotaped them to his window and went downstairs grinning to himself.

'What are you grinning at?' Sheila said. She was changing Claire into her one-piece night suit.

'Who me?'

'No, the feller behind you,' Sheila said. 'You look like that cat that ate the canary.'

'I can be happy if I want, can't I?' he replied. Then he went to the television and switched it on.

'Is work going all right?' Sheila asked.

'Yeah, great.'

'You still like it?'

'It's sound, Mum.'

She ruffled his hair as she passed with Claire. 'I'm glad about that love,' she said.

Just then, the lock turned in the front door and Bobby came in, home from work. 'All right, love, all right son.' He went straight to the baby and kissed her. 'Just in time, eh? Come here you little devil.'

Claire smiled as Bobby took her from Sheila's arms and jiggled her up and down. 'Eh, Bob, she's just had a drink, you'll have her sick.'

But Bobby wasn't listening. In a babyish voice, he said, 'Who's glad to see her dad, then? I'll take her up if you like, love,' he added. He went up the stairs with Claire, continuing to talk nonsensical baby talk. Sheila fondly watched them go.

Damon turned in his seat. 'Was he like that with us lot?' he asked his mother.

Sheila laughed. ' 'Course he was.'

'The times he's belted me round the head. I'd never have guessed it.'

'Maybe he'll have to belt her round the head, eh?' she said, 'You never know. . . .'

Damon grinned. 'He probably hasn't got the strength left. After me and our Barry!'

As Sheila took Bobby's tea from the oven she thought about Barry. He rarely sent a letter, but sometimes he phoned. She hadn't heard a word from him in three months. She hoped he was all right. She didn't even know where he was working.

Nearly a hundred miles away, Barry Grant pulled up outside a run-down three-storey house in a run-down part of the midland city of Wolverhampton and pulled the handbrake on the firm's van. On the passenger seat beside him were two card boxes of Kentucky Fried Chicken. It said 'finger lickin' good' on the box, but Barry didn't

55

have much of an appetite and he knew the girl inside his flat certainly wouldn't. He didn't know why he bothered to buy her some chicken and chips, but he had to do something.

He looked up at the bare bulb visible at the second-floor window. He didn't even know if Jane would be there or not. People like her only seemed to warm up, if that was the word, after dark. As for himself he was tired after a day's work with Harper's Shopfitting Services (Liverpool) Limited. All he needed was some scran and a good kip.

As a precaution based on four months' experience he took out his wallet which contained the last three tenners from the previous week's wages and dragged his metal tool box from behind the seat. He counted the money and locked it inside the tool box. Then pushed the tool box key into a split in the side of the driver's seat. Content with his security arrangements, he got out of the van, locked it, and sprinted up the stairs to his shabby flat. Deep down he hoped Jane wasn't there.

Chapter Five

'Do you think I'm made of money?!'

Crumbs of cake sprayed from Billy Corkhill's mouth. Doreen poured him another cup of tea while Tracy sat expectantly beside her father. Perhaps she should have gone to bed and let her mother ask the vital question.

Tracy had been hinting now for several weeks about the proposed school skiing trip to Switzerland. She'd never been abroad before and most of her school mates had talked their parents into allowing them to go. But more importantly, Peter was going. The thought of them being together in a place as romantic as that ... She had to win over her dad.

But whatever she put forward to push her case was

either treated with sarcasm or ignored. Most of his comments on recent expenditure – like the new fireplace, the decorating, curtains and everything else – were directed at Doreen.

'For God's sake you can do some foreigners,' Doreen said. 'That feller that phoned up last night. He wants a rewiring job, doesn't he?'

'I'm too pushed at the moment,' Billy replied. 'I'm up to me neck in it!'

'Doing what?' Doreen demanded.

'All this bloody decorating. I've still got to sort out upstairs. You've paid out for the gear. I can't let it waste. I'll have to do it!' Tracy felt helpless. She hadn't really considered the costs involved in the family moving to Brookside. She played her trump card. 'If I take me name off the list I'll feel ashamed,' she said. 'You don't want that, do you, Dad?'

'Hard luck!' Billy said. Tracy's face fell. There was a silence. Then Doreen sat down opposite her husband.

'She's going.'

Billy was taken aback. It wasn't often Doreen laid down the law. He tried to protest and ran through the list of expenses again. 'I'm still waiting on that solicitor's bill an' all. Christ knows what that's gonna be. That could be over a hundred. Could be two hundred, easy!'

But Doreen was insistent. 'How much is it, love?' she asked Tracy.

Tracy hesitated. 'A hundred and fifty.'

Billy exploded. 'A hundred and fifty? That's more than a week's wages!'

'It's reasonable,' Doreen said, flatly. 'When the boss's son went to Italy it was something like two hundred and odd –'

'It doesn't matter to the likes of them. Flamin' dentists get a bomb. And I'm not a flamin' dentist!'

'But Italy's further than Switzerland!'

'I don't care if it's the other side of the moon, or this side of the outside bog, she's not going!'

Tracy could feel the tears coming. School holidays were terrible, not being able to see him every day. She couldn't stand Christmas stuck at home, knowing he was over there in the Alps. Her mates seeing him, spending time with him and not her.

Billy was still ranting about money and the bills he had to cover when Doreen silenced him by banging her hand on the table.

'I don't care if I have to borrow the money, Billy. I want her to go. I know we've moved into a new place, but I'm not having anyone talking about me saying we're depriving the kids just 'cause we're got a mortgage and our own house....'

Billy sighed. Here we go again, he thought, the airs and graces just because they now had their own house.

But Doreen continued, 'I don't want people pointing at me.' She turned to Tracy, 'You can go, love....'

Billy opened his mouth, about to protest, but Doreen stopped him, 'She's going and that's that!'

'Can I, Dad?' Tracy waited for another explosion, but none came.

'I'll think about it,' Billy said quietly, the thought of the cost horrifying him.

Tracy seemed no further forward. The tears began to come. She left the room quickly, ran upstairs and sat on her bed, letting them come. Moments later she was joined by Doreen.

'Don't be getting upset,' she said. Tracy and Rod had both been refused expensive school holidays in the past without any tears or bitterness. Doreen supposed it must be something akin to keeping up with fashion, musical tastes and all the rest of it. Tracy didn't often cry.

Later, when Billy climbed into bed, he met a wife determined to use all her powers of persuasion. But before she could start using them, Billy held her at arms length.

'You're wasting your time, love....'

'Ar, Billy...' It looked like Billy really didn't want Tracy to join the holiday party.

'If it's important enough to make her cry like that, then she can go. We'll find the money. . . .'

Doreen hugged him. 'She'll be made up, love. . . .'

When they finally went to sleep, Billy had forgotten all about expense.

Unfortunately, he was to be reminded of the subject very soon. There was only one letter on the fibre mat behind the front door when he went down the following morning. It was from the solicitor's firm which had completed the sale of the house, enclosing a statement of their fees. With disbursements, land registry fees, not forgetting V.A.T., it amounted to £324.00.

As Billy started to tell Doreen, Tracy got up from the breakfast table and threw her arms round her father and kissed him. 'I won't ask for any more Dad. I'll pay everything else meself, honest.' She ran off to phone the news to her school friend, Paula. Billy showed the bill to Doreen.

'Oh, God,' she said quietly. 'I didn't think it'd be anywhere near this.'

Tracy was chattering away on the phone. Billy looked at her and then to Doreen. 'She can't go after this.'

'Billy, you promised!'

There was nothing he could say. He had promised. He'd have to take every foreigner he could lay his hands on from now until Christmas. And he hoped to God there'd be some good news about overtime. Doreen put her coat on, ready for work. 'Oh, love. Don't forget you've got to pick up the shutters, will you?' Billy looked blank. 'They're at Thompsons Do-it-Yourself. You said you'd pick them up for us. . . .'

'Christ, can't we cancel them? Tell them we don't want them now?'

'I can't can I? Not now. I've paid for them.'

Billy groaned. He remembered the good old days when he only had to find the rent. And if anything needed fixing on the house you only needed one phone call and a bit of patience. Solicitor's bills, skiing in Switzerland, flaming fancy shutters. Why had he bought this bloody place?

Chapter Six

'That's marvellous! I'm really pleased!' Peter Montague wanted to kiss Tracy. But at morning break, even in an empty classroom at the far end of the Language Lab corridor, that was out of the question.

Tracy had been bursting to tell him the good news all morning. He had been asking her every day for the past few weeks. Would she be able to persuade her parents to let her go? Now she had and she was full of it. 'It's gonna be great, really great,' she was saying. 'We won't be stuck with them all the time, though, will we? I mean, we can have some time on our own?'

'Of course we can. You'll love Switzerland. I haven't been for years, but it really is beautiful.'

She smiled at him. That smile. The smile that had started it all off between them. But he had a more serious matter to discuss now. He lowered his voice, perhaps a subconscious gesture in view of what they now had to discuss.

'What did you say about the money?'

'A hundred and fifty pounds,' Tracy said. 'That's right, isn't it?'

Montague nodded. 'Yes.'

'My mum said she thought it was reasonable.'

It was, Montague thought, considering the true cost was £275. 'You didn't show them the letter, did you?'

'Not the first bit, no. Just the notes about the place and that.' She hesitated. 'You will be able to ... to do what you said?'

'Yes. Yes, it's no problem,' said Montague. With the skiing gear she needed and paying almost half of the cost of Tracy's holiday it was going to add up. But she was worth it. He was grateful his ticket was free, an inducement by the travel operator to get teachers to organize school trips.

'I said I'd pay everything else myself,' Tracy said, 'from the job and pocket money and that.... But I couldn't really, not without you....'

'There's nothing to worry about,' said Peter Montague, 'okay?'

She nodded and rewarded him with another smile. The bell for next period rang. Tracy moved to him quickly and kissed him. Montague's smile vanished instantly. He had to restrain himself from pushing her roughly away. 'Don't Tracy, please. Not here.'

'Sorry,' she said. 'I'd better go.'

Sometimes she couldn't help herself. She wanted to kiss him. Just because he was a teacher and she was only fifteen. For the thousandth time she wished she was older. Even sixteen.

Julia Brogan was delighted with Brookside Close. The houses looked so neat and tidy and she thought the woods were wonderful. Everyone had such spacious gardens, too. Doreen had done well to find such a decent place. Compared with the estate less than a mile away, it was a different world.

She'd been disappointed to find nobody at home. She knew Doreen only worked three days a week, but she'd changed just recently and Julia had forgotten to ask her daughter which days she was now working. No matter, though, thought Julia, they won't mind if I look through the windows and have a nose round the back garden.

The Close was remarkably quiet. She could settle in a place like that and it wasn't too far away from Mrs Kerfoot and the other neighbours on the estate she'd known for years. She walked round the front and started to wander along the pavement. Julia always said what she thought and she had no embarrassment either about looking through people's windows.

She peeped into Heather's living room, then into the Collins' front room. As she squinted to see a picture on the wall over Paul and Annabelle Collins' fireplace, she was disturbed by a creaking sound from the bungalow in the corner.

Ralph Hardwick was pushing a sheet metal wheelbarrow containing a fork and spade round the side of the bungalow. He stopped it on the front grass and started to attack the flower border, which, after months of neglect, had sprouted clumps of couch grass.

Julia had only a small garden at her corpy house, but over the years she had spent a lot of time on it. She always read the gardening column in the Sunday papers, and considered herself a cut above the rest when it came to horticultural knowledge. The appearance of Ralph in his wellies and cap gave her the perfect opportunity to speak to a kindred spirit.

'Bulbs?' Julia asked.

Ralph jumped slightly. He'd never heard her approach. 'Eh?'

'New bulbs,' Julia explained. She wondered if he was a gardener, a hired gardener, that is. You never knew, perhaps the people round here actually employed gardeners.

'Well I was thinking of putting some in. A few daffs instead of all these crocuses we've got. He –' he nodded to the bungalow, 'he likes daffs.'

'You're asking for trouble, if you ask me,' Julia said, wondering again if Ralph really was a professional. She nodded at the freshly turned soil. 'It was the first frost last night. They should be in way before the frost. You could end up with nothing, like.'

Ralph hadn't been out of bed early enough to see any frost, but he wasn't going to admit that. 'I missed the forecast last night. Was it?'

'You're risking it, I'm telling you. I lost three dozen crocus one year all because I didn't know about the frost.'

And so the conversation continued. She could certainly talk, Ralph decided, but a bit of female company was enjoyable and he didn't complain. In fact, they soon got laughing and joking and Julia was full of the fact that her Doreen and Billy had moved into Brookside.

'Oh, the new family?' Ralph said. 'I haven't seen that much of them yet.'

Julia was only too glad to fill in the details. Their Doreen had to get married, she confided. Billy wasn't her perfect choice as a son-in-law, but . . . well, he hadn't done too bad. He'd bought Doreen a nice place. What more could a woman ask? At least he was a cut above the rest of his family. Ralph leaned on his spade fascinated as Julia gave him a run down on Billy's brother Jimmy and their now dead elder brother, Frankie. Billy might have kept his nose clean, but Jimmy, the youngest, was still a tearaway. And one for the women. He had brought one round to Julia's house looking for Billy the other week, she couldn't have been more than eighteen.

Ralph was fascinated to hear about Frankie Corkhill. Julia didn't spare him any of the grisly details about the night in a club off Duke Street when Frankie and his brothers had gone looking for whoever had attacked young Jimmy in the same club a week earlier. Someone had tipped the wink to Joey Jenkins and he was waiting as the Corkhills and their mates walked into The Zanzibar. Frankie had copped the worst of the action and when they got him to Walton he didn't have enough blood left to take his blood pressure.

'It was a waste all right,' Julia said. 'But he'd have been a real bad'un if he'd got any older. At least it put our Billy on the right track, seeing all that.'

Ralph was just about to ask a few more questions when Doreen turned the corner into the Close. 'Here's your daughter now,' Ralph said.

Julia turned, 'Cooee, Rene . . . I'm over here, love.' She turned back to Ralph. 'That Joey Jenkins is still in, I think. He got life for it. . . .'

Doreen overheard her mother's last few words as she arrived at the Crosses' front garden. She nodded to Ralph, then grabbed her mother's arm. 'Come and have a look at the house, mam,' she said, insistently.

'I'm just talking to Ralph, love,' she said.

But Doreen was insistent. Julia followed her, delaying long enough to call over her shoulder, 'Remember what I said about them bulbs now, eh?'

'All right, Julia,' Ralph said.

Doreen winced at their familiarity. When she got Julia out of earshot, she let rip. 'I heard what you were saying. We move to a decent place and you're telling everyone about what happened years ago. I'm not having it. Do you hear?'

'It wasn't everyone, love, just Ralph.'

'How long do you think he's gonna keep juicy stuff like that to himself, eh? And Ralph? We've been here weeks and I don't even know his bloody name!' She hauled Julia inside, continuing her lecture on keeping Billy Corkhill's family background to herself.

'This isn't much of a welcome, is it?' Julia moaned.

'Any more of that and it'll be the last time you're welcome here,' Doreen snapped back.

Across the Close Ralph waited till the Corkhills' front door slammed. He could do with a cup of tea. He jammed his spade in the flower border and went inside. He couldn't wait to tell Harry about the Corkhills.

Tom Curzon drove up from Colwyn Bay that morning and met Heather at Hamilton Devereux's Liverpool office. 'You haven't arranged to go out with Joyce, or anything?' he asked.

Heather was cool towards him. 'No,' she said.

'Then how about lunch with me?' As usual, he took it for granted Heather would join him, for as soon as she'd accepted, he revealed that he'd booked a table at Jenny's, off Fenwick Street, just half an hour ago.

Heather was quiet in the car on the way to the restaurant. She let Tom go on about the details of Rowena's appendicitis. She had gone to the operating theatre at seven o'clock the night before. The operation had been successful, but it had given Rowena a nasty shock. Apparently, she'd collapsed with severe stomach pains during lunch at her private school on the North Wales coast.

Tom had ordered before he apologized about his absence. 'I'm not concerned about me. How about your father?' Heather replied.

'I left him a message at the pub,' he protested.

'Then he didn't get it,' Heather replied. 'He was at my house when I came home.' Then she told him about the slip up with the ansaphone. Tom's face drained.

Then he bombarded her with questions. Why hadn't she switched off the machine? What did he hear? Did she think he realized? Did he hear Rowena's name?

Heather's replies were terse. Tom realized she was very upset at being obliged to lie to Jim. 'The times I've wished I could return in time, or something,' he said, seeking her understanding. 'But there's nothing I can do. I can't tell me dad.'

'Neither can I. I have to live a lie too.' Heather's voice cracked a little, 'I wish I'd never seen Rowena that day.'

'You wouldn't let that drop,' Tom reminded her. 'You had to know who she was.'

Tom was right, but it was an awful secret to have to share. Tom pressed home the point. 'It was a long time ago, Heather. We have to live with it now. I know I made a mistake not telling them, but at the time I couldn't help it.'

For a moment she pondered on how long Jim Curzon might live. How long such a secret might have to be kept. Tom squeezed her hand and slowly she returned the pressure.

'Will you pick us up from work, love?' Doreen asked.

'Eh?' said Billy. He was reading the sports page of *The Sun*, but his eye had been drawn to an ad in the bottom corner for a loans company. The gist of it was that you could borrow to pay off all your financial commitments and just make one payment a month to the loans outfit. It sounded a good idea. He looked at the repayment table. Fifty quid a month for all that, he thought, sounds okay. Then he looked again. It was fifty quid a week – or two hundred quid a month. He was wondering how many mugs fell for it, when Doreen repeated her question.

'Sorry. What?' he said, putting the paper aside.
'Will you pick us up from work?' she repeated.
'All right.'
'Can you put the shutters up?'

Billy groaned. He was on nights, but although he'd just switched, he still wanted an easy day.

'It's not gonna take that long, is it?'
'I haven't got the screws and stuff. An' I'll need a new bit for the drill.'
'You can get them this morning can't you?'

He had to put up the new shutters or there'd be no peace. 'All right,' he said. 'I'll get them this morning before I collect you.'

She kissed him and went out.

Later, when Doreen came out of the dental surgery she found Billy rooting in the tool box he kept in the boot of the Renault. 'What are you looking for?'

'I'll have to take the by-pass off your mam's meter.'
'Is it still there?'
'It'll only take five minutes.'
'Never mind that, he was at our house yesterday. He'll be doing hers today. Jesus, Billy, what did you leave it for?'
'Stop panicking, will you? There's thousands of houses between us and her.'

They got into the car. Billy continued, 'I think I'll put it on ours. We could do with making some savings.'

'What!' Doreen was horrified. Billy looked at her. She'd never objected before. 'We can't go doing that! Not where we are now!'

'Why not?'

'Because we've left all that behind.'

'What behind?' he asked.

'All that kind of thing. . . . You know what I mean. . . .'

Airs and graces again, Billy thought. If ever they did need to fiddle the electric meter it was now. If only he could by-pass the rates and the mortgage and that bloody skiing holiday.

He turned the car into the road where Julia lived. As he pulled up Julia's front door was open. 'Don't tell me,' said Doreen. 'She's got Mrs Kerfoot round again.'

They got out of the car and Billy went to the boot to fetch pliers and screwdriver. As Doreen went through the gate, an electricity board official came out of the house, tucking a clip board under his arm. Julia appeared behind him.

'I'm only a widow,' she said in a pathetic voice. 'You could put a word in for me, couldn't you?'

The electricity board official stopped. 'That's something for the court, madam. All I do is report the offence.' He stalked to his car passing an open-mouthed Doreen. Billy, quicker on the uptake, was hurriedly putting his tools back in the boot.

Doreen ran up the path. 'Mam, what's happened?'

Billy was dawdling up the path, watching the electricity board man out of sight.

'I'm only being reported for fiddling the meter, aren't I?' Julia said. Then she turned her anger on Billy. 'I'll bloody kill you Billy Corkhill! What did you leave it on for, eh?!'

'I was just coming to take it off. I didn't know –'

But Julia butted in, 'I said you and your family were no good. I said they'd give us a bad name. Now look what's happened!'

'Get her in, for Christ's sake,' Billy said to Doreen. And Julia was pushed inside, half-angry, half-sobbing.

'I can't pay a fine. How am I gonna pay a fine? Eh?'

Doreen turned to Billy, 'Look at the state of her! Why the hell didn't you take it off?!'

'I told you, I forgot.' This was all he needed. 'Look, Julia,' he said, 'they're not gonna do someone your age. I mean it's not like it used to be.' He was thinking frantically. He had to find an excuse for a pensioner being found by-passing the meter.

Julia sobbed. Her sobs were mixed with allegations about the criminal pedigree of the Corkhill family and her concern for her good name. Doreen tried to comfort her, but her eyes were accusingly on Billy.

'Look,' Billy said, 'you'll have to tell them you didn't do it. Say a feller came knocking at the door and said he could save your 'lecky bills if you gave him ten quid.'

'I can't tell them that! I'm not a liar!' Julia protested.

'You'll have to,' Billy said. 'Tell them ... tell them you thought it was all okay.'

Gradually, Julia calmed down. She was becoming more confident that her age would mean her escape from prosecution, especially if it was backed up by the story about the kind man who knocked on the door offering fuel-saving advice.

Billy was full of guilt. After the umpteenth rebuke from Julia for landing her in this mess Billy said, 'Look, Julia, if it comes to the worst and you get a fine, we'll pay it.'

'It's the least we can do, Mam,' added Doreen, giving Billy a dirty look.

'Daddy! Daddy!'

Six-year-old Rebecca and her little sister, Emily, three, squealed with delight as they saw their father clear Customs at Liverpool Airport and walk into the Arrivals hall. They hurled themselves at his legs, each clamouring to be kissed and picked up first. His wife Penny crossed the polished floor towards James. On her face was a huge smile. She kissed him. 'I'm glad you're home, love,' she said quietly.

'So am I,' James replied. Already reality was seeping back into his life. Just seeing his children, dressed in pyjamas and outdoor coats because it was way past their bedtimes, made him realize where he really belonged. He collected his case and the Fleming family walked out of the Terminal building to where Penny had parked the car. The children bombarded him with questions about his flight and was he staying home for good now. But they were soon silenced by Penny. 'Daddy's tired now. Ask him tomorrow.'

As Penny drove towards the suburbs, James sat back in the passenger seat. He was tired – and emotionally drained. Hours before, he and Lucy had slept together for the last time in his hotel room at Fontainebleau. Her passion had frightened him. He'd spent the past three days gently trying to disentangle himself from the affair, desperately talking Lucy through her constant crying jags. That afternoon, all he had accomplished was lost. Lucy was swearing her undying love for him. Hopelessly, he had held her head to his shoulder. He hated the thought of her crying after he'd caught his flight. He now realized it was an infatuation and mainly a physical one. He had tried to get her to think of the affair in the same terms, but it was not to be so.

'If I come back to Liverpool will you still want me?' she said.

James hadn't considered the possibility. He paused before answering. 'Of course I will,' he said, knowing from an earlier conversation that she had no plans to return home. She seemed to be comforted by his insincere talk, but their parting had been awful.

She wouldn't go into Paris and they'd said goodbye outside the hotel. Lucy's face streamed with tears. She'd clawed at him as he got into the taxi. All the way through the Paris suburbs he had felt sick with guilt. Only when the plane rushed down the runway and took off did he start to feel some relief.

Now, as the car moved northwards out of Liverpool, passing Aintree Racecourse and the headquarters of one of the big football pools firms, did he begin to feel more relaxed. The children were now dozing in the back seat. Penny turned to him and smiled. He smiled back. Consciously, he decided to put Lucy Collins completely out of his mind. He was home.

When Tom Curzon asked Heather if she fancied the idea of being Mrs Curzon, she was flabbergasted. Then Tom had started laughing. 'I only mean for an evening,' Tom said. He was meeting an American electronics man and his wife and wanted Heather to play the part of his wife for appearances.

'As long as it's only for one night,' she joked, and said she'd look forward to it. Unfortunately, it was not to be as Joyce ducked an evening appointment with one of H and D's clients and landed Heather with the job. Giving Tom a taste of his own medicine, she'd phoned his secretary and told her she'd have to let Tom down.

She was expecting a comeback in the form of a sarcastic remark from Tom when he called round, but he couldn't have been in a better mood. She noticed, also, that he was wearing a new suit.

'Planning something special?' she asked.

'Taking you out to dinner,' Tom said. But there was nothing unusual in that. A relationship with Tom seemed to revolve round lunch and dinner in a dozen or so of his favourite places. 'So get those jeans changed and put your party frock on.'

Heather guessed his game. She went to him accusingly. 'I know what you've done. You've rearranged things with Mr and Mrs Gersheimer, your American friends.'

Tom laughed. 'Cross me heart.'

'Oh, Tom,' she said, 'you'd better tell me the truth. I don't know what to wear. Where are we going?'

'The Millbrook, but I put the Gersheimers back on the plane for Los Angeles this morning, so they won't be there.'

The Millbrook? Heather was intrigued. It was Tom's place for special occasions. Heather wanted to know immediately why he had booked a table there.

'Wait and see...' he said, enjoying her curiosity.

'I won't wait and see....' She held his lapels. 'If you don't tell me why we're going to the Millbrook now I'll insist on wearing these jeans.' She poked him in the chest playfully. 'Just to embarrass you!'

Tom laughed. 'Come on, we'll be late.'

But Heather kept pressing him. Why the Millbrook?

'Okay, you win,' Tom said, sitting down on the settee. 'I like the food....'

Heather picked up a cushion and hit him across the face. 'I know you like the food. So do I. Now tell me!'

Tom gently took the cushion from her. 'I thought it was just the place to ask you to marry me....'

Heather couldn't speak for a moment. 'This isn't a joke?'

He shook his head. He hadn't planned it quite like this. The vintage champagne was already on ice at the restaurant.

'I'm still legally married to Roger....' Heather said.

'Not for much longer, surely?'

'No,' Heather said. Then, smiling, 'This isn't a joke at all, is it?'

'Nope.' He was grinning. 'This suit's too good to go kneeling down in, so I'll do it where I am....' He took her hand and pulled her down to sit beside him. His thumb stroked the back of her hand. He didn't look her in the eye. For once, the confident company chairman was a little out of his depth. 'Heather, will you marry me?' he said.

Heather laughed. Tom looked at her. 'I am being serious,' he said, without edge.

'I know,' she replied. 'And I'm being serious, too. There's a lot to discuss.'

'We can get through the arrangements inside a week, no problem,' Tom said.

'I didn't mean that. I mean, we only met in April and ... well, you've taken me by surprise.'

'Your fault, not mine. I was going to lead up to it

slowly.' He was more relaxed now. 'So are you going to say "yes"?'

'There's more to it than just saying "yes" Tom,' Heather said, 'I want to be sensible about things. I need to think – at least for a couple of weeks.'

'Two weeks?'

'If you want me for life, Tom, two weeks isn't long to wait, is it?'

He nodded. Then, 'I didn't plan it like this at all!'

They laughed. Heather said, 'Do you mind if we have an evening in? I mean, why waste your money on dinner for two? You've already asked . . .'

'Always the accountant, eh?' Tom chuckled. Then he pulled her to him and kissed her.

Next morning, Heather discovered that the first impediment to her marrying Tom Curzon had now disappeared. In a long, thin envelope came official confirmation that she had now been granted her decree absolute. Her divorce from Roger Huntingdon was complete.

She sat for a long time looking at the legal jargon. Just three years ago they had been so happy. He was working hard, hoping to be granted a partnership in the legal practice. She was busy studying for her accountancy examinations and spending her days at the small, rather old-fashioned firm of Hargreaves. She'd never noticed at first that his hours became longer and longer. She was too busy studying. Then came his mysterious absences at weekends and equally mysterious weekend business trips.

Into her mind came her memory of the day she caught him talking on the phone to that bitch Diane McAllister. For the first time in her life, she reacted violently. It was hearing the betrayal of Roger telling his so-called client that he loved her. Brimming with anger she had literally pushed Roger out on to the street. She had thrown his briefcase after him and told him it was over. Now it was over, not just emotionally, but legally.

She loved Tom Curzon, she was sure, but at one time

she had loved Roger, too. She had never anticipated his infidelity. There was never any sign of his wandering. Would Tom change if she married him?

It was later that day, when she invited Sheila Grant in for a coffee, that she voiced the same fears to her neighbour.

'From what I've seen of him – and what you've told me – he seems a decent kind of bloke,' Sheila said.

Heather agreed.

'But it's whether you're willing to spend the rest of your life washing his mucky socks, that's what matters.'

Heather laughed. At least with Tom she probably wouldn't have to do that. He'd hinted the night before that marriage would mean their moving into a large house which would mean employing a maid.

'It's work, too,' Heather explained to Sheila. 'I know Tom will expect me to be available. And I know he wants children. I've worked so hard to get to where I am . . . I don't know whether I want to give it up to be married.'

Sheila, herself conscious of the clash between domestic work and her own limited attempts at an outside life, was sympathetic. But, she pointed out, Tom was a wealthy man. Couldn't they employ a nanny if they were to have children?

'I suppose so,' Heather replied.

Claire was getting restless. Sheila had to leave. 'I'm sorry I can't help you,' she told Heather. 'But I understand how you feel. . . . Once bitten, twice shy. When do you have to tell him?'

'Two weeks,' said Heather.

'Perhaps you need a bit longer than that. . . .' Heather nodded, but she couldn't see Tom agreeing to it. He already thought two weeks an eternity. Sheila continued, 'I know they're in Ireland and that, but have you thought of having a word with your mum and dad?'

Heather hadn't told her mother about the proposal. Had she been totally sure she knew she would have telephoned immediately. When Sheila and Claire had gone, Heather picked up the telephone and dialled the hotel near Belfast managed by Mr and Mrs Haversham. She was going to suggest flying over that coming weekend, but when her mother heard the news, she insisted on coming to Liverpool.

While Heather felt worried, Mrs Haversham was bubbling with enthusiasm. Perhaps she should have made her decision alone. Heather said goodbye to her mother and tried to envisage life as Tom Curzon's wife.

Chapter Seven

'For heaven's sake, come away from that window,' Annabelle said. She had just come in from one of her regular jogging routes through the woodland which surrounded the Close. 'People will think you're the new Harold Cross.'

Paul moved away from the window. All week he had been looking out at the Corkhill's house. With the soccer posters and those dreadful, Spanish-style shutters, the house had become an eyesore, he thought.

'It's those damned shutters,' he said. 'They're totally out of step with every other house. I suppose their house on the council estate had little cartwheels bolted to the walls. . . .' 'I'm sure it must be against the rules, you know, the ground lease. If I remember rightly it prevents the addition of car ports, window boxes, anything like that.'

'Well if you're that concerned why don't you approach them?' Annabelle replied.

'Aren't you at all concerned?' Paul asked, 'I seem to remember your one-woman battles against at least two planning applications in Heswall. . . .'

'Of course I'm concerned. But it's no use just standing there grumbling. If you feel so strongly about it, tackle them.' She opened the door to the hallway. 'I'm going to get changed.'

Paul peered out at the football posters and the offending shutters. 'I might just do that,' he said aloud.

The passengers on the plane were mainly businessmen and Lucy Collins, dressed in her brown suede suit and boots, drew many appraising glances from the moment she cleared passport control at Charles De Gaulle Airport for her flight to Liverpool.

The past few days had been awful. She had done her best to appear as normal as possible, but inside she felt wretched and empty. Without James there seemed to be no purpose in anything. Over three days, one of them spent retracing walks they had enjoyed together, Lucy had come to the decision that the only way to have James for good was to give up her life in France. She had to be with him in Liverpool.

James had spoken little of his wife and daughters. But Lucy had noticed that he had never flown home to Merseyside for a single day during his four-month visit to Fontainebleau. Surely, if he loved Penny and the girls, he would have made some attempt to see them during such a long period away from home? She remembered too a light moment one evening when he'd joked about making her his secretary, so they could be together every day. Was it a joke, she wondered? Or did he, deep down, love her and want to be with her?

On the fourth day. Lucy telephoned the airport and packed her suitcase. She announced to Gordon and the Dubois that she wanted to go home for a while. The ever-kind Gerard assured her that she would always be welcome to return. They drove her to Paris to catch her plane and Monique suggested she ring Annabelle to arrange for her to collect Lucy on her arrival at Liverpool.

'Oh, no. Don't do that. I want it to be a surprise,' she smiled for the first time in days. Soon, she would see James again.

Throughout the flight, as she got nearer to Liverpool

and James, her spirits rose. She bubbled with excitement as she waited to pass through Customs and in the queue to use the telephones. James worked in the centre of Liverpool at an office not far from the Liver Buildings, where the two great mythical birds, the symbol of Liverpool, look out over the Mersey estuary.

'Can you put me through to Mr Fleming ... James Fleming?' she asked the switchboard operator at Holcroft International.

'Who's calling?'

'It's personal,' Lucy said.

A moment later, James was on the line. 'Hello?' His voice sounded suspicious.

'James. It's Lucy. I'm here ... in Liverpool.'

Paul was pleasantly surprised at Doreen Corkhill's attitude when he pointed out that the 'window decoration' was in contravention of the ground lease. She was very reasonable. 'I'll get my son to see to it,' she said, presuming Paul meant the soccer posters.

'That's very good of you,' Paul said, presuming she meant the window shutters. 'I hope you didn't mind me calling across.'

'Well, if you can't be told politely by a neighbour ...' Doreen said.

Paul smiled. 'Well, it might have been embarrassing if the builder's agent had called round in person.'

Doreen was quite impressed having a conversation with Paul. She believed he was an important business executive. She made a point of speaking as well as she could, smoothing off some of the rough edges of her usual Liverpudlian accent. She told Paul that as they'd actually bought the house surely they could do whatever they wanted with it. But Paul told her the pitfalls of going against the terms of the ground lease. 'Oh, don't worry,' Doreen said, 'we'll see to it as soon as we can.'

Paul gave her a final smile. 'Goodbye, then, Mrs Corkhill.'

Doreen watched as Paul walked back to his own house. Back on the estate, she mused, any complaint by a neighbour invariably ended up in a row or even a feud. Things were different in Brookside. People acted differently.

'Dad!'

Doreen was shaken out of her thoughts by the sight of the tall girl with curly brown hair, who was stepping out of a taxi. She was calling Paul Collins.

Paul turned and looked. 'Lucy!'

Lucy beamed at him. Paul hurried across to pick up her case. He paid off the cab driver. 'This is a surprise!'

Lucy kissed him on the cheek. 'That's what I planned – a surprise!'

'Your mother'll be delighted,' he said opening the door.

Along the Close, Rod and Tracy had appeared by their mother. 'Who's she?' said Rod, his eyes firmly on the back view of the leggy brunette.

'Mr Collins' daughter by the sound of it,' Doreen said.

Inside the house, Paul took Lucy's coat as she looked around the living room. Nothing had changed. Paul ventured, 'Everything is . . . well, there's nothing wrong is there?'

Annabelle came in from the garden. Her eyes lit up when she saw her daughter. 'Why didn't you phone?'

'It was a sort of spur of the moment decision,' Lucy said.

'There's nothing wrong is there?' Annabelle asked.

'Mum, Dad's just asked me that. Why should there be anything wrong? Things couldn't be better!'

One of their children had come home. Paul and Annabelle couldn't agree more.

'Why can't I?' Rod Corkhill asked again.

'Because I don't want anyone learning in my car, that's why? It's in a bad enough state already!'

For days, Rod had been pestering his father to teach

him to drive. Some of the other lads at school had already passed their driving test. At weekends they borrowed the family car to go out in. Often, Billy's car was parked outside all weekend and to Rod that was a waste. He dreamed of the convenience of being able to drive to away games, not to mention the fillip being able to drive would give to his attempts to pick up girls.

'Well book us some driving lessons then,' Rod said. 'I wouldn't go near yours till I'd passed me test.'

'They cost a bomb, lessons,' Tracy said.

'How much?' said Doreen.

'I've phoned up a few places. I can get a course for just under two hundred pounds.'

'You can forget that,' Billy said, stuffing chips into his mouth.

'It's too much, Rod,' said Doreen.

Rod was outraged. 'That's tight, that is. You don't mind spending more than that for her to lean skiing in Switzerland.'

'Yeah, but that's only a hundred and fifty quid.'

'Only, she says,' Billy observed, sarcastically.

'Who says it's only a hundred and fifty?' Rod said. 'I've seen the poster on the wall in school. With equipment and that it's nearly twice that much.'

Tracy was beginning to panic. She fought to stop herself going red.

Billy and Doreen were straight at her with questions. Was that true? Why didn't you tell us? What's going on? Billy was all for her getting back what had been paid in that week. But Doreen was more concerned with Tracy not being straightforward over the holiday and its cost. 'Why didn't you tell us? I mean, where are you going to find that sort of money?'

'I've got some savings. Then there's the job. I'll have it easy by Christmas, I've worked it all out.'

'Maybe you will, girl,' said Doreen, 'but why weren't we told?'

'I knew you were hard up. I knew you'd say no if I

gave you the proper price. I can pay the rest of it, honest.'

'I don't like you lying,' Doreen said, 'even if you thought it was for the best.'

'I wasn't lying,' Tracy replied. Again, her hopes of a holiday with Peter were in jeopardy. 'I'm sorry, Dad. You won't have to help with any more money. I'll earn it all and use all me savings....'

'You better had do,' Billy said. 'I mean it. It's cost me enough already.' Billy got up from the tea table and picked up his newspaper. Doreen started to clear away the dirty dishes.

Rod whispered to Tracy. 'Who says you've got the money? I've seen your Post Office book. There's sod all in it.'

'Mind yer own business,' Tracy said. 'I said I'd get it, didn't I?'

Doreen turned round. 'What are you two saying?'

'Nothing,' Tracy said.

'It's still not fair,' Rod grumbled. He looked at Tracy. She only earned about six quid every Saturday. She'd never find that much by Christmas.

Carol Thompson had heard a lot about Lucy Collins. While she cleaned and helped Annabelle with the catering business, Annabelle had often spoken about her and the kind of life she enjoyed with the Dubois family. So, when Carol let herself in at the Collins' house the following morning, she was surprised to find Lucy there. She recognized her immediately from the photographs Annabelle had brought back from the couple's recent holiday in France.

Carol always came in through the back door. She was very professional in her attitude to being a cleaner and never liked to intrude. As Lucy was on the phone, she didn't walk straight through to go upstairs and start on the bedrooms. She took her coat off and hovered in the kitchen.

Lucy was talking to someone called James. Carol tried to force herself not to listen, but it was impossible. Carol started to lift some dishes into the sink. Lucy became aware of her presence and curtailed the call.

'After work then?' she said. 'You can fix it?' Lucy lowered her voice. 'Perhaps we could go for a drive. . . . Bye. . . .'

Carol came into the living room. 'Hello.'

'Hello,' said Lucy. 'Can I help you? Oh, you must be Carol, I'm Lucy.'

'I recognized you from the photies, your mum showed me them,' Carol said. Then, 'I'm sorry I walked in when you were on the phone.'

'Just ringing a friend,' said Lucy.

'I'd better get on with things then,' Carol said.

Just then, Annabelle came in. As usual she'd been jogging. 'Oh, you two have met, have you? This is our long-lost daughter,' she said lightly. 'She gave Paul and me a big surprise by knocking on our door the other night. She seems to have fled from France on the spur of the moment.'

'Oh, really, Mother,' Lucy said. 'Why do you have to make it into a mystery?'

'It's all right, dear, just a joke,' Annabelle said. Then to Carol, 'It was a marvellous surprise. But she still won't give us any reason to why she should turn up out of the blue like that. . . .'

Carol smiled politely. Annabelle might have a better idea if she had overheard the conversation with a man called James.

When everyone had left the office that evening, James sat thinking. He had been shaken to receive Lucy's call from the airport. Thank God there had been nobody in the office at the time. Lucy had been insistent on a meeting and so he'd picked a pub near to the office but not frequented by his colleagues. Eventually, he telephoned Penny at home and told her something had cropped up, he'd probably be an hour or two late. There was nothing suspicious in that for the office was in the throes of an internal reorganization, out of which James hoped for a promotion. And Penny was as keen as he to get that promotion. He deserved it after France.

He thought of standing Lucy up, but decided against that course of action. He had to cool things down. He couldn't take any risks back in Liverpool and it was better to keep Lucy at arms length until he could end their affair.

He walked into the pub anxiously, quickly double checking that there were none of his acquaintances at the bar, or in any of the small cubicles into which the pub was divided. He found her at the far end of the pub. Her face lit up when she saw him and she stubbed out her cigarette and moved towards him. James panicked as she kissed him.

'Oh, James,' she said, and kissed him again.

He carefully extricated himself, looking over his shoulder to see if anyone had witnessed their embrace. He ushered her back to her seat and sat beside her. She couldn't keep her hands away from him. What he had found flattering in France now seemed embarrassing and fraught with risk. But despite these feelings, he couldn't help experiencing a longing for her. Impressions of those times in France flickered through his head. Lucy did excite him.

Later, they drove along the road through the sand dunes outside the city. They walked down to the sea. He kept trying to tell her they couldn't continue the relationship, but the words died before he could speak them.

Back in his car they made love. Neither of them had done that before. Something which either of them in different circumstances might have described as sordid was, in fact, exciting. Lucy was happy.

That night James lay awake, thinking over the events of the evening. Penny lay asleep beside him. He hated himself for it, but he was hooked. Perhaps he could handle the affair here at home in Merseyside. But his biggest problem concerned his promise to Lucy. He had let her talk him into offering to find her a job. In his company. If he was found out . . . But James preferred not to think about that risk. It was another hour before he fell asleep.

Paul wasn't in the habit of giving lifts to his neighbours. People like Harry Cross, for instance, would soon begin to take advantage. But he made an exception when he saw Doreen Corkhill struggling towards the Close with a carrier bag full of shopping.

Doreen admired the plush interior of Paul's car. It was a far cry from the scuffed and grubby interior of Billy's Renault. She wondered if it actually belonged to Paul, or if it was a company car. But she thought it prudent not to ask. Meanwhile, Paul asked polite questions on whether she liked living on the Close. Doreen, of course, made the point that she liked the neighbours.

Paul pulled up outside the Corkhills' and Doreen got out, thanking him profusely for the lift. She noticed that Rod had taken down the posters on her request and pointed the fact out to Paul.

Paul was horrified. No wonder she'd been so cooperative. She hadn't realized he meant the shutters. 'I meant those things, those awful shutters.'

'Awful?' Doreen said. 'Do you know how much they cost?'

'I don't and I'm not interested. They're in contravention of the ground lease and they'll have to be taken down.'

Doreen bristled. How dare he call her shutters awful! 'I don't care. They stay where they are! We paid good money for them and they look nice. It's just what I always wanted.'

'But the ground lease can't just be ignored,' Paul protested.

'Well I'm ignoring it,' Doreen said, firmly. 'It's our house and if we want shutters we'll have them!'

Paul spluttered. He didn't know what tack to pursue.

Doreen didn't give him a chance to continue. 'Mind your own business if you don't mind,' she said. And slammed shut the passenger door.

Paul watched as she strutted indignantly to her front door, then drove off, hoping none of the other neighbours had heard. Mind you, they'd probably be on the Corkhills' side. Why on earth did they stay here? Sometimes it was intolerable.

Inside, Billy was sitting at the kitchen table fiddling with a yellow plastic box.

'Do you know what that Collins feller's just said about the shutters?'

'What?' said Billy preoccupied.

'He said they're awful. He wants us to take them down!'

Billy looked up. 'What?'

'He says they're against the ground lease. Did the solicitor say anything about that?'

'Not that I know of. If I want shutters I'm having shutters. Did you tell him where to get off?'

'I told him to mind his own business, yeah.'

'Why don't you go and sort him out, Dad?' asked Rod.

'Eh, eh! I don't want any of that,' Doreen said.

'Yeah, sod him,' said Billy. He held up the yellow plastic box. 'At least you've got something they haven't got, love.'

Doreen came to him. 'What is it?'

'A burglar alarm....'

'A burglar alarm,' Doreen repeated, taking hold of the box. 'Fancy us having a burglar alarm.'

'You can't be too careful now, can you?' Billy said.

Doreen examined the yellow box, turning it over. 'Hang on, where's the works, the bell and that?'

Billy looked a little sheepish. 'Well it's only a sort of dummy like.'

'What good's that?'

'It'll frighten them off just the same.'

'Where did you get it?'

Billy hesitated. 'Off our Jimmy.'

'I might have known,' Doreen said. 'A burglar alarm sold by a crook!'

'I'm not made of flamin' money, am I?' Billy said.

Doreen shoved the burglar alarm back into his arms. 'I suppose he goes round and burgles people after he's sold them duff alarms, does he?'

'Gerroff!' said Billy. 'None of our family's ever done anything like that.' He turned to Rod. 'And you listen to this an' all, lad. The Corkhills might have had a bad name at one time, but they never robbed anyone's house.' He pointed at Doreen. 'Right?'

'Where did he get the alarms from?'

'I don't know, I didn't ask,' Billy said.

'As long as you've got him for a brother you'll never make a good name for the Corkhills.'

Billy bit his lip. Airs and graces again. She mightn't like Jimmy, but he was her brother-in-law. Just because he'd been in jail. There was no need for him and Doreen to feel ashamed over that. He examined the alarm box. He didn't care where it came from, he was going to put it up.

Harry Cross tapped the table to emphasize his words. Damon Grant and Rod Corkhill listened carefully. 'Each Saturday night I want you here with your programmes. No programme's valid till I've signed and dated it, right?'

'Right,' said the lads.

Harry continued, 'The one who's been to the most matches – home or away – at the end of the season, as proved by my signed programmes, is the winner. Right?'

'Right,' said the lads.

'There's just one more thing . . .' Harry paused. The lads waited, 'There's no point in having a bet unless there's a stake.' He turned to Ralph, who was reading the paper, 'Isn't that right, Ralph?'

'Right,' said Ralph. Then added, with a smile, 'If Edna could see you now she'd have a fit. Or a good laugh!'

Harry looked at him. 'I'm the banker. These two are the punters. At least it's more sensible than that mug's game you and her used to get yourselves involved with....'

He turned his attention back to Rod and Damon. 'So ... every Friday from now on, you knock at this door with a quid each. I'll keep me eye on that and the winner takes all come next May.'

The lads looked at each other. A nod of agreement. 'Right,' they said.

'Right,' said Harry, standing up. 'And as you're both here now I'll save your legs for Friday. Come on – a quid each....' He held out his hand. Rod and Damon each produced a pound. Harry pocketed the money. 'Should be a fair sum for one of you to pick up by the end of the season.'

As the boys left, Rod turned to Damon and said, 'It's all right for you, you're working. How am I gonna find a quid every week? And there's the tickets and the programmes!'

'You started it,' said Damon. 'You put the posters up first. This'll prove who's the best supporter.'

Rod joined his father who was just climbing down a ladder at the front of the house. On the wall hung the yellow, dummy burglar alarm.

Doreen stood watching with her arms folded.

'Well?' said Billy.

'I quite like it now,' she said, 'It looks quite ... you know, classy.'

Billy smiled.

'It looks like a dummy to me,' said Rod.

Heather was surprised at her mother's attitude to Tom's proposal of marriage. She had expected her to dwell on the emotional side of things – whether she was ready for marriage after the experience with Roger, whether she was in love with him, or not. But Mrs Haversham's main concern seemed to be the money; the fact that Tom Curzon was a reputed millionaire. She pointed out that money worries caused far more divorces than infidelity. And that money can help to smooth the way when there are problems.

Heather appreciated the point, but she was more concerned about the matter of Rowena. Her mother listened to her calmly as she explained about Tom's 'secret daughter'.

'Have you met her?' Mrs Haversham asked.

'Not yet, but I suppose I will before we're married. . . .'

'It can't have been easy for him. Seventeen years is a long time to keep a secret like that.' Mrs Haversham paused, then, 'You're frightened he may have other secrets?'

'Not really, no. At least . . . Well I'm sure he has no others,' Heather said.

Mrs Haversham sipped at her coffee, then asked, 'Do you think he'd have told you if you hadn't seen him with this daughter of his?'

Heather had thought about it many times. She was convinced Tom would eventually have told her about Rowena. 'Yes, I think he would.'

'I think you're sure enough then,' said Mrs Haversham. 'You love him, he has the money that can make life much, much easier and you're not concerned about the daughter . . . so. . . . Are you going to marry him or not?'

Heather smiled. 'Yes. . . . Yes, I am.'

'You've still got another week to decide . . .' said Mrs Haversham, 'and I've got another day here. Do you want me to talk you out of it?'

Heather laughed. 'Thanks.'

'Listen, darling,' said Mrs Haversham. 'I think you'd made up your mind before I got here. I came over just to back you up, whichever path you'd chosen.' She sat back, already looking forward to the wedding. 'And I think you've chosen the right one.' She paused, then with a smile, 'Hadn't you better phone him?'

'Are you sure you wouldn't like to phone him on my behalf?'

Mother and daughter laughed. Heather phoned Tom and told him the answer was yes. He came straight round and convinced Mrs Haversham that her daughter had made the right decision.

The following day, Mrs Haversham had expected to spend the day in Heather's house waiting for her flight-time back to Belfast. But Tom had insisted on lunch out – this time reordering vintage champagne at the Millbrook. Later, he announced they would be going shopping to find an engagement ring. Mrs Haversham had demurred, but Tom had insisted she accompany them. 'I just pay the bills,' he said. 'You'll be much better advice than me.'

Tom took over the ring hunting as though it was a military exercise. They found the right one in a small shop in Chester. A diamond cluster costing £9,000. Heather was horrified at the cost, but Tom didn't bat an eyelid and promptly placed an order for a matching wedding band.

If Heather had allowed it, Tom and her mother would have gone off hunting for a wedding gown. But Heather reminded her of her flight-time. Tom drove them to the airport and stood on the observation deck to wave off Mrs Haversham.

As she kissed Heather goodbye, Mrs Haversham whispered, 'I like him. I think you'll be very happy.' Tom was delighted when he too received a kiss from Mrs Haversham.

Later that evening he surprised Heather by fixing a wedding date a week before Christmas.

Chapter Eight

Julia Brogan was terrified of telling the neighbours and she hadn't told Doreen, either. The day the electricity board official called he had cut off her power supply. Fortunately she had a gas cooker, but since that day she had been without light and even her TV set.

She had discouraged friends and neighbours from calling after dark and dreaded Doreen or Billy coming round. She used candles for light, drawing solace from the fact that she wasn't getting any deeper in debt. She couldn't bear to think what she might eventually have to pay back to the electricity board – never mind what she might be fined.

By subtle questioning of people she met at the shops, she discovered that pensioners stood a good chance of being let off for by-passing the meters. She certainly hoped they would take that line with her. It wasn't just the fine, it was the shame. What if her name was printed in the *Echo*?

As Julia sat in the firelight reading by candlelight, she hoped the electricity board would write to her soon. She couldn't stand living like this, not knowing what was going to happen.

Lucy Collins drove her mother's Maestro into the Close, got out and carried in the shopping. She'd volunteered to do the shopping, so that she would have an excuse to go out and call James from a public telephone. Unfortunately, he had been out, but she'd left a message with his secretary, in the name of Miss Collins from the agricultural estate agency in Fontainebleau.

She had seen James regularly the past few days, but she was unlikely to be able to today. For it was her nineteenth birthday and her mother had planned a special family dinner at home. Lucy had rashly offered to help her to keep on top of the catering business. With summer holidays long gone, business was starting to build up.

As she entered the kitchen, Annabelle said, 'Get everything?'

'Just about. What are you planning?'

'I've not decided. Do you want French or English?'

'I'm not bothered. Don't feel obliged to cook anything French. Don't forget I've been over there for two years!'

Annabelle smiled. 'Yes, well it's nice to have you back.' Annabelle was hoping for a similar view from her daughter, but the telephone rang. Lucy moved quickly into the living room.

'It'll probably be Mrs Curtess about the twenty-first birthday tomorrow. She won't leave me alone,' Annabelle said. She dusted flour off her hands and moved towards the doorway, but the caller was obviously someone Lucy knew. Lucy's voice was low. Annabelle couldn't quite make it out.

Lucy was delighted. She put the phone down. James could get away that evening and Penny didn't expect him back from a 'trip to North Yorkshire' until very late. Her only problem was how to break it to her mother that she'd be going out that evening. She returned to the kitchen considering her approach when Annabelle asked nonchalantly who had rung.

'A friend,' Lucy said. She hesitated. 'I'm sorry, I really am, but I have to go out tonight.'

Annabelle was aghast. She and Paul were looking forward to the celebratory dinner with Lucy. 'But tonight?' she said. 'Couldn't it wait till some other time?'

'I'm sorry, but it can't,' Lucy said.

'You could at least tell me where you're going. Surely I have a right to know?'

Lucy flared. 'No!' she said, 'you don't.'

Annabelle was staggered. 'No?!'

'I've been in France for two years and you haven't known what I was doing night by night. Just because I'm home why should you have the right to know what I'm doing tonight?'

Annabelle was amazed at the vehemence of Lucy's outburst. She started to speak, but Paul came in through the kitchen door carrying a bottle of Moet et Chandon.

'Congratulations, Lucy,' he said breezily, holding up the champagne. 'Nothing but the best for Miss Collins.'

Lucy turned away. 'Jesus Christ! Do I deserve all this?!' She walked into the living room and slammed her way upstairs.

Paul gaped after her. 'What have I done?' he asked Annabelle. But Annabelle was already crying.

The party at the big house shared by three third-year students was the best Karen Grant had ever attended. There wasn't much food, they had to have two whip-rounds for extra drinks and the heavy metal music wasn't her taste, but she enjoyed it nevertheless. She enjoyed meeting people and she enjoyed talking. She even had the satisfaction of being greeted by name by one or two of the writers off the student newspaper.

She was glad Pam had persuaded her to come along and felt no qualms about going without David. In fact, she hadn't seen him for almost a week and when she had seen him he had not mentioned her abrupt disappearance from the common room. She was convinced now that she didn't really care whether she went out with David or not.

Of course, Pam was trying to foist her on practically anyone in trousers. As soon as Karen was busy talking to anyone, Pam would slip away and break in on some other group. The next thing Karen knew Pam was dragging across some other guy to meet her.

When she had extricated herself from a conversation with a boring second-year from Leeds who was obsessed with pollution by agrichemicals, she grabbed Pam. 'Eh, no more match-making if you don't mind,' Karen said. 'How would you like to spend all night talking about antibiotics getting into food chains and water courses?'

'I thought he was very interesting,' Pam said with a grin.

'Oh, yeah. Then how come you disappeared as soon as he started talking to me?'

Pam laughed. Then off she darted as Karen nipped to the lavatory to escape the attentions of the ecology maniac from Yorkshire. Away from the noise and the activity she suddenly realized this was the first party at which she'd ever exchanged more than small talk.

She was on her way down when the doorbell went and one of the hosts let in a good-looking lad of about twenty. He held a two-litre bottle of wine over his head and was welcomed by a horde of students with empty foam cups.

'Hey, Guy!' The voice was Pam's. She came out of the kitchen and grabbed his arm.

'Pam!' he said. 'Here get some of this plonk before it all goes.' He grabbed the bottle back from a drunken girl with a spiky haircut. 'Got any glasses?'

Pam produced two foam cups. Karen approached. Pam spotted her. 'Karen, this is Guy Willis.'

'Hi,' Karen said.

'Do you want a drink?' Guy asked. Karen nodded. 'Tell you what,' he added, 'you have this and I'll have a swig out the bottle. I think I've had enough already.'

It transpired that Guy had come on from another party. He seemed to know Pam quite well. After a while he said to Karen, 'Aren't you going out with David Hargreaves?'

'Not tonight!' Pam interrupted, winking at Karen.

Karen was embarrassed. 'Yes, I am.'

Guy, she discovered, was also in the second year like David. In their first year they had been inseparable friends, but did not spend so much time with each other now. 'The thing is, you keep meeting new people,' Guy said, 'and if you don't live in Hall, or share a place like this, you never seem to fit in.'

Karen explained, with a touch more embarrassment, that she lived at home. 'Well at least you're here,' he said, with a grin, 'which is more than Dave ever is. He never seems to turn up at anything.'

Despite odd interruptions from people he knew, Guy and Karen spent the remainder of the time together at the party. Finally, the time came when Pam wanted to leave. She asked Karen to walk with her. Guy said goodnight and drifted off to talk to two of the party hosts, who were trying to start a card school.

'What time is it?' Karen asked.

Pam glanced at her watch. 'Twenty to three,' she said.

'God it's not, is it?' Karen was mortified. She might be at university, but her mother and father would go mad if they knew she was still out. She hoped they'd gone to bed early.

Bobby and Sheila had not gone to bed early. It was after 2 a.m. when they finally went up. But neither of them had gone to sleep. Bobby dozed while Sheila sat up, a cardigan around her shoulders, straining to catch the smallest sound outside.

Earlier, they had discussed Karen's safety. Not far from the university in recent months there had been two particularly nasty attacks on women, one of them on a student going to catch a bus back to the Halls of Residence. That had prompted the university authorities to issue a leaflet to all female students warning them to take care, especially after dark. Since Bobby and Sheila had seen the leaflet, they had constantly warned Karen themselves to watch out when she stayed out late. But this was the latest she had ever been home.

'I'll murder her when I get my hands on her,' Bobby said. He didn't continue. It was a stupid thing to say. He could tell Sheila's imagination was already in overdrive.

'Go down and phone the police, Bob,' she said.

Just then, they heard a car drive slowly into the Close. Bobby went to the window. It wasn't Karen. Lucy Collins was being kissed by the driver of the car. After a moment, she got out of the car and went inside.

'It's only Lucy Collins,' Bobby said.

'At this time of night?' Sheila replied.

'At least she's home earlier than our Karen.'

Bobby got back into bed. Sheila turned to him, 'I think you should phone the police.'

'Ar, eh, love. We could end up looking idiots. She is an adult now, you know.'

But Sheila was insistent. Bobby called the police.

Across the Close, the Collins, too, had gone to bed late. They had tried to make the most of it with Anna's special birthday dinner and the vintage champagne. Paul had drunk most of the champagne and graduated to whisky. As a result, he'd announced, 'To hell with my children, both of them,' and staggered up to bed. Annabelle had followed later, not drunk, but in tears. She had lain awake long enough to hear Lucy safely inside the house, but not long enough to hear the arrival of two giggling girls.

The wine at the party had affected Karen Grant and she had been expansive enough to invite Pam to stay the night at Brookside. Now, as she and Pam arrived in the Close, Karen was giggling like an idiot.

They joked about waking up the neighbours, playing 'knick-knock' – knocking on doors and running away – but decided that was too crude. It was Pam's idea to set off the Corkhills' burglar alarm. They got a clothes prop from behind the house and Pam belted the alarm. To her surprise it fell off the wall and thudded on to the grass. 'It's a dummy!' Pam said, and started giggling again. 'If we can't get it ringing, we can swipe it.' Karen was horrified, but Pam said, 'Only for a giggle.' They took the alarm and fled into the Grants' house.

Karen was making up a bed for Pam on the settee when Bobby came downstairs, woken by Sheila who had heard the door open. He didn't see Pam and demanded to know where Karen had been to this hour. As Pam sat up on the settee, Bobby was calmed, but only slightly. Seconds later they were joined by Sheila. Together Bobby and Sheila went through all the usual questions asked of daughters who come home late.

Karen was mortified with embarrassment, but she was able to defend herself by pointing out that if she had gone to Manchester or London University, in fact anywhere away from Merseyside, her parents would never have worried over her whereabouts.

When a relieved Bobby and Sheila finally went back to bed, Karen and Pam were again taken by a fit of giggles.

Later that morning it was Damon who found the burglar alarm stuffed in the cupboard under the stairs. Unfortunately, he dangled it in front of a concerned Karen and Pam just as Bobby walked in to get his breakfast. They had to explain what Pam called a 'student prank'.

Bobby insisted it was stealing. Damon, putting in his two-penn'orth, described it as vandalism. Pam insisted she wouldn't call it either.

'Why not?' Bobby said. 'Because you're at the university? Because your old man has a good job? Can't you get middle-class vandals?'

The whole family had noticed Pam's accent and they knew she came from the Home Counties. Karen warned her father off. She was again embarrassed.

Sheila stepped in. 'I think we've all said what we think it is. The main thing is how to get it back without upsetting Mr and Mrs Corkhill. And I don't want you two doing anything like this again! Right?!'

Bobby suggested owning up and taking it back across the Close. But the girls didn't fancy that approach. They were both sorry they'd done it. It was Damon who came up with the most appealing idea. He volunteered to take it back, and the girls jumped at the chance. Then Damon introduced his condition.

'It'll cost you a fiver.'

Pam and Karen swapped looks. 'Okay,' Karen said, 'But what will you tell them?'

'Nothing. I'll nip over after dark and stick it back up. Easy.'

The deal was settled. There was just one embarrassment left for Karen after her late night. The phone rang and when she answered it, it was the local police station. She realized her parents had reported her missing. She sighed and, looking at Pam, rolled her eyes heavenwards.

When Doreen Corkhill went out to work and noticed that her new burglar alarm was missing, she went mad.

Billy came out to see what was wrong. He was amazed.

Doreen said, 'I've a good mind to get the police on this!'

But Billy would have none of it. 'I don't want any bizzies round here.'

Doreen was immediately suspicious. 'Because it was knock-off?'

'I'm not saying that.'

'Well why not call them? I've nothing to worry about.'

Billy tried to sidetrack her. 'You don't want to fall out with the neighbours. How do you know it wasn't old Collins?'

'Him?' Doreen said, incredulously.

'He's got a grudge. The shutters and that.'

'Oh, don't be soft. He wouldn't do anything like that,' she said. Then to Billy pointedly, 'I'm not sure I'm that bothered anyway. I like to know where things come from.'

The atmosphere in the Collins' house was strained, but courteous. Paul, nursing a hangover, had sniped at Lucy a little, but when he had eventually taken himself off for a lie down, Lucy had apologised to her mother for missing her birthday dinner.

'It's all right,' Anna said, 'it's just that when you're so secretive we get upset.'

'But I shouldn't have to tell you,' Lucy replied. 'I've been looking after myself for two years now. I don't want anyone putting ties on me.'

'We don't want to tie you down, we just . . .'

But Lucy cut her short. 'That's good.' She smiled at her mother with a glint of triumph in her eyes. Annabelle went back to her magazine.

Terry Sullivan sat by the telephone feeling sorry for himself. In two weeks, he and Pat had done three jobs in the van, earning less than fifty pounds between them. On top of that, things were strained in the house because of Sandra's smoking. Terry had been nagging Pat to get her to stop, and when Pat had objected to her smoking cigarettes in their bedroom she had kicked him out. Now Pat blamed Terry for his three-night sojourn on the sofa in the living room.

Sandra, of course, knew who had put Pat up to the anti-smoking message. In Terry's presence, she said, 'Perhaps if you get yourself a proper job, I'll give up smoking.'

As far as Terry was concerned, running the van was a proper job. He was determined to make it a profitable business, even if he had to work seven days a week. He was thinking how he might boost business when Pat came in from changing the plugs on the van. He was carrying an envelope. 'Here, Terry, open this, will you? Me hands are filthy.'

The letter carried the crest of the bank from which they had borrowed the money for the van. 'Eh, the loan is paid up to date, isn't it?'

'Yeah,' Pat said, from the kitchen. 'Just.'

Terry opened the letter. His heart sank even deeper. It was signed by the manager and, in two sentences, asked them to call in as soon as possible to discuss the business. Terry read it out to Pat.

'Jeeze,' he said, examining the letter, 'you don't reckon he's going to repossess, or anything?'

'You said it was paid!' Terry was beginning to panic.

'Nah, it can't be that. I've definitely paid and we haven't missed a payment yet.' He paused. 'Though it might be a different matter next month.'

Terry got up. 'I think we'd better go and see him now, get it over with.'

Mr Simmins, the bank manager, kept them talking on what seemed unimportant matters for about five minutes after Terry and Pat had taken their seats in his plush office. They were both nervous.

Terry had taken his Woolworths account book with him and had pushed it across the desk. Mr Simmins perused it for a moment, then looked up. 'Do you always charge these kind of rates?' he asked.

'Well not always,' said Terry.

'No, sometimes it's less. Quite a bit less,' added Pat.

They had both jumped to the wrong conclusion. They thought Mr Simmins thought they were two racketeers.

Mr Simmins ran his finger down the accounts columns. Pat and Terry waited nervously. Mr Simmins shook his head and tutted to himself. 'They're not nearly high enough. You need at least another thirty per cent on top to make the business viable.'

Pat and Terry couldn't believe it. 'You asked us in to tell us we aren't charging enough?' Pat said.

'Well I do keep an eye on what goes through the accounts,' Mr Simmins said. 'But no that wasn't the only reason.' He told them his wife had just bought a stripped pine wardrobe and he wanted it transported to their Liverpool home.

Pat and Terry were delighted to be given a job by the bank manager.

Mr Simmins asked, 'Perhaps you could give me an estimate?'

Pat and Terry looked at each other. The thirty-per-cent figure flashed through their minds.

'Twenty,' Terry began.

'Twenty-five,' Pat said.

Mr Simmins grinned. 'I suppose I asked for that, didn't I? Okay, twenty-five it is.'

Pat and Terry made to go, determined to collect Mrs Simmins' wardrobe immediately. But the bank manager waved them to sit down again. Was this some sort of cat and mouse game? Mr Simmins handed them a business card from a company called 'Hentytainments'. They laughed at the name, when Mr Simmins told them it was run by a friend and customer of his called Henty who supplied pubs and clubs with video games machines and gaming machines.

'He's looking for a solid, reliable little business like yours to carry these machines around,' said Mr Simmins. 'Go and see him and mention my name.'

Pat and Terry were full of enthusiasm as they drove round to Henty's back-street address. They were even more delighted as they drove back. Henty had taken them on there and then, giving them a guaranteed £100 a week.

'I've been let down pretty bad by the other outfit I've been using,' he told them. 'They think they can mess me around.' He looked at Pat and Terry seriously and added, 'If I'm paying out a ton a week guaranteed, I come first. I don't want any of this "We can fit you in tomorrow, Mr Henty" business. Right?'

'Right,' said Pat and Terry. That day they delivered ten machines to clubs across North Liverpool. Business was looking up.

The firemen had gone. Julia and Mrs Kerfoot had spent an hour and a half doing their best to wash down the smoke-blackened walls of Julia's living room. The damage had not been as bad as it could have been, but Julia was lucky not to have been overcome by the smoke.

All the windows and doors had been opened to let out the stench. A moment's carelessness with a lit candle at half past six that morning had started the fire. Mrs

Kerfoot had been curious to know what Julia was doing lighting candles and Julia had been obliged to confess that her electricity had been cut off for fiddling.

That had been bad enough, but while they were cleaning out, the postman had brought Julia a long, official-looking envelope. In it was a summons from the magistrates' court asking her to appear in eight days' time to answer a charge of fraudulently abstracting electricity. She showed Mrs Kerfoot.

'You'll have to tell them now, love,' Mrs Kerfoot said. She was right. Julia should never have hidden from Doreen and Billy the fact that she was now without electricity. She decided to go round to Brookside immediately.

She couldn't have picked a worse time. Doreen was going through a period of depression brought on by a reminder from the solicitor's firm about their £324 bill. In addition to that there had been the unpleasantness with Paul Collins over the shutters – and now the theft of their burglar alarm. She worried that the neighbours didn't like them. In conversation with Harry Cross, she had also learnt a little of the history of their new house. Harry had delighted in telling her about Gavin's death, Petra's suicide and the imprisonment of George Jackson. 'I reckon it's got a jinx on it, that place,' Harry had confided, not realizing the depressing effect it might have on his new neighbour.

Billy had dismissed the idea, even threatening to go and give Harry a telling off. He'd spent a lot of money on buying the house and he wasn't having anyone making Doreen unsettled.

As Doreen sat fingering the reminder from the solicitor's, Billy touched her hand, 'I'll see the solicitor,' he said. 'I'll find out about this shutters business and ask him for a rebate. If he couldn't tell us about ground leases, why should we pay him all that, eh?'

Doreen smiled. Billy telephoned the solicitor's and

made an appointment for the next day. He'd just put the phone down when a distressed Julia arrived. Breathlessly, she told them about the fire. Doreen was horrified. Billy was despatched to make some tea.

'I've told you before. You'll throw any old thing on that fire!' Doreen said.

Julia looked shamefaced. 'It wasn't the fire started it. It was the candle.'

She explained about the electricity being cut off. Billy's guilt over the meter fiddling deepened, 'You've had no light since then?'

Doreen was appalled. 'Why didn't you tell us? I don't know! Me own mother living with just candles!'

Julia was now in tears, but the worst was yet to come. She showed Billy and Doreen the summons. 'I thought with me age, you know . . . they'd leave me alone,' Julia sobbed. 'How am I going to pay any fine?'

Billy felt awful. 'It probably won't be much. I mean, you being a pensioner and that.'

Julia snapped back at him, 'I wish you'd taken your wires and fiddling with you when you went, Billy Corkhill!'

He took the slight, but tried to comfort Julia. 'Look, I'm on nights this week. There could be some ovies coming up and a few foreigners. We'll pay.' He turned to Doreen. 'Won't we love?'

'Yes, don't worry about that, Mam. You've been through enough. The main thing is to get the house straight and the lecky back on again.'

But Julia wasn't keen on the idea. 'I don't want to bother about that. I owe them enough already and I'll have to pay back what was fiddled.' Then Julia dropped her bombshell. 'The house is like a midden. I think I'd sooner stay here for now.' Billy groaned inwardly. Julia continued, 'Just till I go to court, like. You don't mind do you, Reenie? I'd feel much better.'

'Of course you can,' Doreen said. 'You're me own mother, aren't you?'

Mother and daughter smiled at each other. Billy felt

sick. He felt guilty over the meter fiddle, yes, but he didn't fancy Julia staying with them. Not when he'd got used to the privacy of their own place.

Chapter Nine

For the second time that day, Lucy Collins sat chain smoking in the cubicle at the far end of the city centre pub she and James used as a regular rendezvous.

James had failed to turn up at lunchtime as arranged. Lucy was now waiting in the hope he could call in before going home to Penny and the children. She'd been hanging around Liverpool all afternoon, browsing in book shops and drinking coffee, until the pub reopened at five o'clock. She hadn't wanted to go home for the afternoon. That would have meant keeping her mother company and endless questions about her job interview. That morning, Lucy had recklessly told her mother that she had the chance of a translator's job in Liverpool, which would give her the chance of travel to France and Belgium.

Anna, mindful of Lucy's warnings to her and Paul not to interfere, had been circumspect. But she had been bursting to ask more questions. Lucy had been dismissive. She certainly couldn't tell her mother that James was trying to arrange the job on her behalf. Lucy had left the house hurriedly, telling Annabelle she was meeting her old school friend, Janice.

When James came in he was quiet. 'I'm sorry about lunchtime,' he said. 'I couldn't help it.'

'Not like France, is it?' Lucy said.

James agreed. 'Three-hour lunches and no one on your back.'

Lucy looked at him. 'Who's on your back?'

James explained that the restructuring of the office had meant incessant meetings.

'Oh, I thought it was the usual secretary's brush off,' Lucy said. 'When I rang they said you were in a meeting.'

James was alert. 'How many times did you phone?'

'Just once – before I got you.'

'Oh,' he said.

'Don't you want me to phone?'

'It's all right,' James said.

Lucy said quietly, 'I won't phone if you don't want me to. . . .'

James said it was okay, but added that perhaps while the restructuring was continuing, it might be as well not to phone him at the office. To Lucy, James seemed very edgy these days. She didn't press the point. 'I told my mother about the interview,' she said, eventually.

James reacted immediately. 'You told her about me?'

'No, of course not,' Lucy said.

He nodded, thankful that she hadn't. He didn't want any security leaks.

Lucy was continuing, 'She was a bit suspicious about where I'd been on my birthday, but she doesn't know. When do you think you can fix up the interview?'

James was very uncomfortable. After a moment, he turned and said, 'I'm afraid it's been shortlisted already.'

'But you said you'd put a word in.'

'I'm sorry. I was a couple of days late. Everything's changed.'

'So where does that leave me?'

He covered her hand with his. He wanted her. 'I'm working on it,' he said.

'But you said it was as good as fixed.' There was a hint of whining in her voice.

'It will be . . . I promise,' James said. Lucy sat back, her lips tight. 'I promise,' James repeated.

She smiled at him. But he didn't smile back. What could he do?

Heather was worried about Tom's attitude to the wedding

arrangements for the service, reception and honeymoon. She had invited him round for a leisurely chat about it all, but he seemed to have done everything with the assistance of his secretary. Heather had wanted the reception at her parents' hotel in Ulster, but Tom had not been keen because some of his business guests might not have been able to manage a time-consuming trip to Ireland. Then when she broached the subject of a honeymoon, Tom jumped in to say Josephine had already arranged for them to spend it at a villa in Kowloon belonging to an old business contact of Tom's in Hong Kong. There was another surprise when he announced that he had already made a provisional booking for the reception to be at a stately home in Cheshire with a four-poster bed for the wedding night.

When Annabelle Collins called round they hadn't even discussed who should be invited. But Tom blithely invited Annabelle and her family to attend. Heather had looked on helpless as Annabelle had gushed her thanks and congratulations.

The next disagreement came the following evening when Heather had already started on the guest list. Tom looked over her shoulder and spotted the top name on the list – 'Miss Rowena Curzon.' Tom had exploded. 'What the hell is she doing on it?'

Heather was taken aback. 'Sorry?'

'There!' Tom jabbed his finger at the list. 'You've got Rowena's name there – top of the damn list!'

'She is your daughter,' Heather replied.

'Are you mad?' he said. 'Me dad's going to be there.'

'But this is your wedding – our wedding!'

'Never mind that – cross her off!'

Heather was appalled. 'Tom, you can't get married and not invite Rowena.'

'I'll tell her it's a quiet do. It's no problem.'

'But it is a problem,' Heather said. 'You've planned the wedding of the year and you're going to keep your own daughter away. It's so cruel.'

Tom sat beside her. 'It isn't cruel. I'll talk to her. I'll get round it. I just can't have her meeting my dad.'

'I've lied before. Can't we just tell your dad she's a friend?'

'Jesus, Heather, it's just too dangerous!'

'We could say she was one of my friends, or one of the neighbours....'

But Tom was adamant. 'We can't! She's not got to know about my dad!'

Heather felt a flicker of suspicion. Calmly, she said, 'And why is that?'

Tom did not want to reply. She pressed him. 'Why, Tom?'

Eventually, he said, 'She thinks he's dead.'

Tom refused to discuss this other lie in his life. The choosing of other guests had gone on in a desultory fashion. Then the taxi had arrived. Heather went to answer the door. She knew nothing about a taxi. Tom, putting on his coat and picking up a suitcase from the hall, had explained the cab was for him – he was catching a plane to America that night.

'You never said a word about America!' Heather said.

Tom was dismissive. 'It's just something that cropped up this morning. I'll only be a week.'

Heather was horrified. 'A week? At this time?'

'It's business,' Tom said.

'There's so much to do!'

'Do it,' Tom said. It was an expression he used when talking to subordinates. 'You're always saying I make decisions for you, here's your chance.'

Heather followed him, out on to the Close. The taxi driver was waiting with the engine running and the door open.

'But it needs both of us.'

'Get off!' Tom said, grinning. 'If you need your hand holding get Josephine in on it all.'

'I wanted to do it together,' Heather said.

But Tom was again dismissive. 'This happens to be an important trip.'

'Don't you think we should talk this over about Rowena?'

'We've made a decision on that. I'll phone her sometime.' He was more concerned that Heather phoned his secretary the following morning to make some final arrangements for the trip to the States. As he got in the taxi his final remark was, 'You can handle it. You don't need me to write a few invitations. I've done the business list and the VIPs.' From the window of the taxi, he added, 'Take care now. And don't forget to get Howard Drucker to call me. Tell him it's the usual hotel.'

Heather waved half-heartedly as the taxi carrying Tom left the Close. She turned back to the house, feeling flattened. This wasn't her idea of how to arrange a wedding.

Karen had been hassling Damon for days. He had been given a fiver by her and Pam to replace the Corkhills' burglar alarm, but it was still in his bedroom. Now he had been given an ultimatum by his sister, 'Put it back tonight or I want a fiver first thing in the morning.'

When his alarm clock went off at five a.m., Damon was ready. His socks, jeans, trainers and jumper were spread out neatly on the floor. In a minute or two he was dressed and outside in the back garden. He picked up his father's aluminium ladder and sprinted with it across to the Corkhills'. Between his teeth he gripped the plastic burglar-alarm box. Carefully, he put up the ladder, looking round anxiously, in case he had made a noise. It was an awkward job putting the alarm back.

Inside, Doreen was sleeping alone as Billy was on nights. Tracy was in her own room at the back of the house and Rod was reluctantly sleeping on the settee as Julia had taken over his bedroom. The settee was uncomfortable and Rod had slept fitfully. As Damon struggled to put the alarm back, Rod turned in his sleep. Suddenly, he was awakened by a grating sound, followed instantly by the sound of footsteps. He sprang up and looked out of the window. He couldn't see anything. So he rushed upstairs and woke Doreen. She followed him down, in the process waking up Tracy, then Julia.

Outside they all looked round the house. There was no sign of anyone. But Rod spotted a light across the Close. It was in Damon Grant's room. Before he could tell Doreen, the light had gone out.

'It's Damon Grant,' Rod said. 'I bet he was messing about.' He accused Tracy of telling Damon he was sleeping on the settee that night.

'Get off,' she said, 'I wouldn't even talk to him!'

Eventually, they went inside, not noticing that the yellow plastic burglar alarm had been replaced. That didn't come to light till next day when Doreen felt obliged to report the 'prowler' to Annabelle. In conversation, Doreen mentioned the incident of their burglar alarm going missing. When Annabelle glanced up at the house and pointed to the alarm – hanging on the wall as good as new – Doreen had been speechless. Doreen went red with embarrassment as Anna drily commented, 'Whatever next?'

Billy had gone to see Harrison, the solicitor, determined to get a reduction on his bill over the ground lease. 'The job hasn't been done properly. We knew nothing about this ground lease business. I put up shutters for the wife and I've got some bloody toffee-nosed neighbour going spare about it.'

'Calm down, Mr Corkhill,' Harrison said. 'In the first place the job has been done properly and, secondly, all new property has ground lease conditions.'

'And do they all say you can't have flaming shutters? We want to make something out of that place. Do I have to see the likes of you every time I want to change a bloody washer on the tap?'

Harrison tried to explain that it was only a planning formality, that he could handle it on Billy's behalf.

'No chance,' Billy said. 'I'll do it myself and save a few

bob.' Then he got to the reason for his visit. 'Anyway, we didn't know about the ground lease. I reckon we should get something back on this bill!'

'That's not possible,' Harrison said.

Billy argued, but he couldn't get anywhere. He suggested that Doreen had been so upset about the shutters they should have some sort of compensation.

'I understand that, but I'm afraid there's no question of any reduction,' Harrison said.

Billy realized he couldn't win. 'Okay,' he said. 'But there's something else I'd like to ask you while I'm here.' He explained that he needed legal help for Julia's court appearance.

Harrison nodded, then apologized. 'I can't help you on that. That's criminal law. I'm a conveyancing clerk.'

Billy was outraged. He'd paid for a solicitor, he said, not a clerk. 'I've had second best.'

Harrison winced at the slight, but pressed on. 'I can refer your mother-in-law's case to someone else in the office.'

'Oh, aye, and get robbed soft again,' said Billy.

Patiently, Harrison explained that Julia might qualify for legal aid. But Billy saw it as Harrison being patronizing. 'Never mind legal aid, I'll pay,' he said, truculently.

'That could prove expensive,' Harrison said.

'I'm not rubbish,' Billy replied. 'Perhaps this time I'll get what I pay for! I don't care what it costs as long as I'm paying for someone who does a decent job!'

Harrison gave him a withering look and went out to see if one of his colleagues was available.

Billy put his head in his hands. He'd made a mess of that interview, all right. He came to save money and now he was going to have to spend more. Just because of his carelessness over Julia's meter. He sat back and waited.

James had been successful in his attempt to get Lucy an interview for the translator's job. Lucy was delighted. She wanted to know all the arrangements and studied the job description enthusiastically.

'We'll have to be careful,' James said, 'when we're working together.'

'You reckon I'll get it?' Lucy asked.

'I can't make any promises, you realize that?' he replied.

Lucy was happy. But only for a few minutes. James had to go home. He couldn't spare the time to drive to the beach.

Heather's head was full of troubled thoughts over Rowena as she drove home from the office. Leaving the city centre, she wasn't quick enough when the car in front of her suddenly braked. She ploughed into the back of it. Fortunately the damage wasn't great. But the driver was annoyed. As he got out Heather was already at his side. She apologized profusely and they came to an agreement not to involve the insurance company. Gradually, Nicholas Black's annoyance disappeared. There was an air of amused forbearance in his manner.

Heather told him about the wedding. He'd sent her up with chat about looking into the future, rather than ahead of her. Heather had liked his manner. And his looks. They'd agreed that she send him a cheque by return as soon as the repairs to his car were finished and he received the bill. Nicholas watched her as she drove off.

But the accident and the meeting with the good-looking Mr Black were soon pushed from her mind when she arrived home to find Jim Curzon walking down the Close to her house. He offered his congratulations over the wedding and his help with the arrangements.

Heather invited Jim to stay to eat. While she busied herself in the kitchen, he sipped a drink in the living room. He couldn't help himself when he saw the two lists of wedding guests on the telephone table. He picked them up and started to read. Tim's typed list was full of VIPs and business contacts, while Heather's was handwritten with question marks and crossings-out.

The name 'Rowena' jumped off the page at him. The name of Tom's ex-secretary whom he visited that time in Colwyn Bay. It was at the top of Heather's list with a query mark beside it. Jim had thought about that incident a few times since and he felt sure there was something odd about it. He waited half an hour until they'd eaten, then broached the subject with Heather.

'I was looking at your list of invitations,' he said, casually. 'I see I might be meeting that Rowena one, the girl who was ill. . . .'

Heather stiffened. 'Oh, her. No, I don't think so. I believe she can't make it.'

'Is that right?' Tom said. He looked levelly at Heather. 'Who is she, love?'

Heather couldn't speak. She didn't know what to say.

Jim thought he had the answer. 'It's some ex-girlfriend, isn't it? You want to put a stop to it now if that's the case. Don't stand for it, Heather, love. Put him straight.'

Heather could have gone along with Jim's daft theory, she supposed, but she wouldn't. 'Just leave it, please, Jim,' she said.

'You're hiding something, aren't you,' he said, quietly.

'No,' Heather said, 'Well, yes . . . I'm doing what Tom asked of me, that's all.'

'You do everything he asks of you, do you?'

'No,' she said, 'but this is different. He asked me because he feels it's the right thing to do.'

'Oh,' Jim sat back. He felt as uncomfortable as Heather, but he was determined to get to the bottom of all this. 'And what's your opinion?'

'He's wrong!'

'Hardly the way to start married life, is it? Having what seems like a serious disagreement just a few weeks before the service.'

Heather shook her head. But Jim continued to probe. Heather had to admit it made no sense for the secret to be kept from Jim. So she told him.

Jim spent the evening asking questions that Heather

couldn't answer. About pictures, about financial provision, whether he could meet Rowena? She was glad when he left. What would Tom think of her? She had promised solemnly to keep his secret.

At the end of that week, Heather received a message from Tom asking her to meet him from the airport on his return from the States. As she was preparing to leave, having taken the afternoon off, Jim arrived at the house, ostensibly to refix some loose tiles in the bathroom.

'I know what he does when he comes back from abroad,' he said. 'He goes into hiding for a few hours at least.'

'Yes,' Heather said.

'I'd like you to make sure he does his hiding here.'

Heather collected Tom from the airport and drove him back to the Close. Making an excuse about shopping she had to do, she left father and son together making a snack. Tom was pleased to find his father had offered to help with the bathroom tile repairs. He felt thoroughly relaxed with Jim, until he asked his father if he'd noticed Heather was a little subdued.

'Oh?' Jim said, sitting down. 'Well I'll tell you about that, shall I?'

Tom felt uneasy. And he grew more uneasy as Jim mentioned first the ansaphone message about Rowena's illness and Tom's sudden trip to Colwyn Bay, then the fact that this mysterious girl's name had appeared on the wedding invitation list. Tom looked at his father. This was the closest they had been to the truth in seventeen years. 'You're saying that you know, then?'

Jim nodded. 'I wasn't going to be fobbed off this time. Heather told me the truth.'

'Christ,' Tom said. 'No wonder she looked strained.'

'I had to pressure her a bit. To get the truth,' Jim said. 'She didn't just out with it and tell me everything.'

Tom gave a snort, then said, sarcastically, 'Don't feel you have to protect her. I mean it was only a promise she made me!'

Jim was angry for Tom trying to push the blame on to Heather. 'It doesn't matter how I found out. I know.'

Tom took a deep breath and decided to tell his father everything.

'Why?' Jim said. 'Why?' He couldn't understand Tom's decision to hide his daughter.

'It made sense at the time,' Tom said. 'When it first started, when Janet was pregnant, it all made sense.'

'But to hide her like that. For all these years!'

'I was trapped, Dad,' he said. 'And as time went on it got worse. Don't think I don't know what you missed out on – and Mum.'

'Thank God she's not alive now to hear this!' Jim said, angrily.

Tom continued, 'But I couldn't do anything. I couldn't tell you without crucifying you.'

Jim regarded his son a moment. 'And you didn't want to look bad, either, did you? Tom Curzon the big "I am", the company chairman, the go-ahead young millionaire. And you couldn't bring yourself to face something like this! Well don't you take this out on Heather. Do you hear me? She's the one with the courage round here!'

Jim went into the living room and sat down on the settee. Tom sat and stared at the two omelettes going cold on their plates. It was nearly twenty minutes before he followed his father into the sitting room.

Tom tried to explain his actions, thinking back to when he was twenty years old and Janet had announced her pregnancy. Then how he had managed to keep his life in compartments ever since.

'Was I so off-putting?' Jim asked. 'Was I so – so distant from you that you couldn't even . . .?'

'You had high standards, Dad. Such high standards.'

'Me?'

'Yes, you. You *and* Mum. She'd have gone on about me marrying the girl and I had a future to think of and . . . Anyway, that's it. You know everything.' They were disturbed by the sound of the car as Heather returned.

111

Jim stood up, pointing a finger at his son. 'Remember, I pushed Heather to tell me about Rowena. If I find out you take it out on her, I'll never speak to you again!'

'We're still on speaking terms, then?'

'I don't see why not,' Jim said.

'You can forgive me? Depriving you of a granddaughter all these years?'

Jim nodded. 'I already have.'

Heather walked in and realized that there had been some sort of agreement reached between them. Tom was sarcastic and cutting towards her, unable to resist the temptation to hit back at her. But Jim's warning glance made him stop. Jim went home, leaving them together.

Much later, Tom told her, 'He's got something on me now. He'll really milk my guilt over all this for evermore!'

'You're wrong, he loves you.'

Suddenly upset, Tom sat down and put his face in his hands. For the first time in their relationship he was close to tears. 'I knew,' he said. 'And I let him down. I've let him down for seventeen years. That's why he made me feel so small . . .!'

Heather had never seen Tom like this before. But all she could say was, 'I'm sorry.'

Chapter Ten

When Julia confessed that she had spotted a love letter in Tracy's room, her granddaughter panicked.

Julia teased her about 'Darling Peter', and Tracy demanded to know how much of the letter she had read. Truthfully, Julia told her she had got no further than the first line. 'I didn't need to read any more, love. I've written a few myself in my time.'

Tracy breathed a sigh of relief. The letter had gone on to thank Peter for the money he had given her to hand in to the school secretary that day. It was a final instalment on the hire of ski boots and thermal gear for the Swiss trip. She'd have to be more careful in future. She and Julia were peeling spuds and chopping vegetables for the tea. Tracy decided the best form of defence was attack.

'Don't you go telling me mam,' she said.

'I wouldn't do that!' Julia said. 'What do you think I am?'

'She's fed up enough with you for telling that Ralph feller about me Uncle Frankie and showing her up.'

'I couldn't help it,' Julia said.

'Then how do I know you won't go telling her about my letter?'

'I won't love, honest. I respect your privacy.'

'I saw you talking to him and his mate this afternoon,' Tracy said. Julia looked guilty. 'If me mam found out about that I don't know what she'd say.... She might not want you here anymore....'

'I won't say anything,' Julia said, remembering telling Ralph and Harry about Billy fiddling her meter.

'I hope not,' Tracy replied. She'd have to be very careful where she wrote letters to Peter as long as her nan was in the house.

Julia went quietly back to her spud peeling. Anyway, minor matters about Tracy having a young boyfriend weren't that important to her just now. She was due in court tomorrow.

There was no doubt in Billy's mind that he had made a mess of the court case. He should have sat at the back of the court and kept quiet. Instead, he had allowed Julia's solicitor to call him to the witness box where he told the Bench that he could help Julia financially.

The decision of the court had been a shock. The fine of two hundred and fifty pound was bad enough. But to have to pay back seven hundred and fifty in fiddled electricity ... Jesus, Billy thought, a thousand quid adrift and the solicitor's bill still to come in.

Billy still felt guilty about his part in Julia's conviction, so he felt unable to protest when Doreen announced that her mother would be staying until between them they could pay back some of the fiddled electricity.

'Our Tracy'll go mad,' he said.

'Yeah, well she's getting a holiday at Christmas. She'll just have to bear with it a bit longer.'

'She's not staying till Christmas, is she?' Billy asked. The thought appalled him. With Tracy away and Rod out he was looking forward to a quiet holiday with some time alone for Doreen and himself.

'She's me mother,' Doreen said. 'And you got her into all this ... Remember?'

Would he never be allowed to forget the fact?

Lucy Collins had a shock that day, too. She had been supremely confident on her way to James' firm's Liverpool office for the interview as a translator. Her French had been judged to be excellent – which it certainly was – but her lack of paper qualifications went against her.

Paul and Annabelle sympathized. Paul explained that she was lucky even to have got as far as an interview. And in job-starved Merseyside, any job was bound to have hordes of applicants. They were pleased to have Lucy back at Brookside, despite the friction of the past few weeks. Now with this rejection they feared Lucy might once again leave for France, or elsewhere.

But Lucy was clear. 'I want to stay in Liverpool. That's why I came back.'

However, she was not as easy going that evening when she met James. 'You promised me it was going to be practically a formality.'

'I said I couldn't promise anything!' he replied.

'I followed you back here for us to be together. I want to work at Holcroft's. With you!'

'Couldn't you try applying for –'

But she cut him short. 'I don't want to work anywhere

else. I want to be with you.' She sighed, then continued, 'I hardly see you. We have to meet like this. I want a good reason to see you every day.'

James promised to see what he could do. The affair was beginning to play havoc with his nerves. He wanted out. With Lucy and the restructuring in the office, the only sanity and normality he could find was at home with Penny and the girls. Desperately, he wanted normality.

Heather looked at the job description and couldn't believe her eyes. Twenty thousand pounds a year, plus car and a flexible twenty-hour week.

'Is this for real?' she asked Tom.

Tom was lounging on the sofa at one end of his plush office, which looked out over the river. ''Course it is.'

'Twenty thousand for twenty hours a week?'

'Better than Drucker's paying, I bet,' he said, grinning. He got up and moved towards her. The upset of Heather telling Jim about Rowena was past, though Heather didn't doubt that in future it might well cause problems. She had taken the afternoon off at Tom's insistence. He said he wanted to show her something.

He held her by the shoulders. 'How are you going to carry on working for H and D when we're married, eh? There's going to be a load of entertaining for starters. Travelling, too.'

He had a point. And the salary and conditions for this part-time job with Curzon Communications were certainly tempting. At least she'd have something to keep her mind working. She asked Tom about the details of the job.

'We can talk about that later,' he said. 'Do you want the job or not?'

'Well, yes, but . . . I'd like to know more.'

Tom, however, was unwilling to continue the conversation. 'Come on,' he said, 'I've a meeting at three. I want to show you something.'

'I've seen it,' Heather said, holding up the job description, 'haven't I?'

'I didn't mean that.' Tom grinned and ushered her out to the lift.

He threaded the Audi Quattro through the city, heading south. Eventually, they arrived at a tree-lined avenue in Grassendale, a residential area on the north bank of the Mersey. A large, Edwardian or late Victorian detached house, set back from the road, confronted Heather. In the front garden stood an estate agent's saleboard.

'Why have we stopped?' Heather asked.

'Look at it,' Tom said, pointing at the house. 'What do you think of that?'

'Very nice,' Heather said. Then the penny dropped. He was suggesting it as somewhere to live after their marriage. She smiled. 'Can we go in?'

'Can't, I'm afraid,' he said. 'The estate agent bloke's a bit pushed. Anyway,' he added, 'there's no need, I've put down a deposit. All we have to do is exchange contracts.'

Heather couldn't believe it. 'But what about my place?'

'Sell it,' Tom said. 'Mind you, I did mention it to me dad. I'd pay you for it and he could live there. It wouldn't be too far from his mates, Archie and them.'

Heather was speechless. Every second of the way, Tom seemed to be rail-roading her. Eventually she said, not without edge, 'I suppose you've ordered my wedding dress, have you?'

But Tom failed to see the sarcasm. 'Oh, that's your department,' he said breezily, as he started up the car. He glanced at his watch, 'Have you decided about the job?'

'Well it seems fine, but I would like to talk, as I said.'

'Why?'

'Look, Tom, my head's spinning with all this. I need time to think.'

'You've got half an hour. You won't be going in to see Drucker till half-two.'

Heather was mystified. 'What? I've got the afternoon off.'

'I was confident you'd say yes, so was Howard. I've fixed you up with an appointment.'

Heather felt that she was being turned into an object. Or some overseas visitor on an official tour. Everything was being done for her. Soon she wouldn't even have to think anymore.

James had to pull more strings than he cared to think about to get Lucy a job at Holcroft's. He worried that people might suddenly start gossiping about this girl called Collins who seemed so indispensable to the company. So he was understandably miffed when Lucy said, almost contemptuously, 'Mainly secretarial?'

'All right, totally secretarial,' James replied.

'Great,' Lucy said flatly.

'This is Merseyside in 1985,' James said. 'Jobs don't grow on trees here anymore. And remember, you've only been out of work for a month.'

It wasn't what Lucy had planned. In her mind, she thought of herself as some kind of personal assistant to James in a job where she would spend more time with him than he did with his wife. Still, it was a job. It would keep her parents quiet.

They celebrated with dinner out and a few hours in a cut-price hotel, where the management didn't bat an eyelid when a couple checked in without luggage and checked out before the night porter had drunk his first cup of tea. James carefully told her that he had a lot of evening work to do and there were family commitments coming up, including his wedding anniversary. They would have to see less of each other.

Since her return, Lucy had been out a great deal, both at lunchtime and in the evening and so Paul and Annabelle quickly noticed when she started spending fewer evenings out. Paul asked her why she was at home so often. 'Cash flow problems,' Lucy replied.

'If you need a loan . . .?' Paul said. He realized that Lucy's new job didn't start till the following week and she might have to wait for her first pay cheque.

'No, it's okay,' Lucy replied. Then rather recklessly

added that she hated being paid for every time she went out; that she'd prefer to pay her way.

Annabelle and Paul picked up on that comment immediately. Who was she going out with? Lucy reluctantly mentioned that she had found a nice bloke. She told them his name. Within twenty-four hours Annabelle was practically having the banns read. Lucy protested that she wasn't about to go rushing into matrimony with someone she hardly knew. But Annabelle immediately came up with Heather as an example. 'A few months ago, Heather seemed to be the committed single woman. Now look at her!'

Lucy had laughed it off. But in her mind she quite liked the idea of being married, as long as it was to James. Unfortunately, things weren't that easy when someone you loved already had a wife.

Mrs Haversham had expected Heather to be on the phone every evening updating her with each stage in the wedding preparations. But Heather hadn't phoned at all and when Mrs Haversham phoned Brookside, her daughter seemed distant. She caught the plane from Aldergrove to Speke the following day.

'It's literally a flying visit,' Mrs Haversham said, when she arrived without warning. 'I have to be back tonight.'

Mrs Haversham discovered that Heather hadn't even bought her wedding dress and there was no sign of the usual panic-stricken arrangements. As Heather pointed out, Tom and his secretary were seeing to all those.

At first, Mrs Haversham pussy-footed round the issue. Then she asked, 'Have you got cold feet?'

'No,' Heather replied. But she didn't sound sincere.

Mrs Haversham asked the same question several times. On the final occasion, Heather was too emphatic in her denials. Mrs Haversham reminded her of an earlier conversation. 'Like I said, whichever way you choose, you know your father and I will back you.'

Heather explained that she loved Tom, they got along marvellously, but . . .

'It's a big but, is it?' Mrs Haversham asked.

Heather nodded.

Mrs Haversham took a taxi to the airport, telling Heather before she left that she had to make a final decision soon, for Tom's sake. When she'd gone, Heather phoned Tom and asked him to come round.

Tom acted as though they were married these days. For him the wedding was just something to get through, like a tricky board meeting. When Heather told him she did not want to marry him, he reacted with anger. He accused her of making him look a fool.

Again and again through a tearful, sometimes angry, discussion, he asked her if she loved him. 'Yes, yes,' she said, 'but not enough.' Not enough to give up all she had worked for. Not enough to be content to be a millionaire's wife. Not enough to pretend that any advances in her accountancy career would be made by her own efforts alone.

Tom offered to change. He swore he'd change. But Heather knew that was impractical. He would never change. He even offered to sell Curzon Communications, to start from scratch again, but as a man and wife team. But Heather knew he wouldn't. Ever.

What started as anger soon turned into tears. For both of them. Tom fought to change her mind, but in the end he knew he had failed. Tearfully, Heather asked if they could remain friends, but Tom would have none of that.

'I love you,' he said. 'Being friends isn't good enough.'

Heather had hurt him and hurt him badly. But it had to be done. When Tom finally left she walked back into the living room and sat down in the settee. She was in a state of shock. She looked round her. The signs of Tom were everywhere. The ansaphone, the remote-control unit for the lights, a pair of battered training shoes. Grief welled up from inside her and the tears came. She cried all night.

The grief Harry Cross felt after the death of Edna had

diminished, largely thanks to Ralph. They had started to go out in the sickly purple Fiesta a little more. They went to Southport, once to the Lake District and, quite often, down to Lime Street Station to watch the inter-city trains pull in and out. On one memorable occasion they retraced footsteps of happier times with a day on the Festiniog narrow-gauge railway in North Wales.

There had been regular visits, too, to the cemetery, where both Edna and Grace were buried. There they would stand – a hundred yards apart – staring down at the headstones of their respective wives. Harry had spent a great deal of money on a marble stone, bearing the words 'Edna Cross, 1920–1985', carefully leaving sufficient space underneath for his own inscription, the money for which was carefully tucked away in his savings account with the funeral fees.

But as the weather grew colder, the days out grew fewer. Together they spent long periods in the house. Self-sufficient Ralph had retrained Harry in the art of housework. But there was only so much housework to be done.

In short, the two old mates were bored.

For Pat and Terry there was no time to feel remotely bored. For two weeks the demands of Mr Henty and his firm had kept them busy several days a week. In between the transport of gaming machines, they had found an increasing number of jobs, mainly as a result of Terry placing an ad for 'Hancock and Sullivan' in the *Echo*.

Mr Henty was so impressed with their efficiency that he made them an offer they couldn't refuse – the whole of the Hentytainments contract on condition it was a good deal. Pat and Terry were only too happy to oblige and secured the contract for themselves by undercutting the other firm. Ten pounds a round trip, as compared with twelve pounds, the rate being charged by Cleary Brothers.

When the lads told Sandra about the contract she was delighted. Terry was pleased that she was beginning to see the van business as a 'proper' job for Pat, obliging her to stop smoking as part of the deal. The only incident which dampened their pleasure at snatching away the contract came with a visit by a good-looking young woman a few days later.

Vicki Cleary came from a long line of small businessmen. The name Cleary made officials at the Inland Revenue and the V.A.T. department shake their heads. Old man Cleary hadn't paid a proper year's income tax in all the years he had run the scrapyard that his own father before him had started. And his sons, Joe and Eddie, were chips off the old block who had been running the vans for years, ever since they'd left school. Before the days of mass redundancies and poorly paid 'moonlighters', when the number of vans and drivers for hire mushroomed, they had made a steady cash-in-hand living from their van. When Vicki left secretarial college, she went through a number of jobs. But she couldn't find anything that suited her. Joe and Eddie eventually persuaded her she'd be better employed dividing her time between the father's scrap yard and the van business. Even if they ran two sets of books, it looked better if the one the accountants saw was nicely set out.

It suited Vicki working with her dad and the boys. And she was as loyal to the two family businesses as any of them. It showed when she turned up on Pat and Terry's doorstep. 'You've taken our job,' was her allegation. 'Henty told us. We know all about it.'

Pat was furious. He reminded her about the free market economy.

'That's crap,' was Vicki's reply. As far as she was concerned, Henty had started them in a cycle of undercutting each other until he could get the services of one firm for buttons. 'That's all he wants,' she said.

'Yeah, well we're carrying on with it,' Pat said.

But Vicki insisted Pat and Terry had no right. 'That's

Joe and Eddie's contract. And this is our area. It has been for yonks. Find something else to do with yourselves.'

'No way,' Pat said.

Sandra backed him. 'They got the job fair and square. This Henty guy asked them. So you can go and find something else to do.'

'I mean it,' Pat said. 'We're sticking with this.'

'Really? Well, we'll see about that!'

Terry had been watching Vicki. He knew she was trying to talk them out of continuing the contract, but he admired the nerve it must have taken to come round to warn them off. She was only a slim girl. He and Pat could easily have turned out to be violent, foul-mouthed louts. He liked the look of Vicki Cleary.

'Eh, come on, let's not start getting nasty,' Terry said. 'Can't we talk about it a bit more?'

'There's sod all to talk about,' Pat said.

Vicki looked at Terry. 'Your mate doesn't seem to think it's worth it.'

'That's right, it's not,' Sandra said.

'Look,' Vicki continued, 'Joe and Eddie don't know I'm here. They haven't had the news off Henty. If they do come round they might be a lot more forceful than me.'

'I don't think there's any need to get heavy,' Terry said.

'Don't say I haven't given you a warning,' Vicki said.

Sandra turned her back on Vicki. 'Bloody cheek,' Pat said, as Terry showed her the door.

Outside, Vicki said she was sorry, but she felt she had to come round and make her point. Terry nodded, 'I know. We need the work, though. We were struggling till we got this.'

Vicki went. She didn't like the Cockney, but Terry seemed all right.

Inside, Pat and Sandra were slagging off Vicki and her nerve at calling round.

'You've got to see her point,' Terry said.

'Yeah, well this isn't a charity we're running,' Pat replied.

'I know, but –' Terry began.

Pat cut him short. 'You fancy her, that's why you're seeing her point.'

'What?!' Terry said. 'Don't be soft.' But Pat had been close. The more he thought about the slim girl with the shock of blonde hair, the more he did fancy her.

Chapter Eleven

Julia Brogan was settling in at Brookside. She wished it was the summer. She could really enjoy herself pottering round in the back garden. But it wasn't. She had to content herself with pottering round the house and spending afternoons down at the bingo hall. She was blissfully unaware of the friction she was causing. She was contributing fifteen pounds a week out of her pension to Billy and Doreen, some for her keep and some towards the fine and the electricity repayment. It left her a little short, but she felt she was paying her way with the cooking and ironing and other little jobs she did.

One afternoon, having arranged to play bingo with Mrs Kerfoot, Julia was alarmed to find herself three pounds short on the money she needed. Mrs Kerfoot knew her circumstances and the fact that she owed a thousand pounds. She would probably offer to pay for Julia. But Julia liked to be self-supporting. Just because she'd been had up for fiddling the meter didn't mean she couldn't pay. It was a question of pride. But the money was a problem. She could hardly ask Doreen or Billy for a loan, not in the circumstances.

As the time of her meeting with Mrs Kerfoot drew near, Julia decided it would be all right to 'borrow' a few pounds from Doreen's whisky bottle in which she saved twenty-pence pieces for Christmas. She counted out the nickel coins. Doreen wouldn't notice unless she counted them. But she got her pension in a day or two. She'd ask for three pounds of it in twenties and slip it back. Doreen wouldn't need to know. Anyway, she thought, she might get lucky at bingo. Then there'd be no problem.

The telephone rang . . . again. It hadn't stopped ringing all morning. Sandra dragged herself out of bed and downstairs. By the time she got to the telephone and picked it up, the line was dead. She left the receiver dangling and went back to bed. How could she work nights if she couldn't get a decent sleep during the day?

Terry and Pat were appalled when they arrived home to find Sandra had taken the phone off the hook.

'I thought you wanted us to get somewhere with this business,' Pat said, angrily.

'You could have lost us half a dozen jobs,' added Terry.

'Yeah, well I'm on nights at the moment,' Sandra said, 'and the last thing I want is a phone ringing when I'm trying to kip. And don't forget I'm still the biggest earner in this house, van business or no van business,' she went on, directing her look at Pat. 'If I get the bullet for being late or too knackered to do the job properly . . . What then?'

It took two of them to do most of the work on the van. What Pat and Terry needed was a telephone answering employee. But they couldn't afford to pay anything more than perhaps a couple of pound a week, despite the upsurge in their income. And there was the complication of them still signing on for the dole. 'Employing someone while we're signing on,' Terry said. 'They'd throw the bloody key away!'

But after some thought, Pat came up with the ideal people with time on their hands. When Terry asked Harry if he fancied being a telephone answering person, he got two telephone answering persons. Ralph volunteered too.

And the terms were easily absorbed. A pound a day and as much tea and coffee as they could drink.

As the end of the Christmas term approached, Karen was getting even more invitations. With the parties to attend and her work-load on the paper, she found it increasingly difficult to write the essays she was expected to hand in. Late nights meant getting up late in the mornings. And once she set foot on the campus, she was roped into the whirlpool of booze-ups and editorial meetings. The most she could spare for her academic work was about an hour a day. Pam was experiencing similar problems, but her unwillingness to work resulted from a growing involvement with the university drama group. She had landed a part in the Christmas review.

Often, Karen would leave home and go straight to Pam's study-bedroom in the Halls of Residence. Pam was usually still in bed. Karen would brew up and sit on Pam's bed to compare notes on the previous evening.

'Are you going to the engineers' do tonight?' Pam asked. 'It's usually good, I'm told.'

'I can't,' Karen replied. 'This essay for Holingsworth. I've got to get it in.'

'Haven't you done it yet?'

'Have you?' Karen asked.

Pam laughed. 'Well yes and no.'

'You have or you haven't.' Karen didn't follow.

'It's an old fiddle. I copied the same essay a second-year did last year.'

'You didn't!'

'They'd need a bionic memory to remember what someone did last year. It's the only way. Look, we've got next year and the year after to start writing our own essays, so why not?'

Karen didn't like the thought. But she had a piece to finish for the paper and she would like to try the engineers' party. 'Whose did you copy?'

'I had a quiet word with Guy Willis,' Pam said. 'He lent me his.'

'But I can't copy the same essay,' Karen replied.

'Look, leave it to me, Karen,' Pam said, 'I'll see Guy and get him to borrow one off one of his other mates in the second year....' She grinned at Karen. 'Unless you want to ask David Hargreaves, perhaps?'

'No thanks,' Karen snapped.

'Okay, leave it to me,' Pam said. 'I'll try and get it today.'

It wasn't Pam who brought the essay to her. She was sitting in the common room when Guy Willis appeared and sat down with her. 'You wouldn't be the lady looking for a certain essay, would you?' he asked.

Karen had seen Guy at several of the end-of-term parties. He had always made a point of speaking to her. Karen thought he was good company. 'I might be,' she said.

'Come on, I know you're desperate,' he said, grinning. 'Pam told me.'

He produced the essay. It was duplicated in purple ink on sheets of typing paper. 'Why's it like that?' Karen asked.

'Oh . . . I just like things legible for revision,' he said. 'If you saw my handwriting you'd think the same!'

Karen scanned the essay. On first glance it seemed fine. 'Thanks,' she said, 'I'll just copy it out in my handwriting and let you have it back.'

'Great,' Guy said.

Karen felt she had to explain. She told him about the student work and all the parties which were taking up her time. 'I hope you don't think I'm some sort of . . . you know, a cheat, like.'

'God no, you wouldn't be the first one to try this kind of thing.'

'It's good of you to let me borrow it.'

'It's no bother,' Guy said. He paused, then, 'You could do me a favour if you like . . .?'

'Yeah,' Karen said.

'It's the end of term soon and I'll be going back to Leicester, my folks' house. Why don't we have a drink of something before I go back?'

Karen looked at him. She didn't mind a bit. 'Yeah ... Yeah, I'd like that.'

Guy grinned. 'That's if you can find time, eh?'

Karen laughed. They made arrangements.

On their first day on answering duties, Harry and Ralph came equipped with a map of Merseyside, coloured map markers and a pad and pencil each. Terry and Pat were amused and left for a day's work lugging round one-armed bandits for Mike Henty.

Harry and Ralph had been warned to expect a busy day. There was a lot of Christmas work coming in with people advertising household items they didn't want, to raise ready cash for the holidays. Van firms could pick up jobs like shifting fridges and washing machines. So Harry was a little disappointed when the only call that came through was answered by Ralph. Still, it was better than sitting in their own house doing absolutely nothing. At least they had free tea and free heat. The only problem was that Sandra was asleep upstairs and they were on strict instructions not to disturb her.

The single call was from a customer who wanted some motor parts taken from Wrexham to Liverpool. Ralph took every detail of the message with great care. When the lads returned home, he presented them with the message written clearly on a page from his pad.

'Just one call all day?' Pat said. 'I thought you'd be snowed under. And we've got a free day tomorrow.'

'It's not that bad,' Terry said, examining Ralph's message. 'A run over to Wrexham isn't a bad earner.'

He didn't feel the same the next day. It took an hour and a half to get to the address in Wrexham. Then after asking a dozen passers-by and eventually calling at the local police station, they discovered that the address they were seeking didn't exist.

Pat shouted at Harry and Ralph, accusing them of cocking-up the message over the phone. But Ralph was adamant. He'd checked every detail with the caller. 'Even this bloody Welsh spelling?' Pat demanded.

'Everything, positive,' Ralph replied.

Harry backed up Ralph's story, then proudly presented Pat and Terry with a message detailing another job. This time it was out to Southport and back to Liverpool.

'I just hope you didn't have your cloth ears on when you took this one!' Pat remarked.

'I was in North Africa and on the railways before you were born, son,' Harry said, pointing a finger at Pat. 'If there's one thing I can do it's take an accurate signal.'

'Is this all you've got all day again?' Terry asked. 'One job?'

Harry and Ralph confirmed that. The phone hadn't rung more than once that day.

Sandra came in on the last part of their conversation. 'Mind you,' she said, 'perhaps it was engaged.'

'What?' Terry said.

'These two have been using the phone,' Sandra replied. 'I heard you. You rang about your paper bill,' she told Harry, 'and you rang up about getting the toaster fixed,' she told Ralph.

They both looked embarrassed.

'Naughty, naughty,' Pat said. 'Any more of it and we'll have to find new people. Right?'

Next morning, as they set off for Southport, Pat suggested they visit the Liverpool end of the job first. He felt suspicious at two long-range runs within two days. Soon his doubts were confirmed. The street they had been directed to didn't have a number 259. They checked and double checked.

Meanwhile, Harry, wishing to ingratiate himself with Sandra, had taken her up a cup of tea. He touched her gently on the shoulder. 'Wake up, love, I've brought you a nice cup of tea.'

Sandra struggled awake. 'Eh?'

'Nice cup of tea, love,' he repeated.

'Great,' Sandra said. 'What time is it?'

'Half past ten, love.'

'Half-ten!' She practically screamed. 'Bloody hell!' She dived back under the bedclothes and Harry almost spilt the tea.

Pat and Terry came home in a bad mood. Again, Harry and Ralph were adamant they got the details correct. 'It must be someone pulling your leg,' Ralph said. 'I mean, it's got to be, hasn't it?'

Pat and Terry looked at each other. It definitely looked that way.

'Those bloody Clearys,' Pat said.

'We can't prove that,' Terry said. He couldn't imagine Vicki doing anything so underhand.

'I'll have a damn good try,' Pat said. He picked up the *Echo* and scanned the column offering vans and drivers for hire. 'I'm checking to see if there's anyone else on the 259 exchange. Yeah, look, here's one. It's the only one apart from ours.'

Pat went straight to the phone and dialled the number. After a moment a voice came on. A girl's voice. Vicki Cleary.

Pat waved Terry to come to the phone. Terry listened. His face fell. He recognized Vicki's voice instantly.

'They're trying to carve us up, that lot,' he said, angrily. 'And you fancy her! Bloody hell!'

Harry, quick to respond, jumped straight in. 'We'll ask for identity or something from now on. A number to call back, too. You won't get any more wild goose chases with us on the job, will they, Ralph?'

'No chance,' Ralph replied.

But Sandra came in from the kitchen. She was carrying a plastic box with wires attached. She went straight to Harry. 'Sorry, Mr Cross, I think we've just made you redundant!'

'Eh?' Ralph said.

'What's that?' Harry demanded to know.

Sandra smiled happily at the two old men. 'It's high

technology. It dispenses with the need for labour ... it's Heather's ansaphone. I've got it on permanent loan.'

Pat and Terry laughed. Harry and Ralph went home.

Something in Terry's mind clicked. He went and picked up the folded copy of the *Echo*. Then looked down the column which contained the Clearys number. 'Guess what?' he said. The others looked. Terry continued. 'There's no advert in. It's supposed to be in all week.'

'They've cancelled it,' Pat said. 'Those bloody Clearys have cancelled our ad.'

Chapter Twelve

It had been a bad day for Barry Grant. That lunchtime he and his mates on Harper's shopfitting contract in Wolverhampton had been given a few hundred pounds each and been told they were laid off until further notice. The men were furious, but what could they do? They didn't belong to a union, the pay was good when the work was there and they could hardly get petulant and threaten to go back to work in Liverpool.

Still, Barry had a few pounds stashed away in his tool box, well away from Jane's thieving hands. He comforted himself with the thought as he left the firm's van at the site and caught a bus back to the flat.

When he let himself in, he expected to find Jane in one or other of her usual states – either restless and beginning to become desperate for another bag of heroin, or 'nodding out', lost to the world in a narcotic stupor, rocking back and forth in front of the electric fire.

But Jane wasn't there. Neither were the few pounds he'd left for some food and neither were his leather jacket and one of Billy Harper's drills he'd been fixing the night before. Anything that Jane could turn into cash to buy smack had to be bolted to the floor to stop it walking. He should have known better.

He walked over to the bed. When they first started living together, that was the scene of some good times. That was before he realized how far into drugs Jane Smith was. Originally, he thought she was just a girl who liked to smoke cannabis and take a few uppers. When she was stoned, she was really great in bed. But heroin. He might as well have slept with a zombie.

Barry looked down at the bed. Grey cigarette ash was rubbed into the sheets and the pillows. In a sticky mess on the bedside table was a bottle of the thick, sickly cough medicine she drank when she was waiting to see the dealer. 'Do not exceed the stated dose' it said on the label. Jane sometimes drank three bottles before she got out of bed.

Barry decided to walk out and stay with one of his mates from the job. He knew which pub to find them in. He left the flat and walked to the bus stop, stopping only to phone his mother at Brookside Close.

He told her he was fine and doing well. But he was due for a holiday. He was coming home for Christmas.

Sheila put the phone down and gave the good news to Bobby and Damon. 'Whose big brother's coming home for Christmas, then?' The baby giggled as Sheila tickled her under the chin. 'He'll see some changes in you all right, madam.'

In fact, Barry hadn't seen Claire since the day after she was born. That was last New Year.

'Is he doing all right? Where is he?' Bobby asked.

'Wolverhampton,' Sheila said. 'He sounded quite happy.'

Lucy had started work at Holcroft's. She might as well not have bothered. The job was dull and repetitive, mostly typing invoices, and the company in the office was pretty tedious too. There were two girls of her own age, but in experience of life, they seemed much younger. Privately, she thanked her parents and the Dubois for giving her the chance to expand and experience a better life during her formative years.

When Margy and Sue chattered on about their social life in the clubs and discos of Liverpool and their endless strings of boyfriends and music, Lucy didn't feel left out. She had a real lover, not an adolescent whose only interest was drinking beer and pawing her in the corner of some tatty disco. She had James.

But she hardly saw James. He rarely came to the transport office, where Lucy was based, and if she wanted to contact him she had to wait till her colleagues were out of the way and use the internal telephone. It wasn't like her dream of working alongside him. At home, the pressure to learn more about 'the mysterious James', as her father sometimes called him, was also continuing.

'You must invite him over for dinner,' Anna said out of the blue one morning. 'How about Christmas Eve?'

Lucy had to think quickly. 'I think he'll be going home for Christmas. To his parents in Leeds.'

Anna wasn't going to let the matter drop so easily. 'Just after New Year then. Be sure to tell him so he has plenty of notice.'

James was aghast at the thought. It was tempting providence. But Lucy gradually convinced him it could be done. You just had to be careful what you said. She quite liked the idea. Secret affairs were all very well, but when you loved someone, really loved them, you had to tell people. Just like two youngsters daring each other to do something silly, James and Lucy finally convinced each other that, if nothing else, it would be a giggle.

The times James was available to meet Lucy grew fewer. He invented excuses, but there were genuine reasons, also. He had to attend family occasions in the run up to the holiday. Mostly, their meetings continued in the little pub not far from Holcroft's office.

It was there one day in December they had a nasty shock. They were sitting holding hands in the corner when a middle-aged man came in with a younger woman.

Lucy and James recognized them – both worked for Holcroft's and James knew the man was married.

Immediately the couple entered, James had pulled his hand away from Lucy. But they had been spotted. Both couples were equally embarrassed.

'I hope he keeps this to himself,' James said.

'He's doing the same, isn't he?' Lucy said. 'Why should he talk?' With a glint in her eye, she added, 'We'll have to keep an eye on them at the office party!'

James had laughed. But he was still uneasy.

White paint was smeared down one whole side of the van. When Pat saw it at eight o'clock one morning, he was furious. 'Right, that's it, I'm going to go round to the Clearys' and bust them.'

'Don't be stupid,' Sandra said. 'What's that going to achieve, eh?'

'It'll stop this bloody messing around. They take our advert out, send us on wild goose chases, now this!'

But Terry was in favour of letting matters die down. 'We can't prove they took the advert out, or this, or anything.'

'That's right, Pat,' Sandra said.

'Oh, come on,' Pat said. 'That Vicki girl threatened us. Who else could it be?'

'We've got Chrimbo coming up, haven't we?' Terry said. 'Work'll go slack. After Christmas they'll probably have forgotten all about us.'

Pat contented himself with taking out his frustrations with a rag and a bottle of paint thinner. Fortunately, the paint had not dried hard. 'All right, but if they do anything else, we do it my way!'

Pat and Sandra shared a look. Then chorused together the Frank Sinatra song.

Pat had to laugh. Terry said, 'Have you two decided what you're doing for Christmas?'

'We're going home,' Pat said.

'Together or separate?'

Pat and Sándra smiled at each other. 'First time we've been apart in months, eh, Sand?'

Pat and Sandra continued that conversation later. 'You don't mind, do you?' Sandra asked him.

'No, but I'll miss you.'

Sandra had noticed that Pat's bad dreams had been fewer lately. Perhaps at last the effects of the siege were leaving him. She hoped so.

Next day the van was intact. There were no paint smears and all tyres were perfect. Since the Southport hoax call, there had been only genuine messages from customers. Pat was beginning to believe that Terry was right about the matter being forgotten by the Clearys. Until Vicki Cleary turned up again. It was the morning that Pat and Sandra were due to leave for their Christmas holiday, he to North London and she to Glasgow. Sandra showed her in.

'When I came round last time I didn't know what was going on. I think we should talk.'

'Oh, yeah,' Pat said. 'If we believe that we'll believe anything!'

'It's the truth,' Vicki said.

But Pat wouldn't accept it. 'How about us seeing what the coppers say about it? We all heard you threatening us last time. Three witnesses against one.'

'You can't prove anything,' Vicki said. 'And anyway I don't agree with what Joe and Eddie have been doing. I want us to talk.'

'I want you out,' said Pat.

'So you're carrying on with Henty?' Vicki said.

'Too right we are. So go home and tell your two tame vandals,' Pat said.

Terry butted in. 'Look, Pat, the last thing I want is World War Three over this.'

'Yeah, well we can do wild goose chases, too. And I for one know a better way to bugger up a van than a bit of white paint.'

Vicki had turned on her heel and left. Terry waited a few moments and followed her, pretending to be going to the shops.

'No need to guess who he's gone after,' Pat said to Sandra. 'Just because he happens to think the sun shines out of her I'm not letting those two walk all over us – or put us out of business.'

'Yeah, Pat, but if he does fancy her – and she likes him – he might just get to settle it.'

Terry caught Vicki as she reached the main road. He said he was willing to talk even if Pat wasn't. He suggested a drink in the Swan and she accepted. They convinced each other that they were both anti-violence and Terry promised to try to talk Pat into perhaps meeting Joe and Eddie.

But the conversation wasn't all business. Casually, Terry discovered that Vicki was unattached. He took the opportunity to tell her he was in the same position. Then he told her a little about his past and his broken romance with Michelle. He was about to leave when Vicki offered to buy him a drink. 'Yeah, ta, just a pint of lager, if you don't mind....'

Vicki smiled at him and went to the bar. Terry sat back. It was Christmas and he'd have the house to himself. Things looked promising.

In his desperation to get rid of Julia, Billy had phoned the electricity board. When he announced the news that everything was now back to normal her reaction was lukewarm, especially when he hinted she might like to be on her own away from the children.

Julia said that it wasn't worth going home so soon before Christmas as they'd all be together at Christmas and Boxing Day anyway. 'And with our Tracy being in Switzerland, well the more the merrier, eh love?'

Billy, still conscious that it was his own fault she was here at all, didn't want to get heavy-handed, but he tried to put pressure on Doreen to persuade her mother to go home. Doreen tried to bring up the matter throughout the day, but she couldn't do it. 'It's our fault, Billy. I can't just push her out. What'd people think?'

'Never mind what people think, get shut of her,' he said. 'I've done all I can sorting out the elecky!'

But Doreen's thoughts were distracted from the issue when Rod returned home that evening. Doreen was horrified when she saw his black eye.

The lad who had hit him was bigger than Rod, but Rod gave him as good as he got. The fight started in the school toilets when a lad called Carter had made a remark about Tracy 'screwing' a sixth-form boy called Brian Moloney. Rod had pulled him up about the remark and Carter had hit Rod first. Rod had forced the lad to say where his information had come from and Carter had sworn it had come straight from the horse's mouth, Brian Moloney. Despite the pain in his eye, Rod had gone in search of Brian Moloney, but he wasn't in school that day.

Of course, he couldn't tell his parents all this. But it was obvious Doreen was appalled at the fact that he'd been fighting. Billy had been more light-hearted about it, asking if he had given the other fellow a shiner too.

'You shouldn't talk like that. What kind of an example is that supposed to be?' Doreen snapped at Billy. 'If it was up to you they'd be growing up like your Jimmy. And we all know what happened to your Frank!'

'Jesus, all lads fight,' Billy said. 'Haven't we got more important problems to think about?' She followed his gaze to Julia, who was making herself useful cooking bacon and eggs.

'What about the neighbours?' Doreen demanded to know. 'If they see him going round like that, what are they going to think?'

Rod was glad to get upstairs after his tea and away from the hassle. It wasn't just that, either. His nan was getting on his nerves too. You couldn't get in the bathroom in the morning and she was forever wandering round the house rooting about.

A little later, he heard Tracy come up to her room. He crossed the landing and walked straight in. She pushed a writing pad away from her.

'I want to talk to you, girl,' he said.

'Do you mind knocking if I'm in here?!'

'Never mind that,' Rod said. He pointed to this injured eye. 'Do you want to know why I got this?'

'I couldn't care less,' Tracy replied, looking away from him.

He pulled at her shoulder. 'I got it trying to defend your reputation – that's if you've still got one.'

Tracy moved quickly and shut the door. 'What's that supposed to mean?'

'I keep hearing people talking about you. The things you're getting up to.'

Tracy coloured. 'What things?'

'You know what things I mean.'

'What's been said to you?' she asked quietly.

Rod felt a little embarrassed. 'About you having sex.'

Tracy flashed a look at him. She felt as guilty as hell. 'Whatever you've heard is lies, right? All lies! So just leave us alone!'

She stormed out of her bedroom into the bathroom. Rod wondered whether he'd said the wrong thing. He couldn't tell whether she was telling the truth or not.

Tracy went out a little later, when Billy and Doreen had gone out for a drink with his Uncle Jimmy and his girlfriend. Rod considered following her, but decided against it. He wouldn't like anyone to do that to him and he had nothing to hide.

Rod was watching television with Julia when Harry Cross knocked at the door. He wanted to know why Rod was five weeks behind in his stake for the football bet with Damon Grant.

'I'll pay you tomorrow,' Rod told him.

'Just make sure you do, son,' Harry answered. 'I might be having to think about making the whole thing void.

And I couldn't have you being beaten by a Liverpool supporter, could I?'

Harry went. Rod had no money. He tried to borrow some off his nan, but she assured him she was broke. 'Don't you get your pension tomorrow?' Rod asked.

'It's spoken for,' Julia said. 'I can't live here for nothing, you know. I have to see your mother all right.'

Rod didn't know what to do, until Julia casually mentioned the untapped mass of twenty-pence pieces in the Christmas fund bottle.

'I can't do that!' Rod said.

'It'd only be a loan,' Julia said. 'To tell you the truth, I owe it three pound meself.'

Rod fell to the temptation and took out five pounds. He delivered them to Harry Cross that evening and determined to replace them by the weekend.

Gradually, Heather had let it be known on the Close that her marriage to Tom Curzon was off. Reactions had varied. Sheila Grant had sat her down with a cup of coffee and listened sympathetically to Heather's reasons for not continuing with the wedding. Heather had told her she might never now remarry. Sheila had told her not to think so negatively, she had a long time ahead of her.

At the other extreme, Harry Cross had called to offer his condolences, thinking Heather had been dumped by this ruthless millionaire, Tom Curzon. Heather quietly pointed out that it was her who had called everything off. Then, speechless, she had listened to Harry ask for the wedding present from Ralph and himself to be returned. Heather had gone straight to the chairful of wedding gifts, picked out the set of cheap whisky glasses, and thrust them into Harry's arms. Ignoring his insincere sympathies, she'd pushed him out into the night.

Telling people the wedding was off was the easy bit. What worried her more was getting her job with Hamilton Devereux back. As soon as she had felt well enough she'd had a word in private with Joyce Harrington. She waited nervously for more than twenty-four hours before Joyce could see Howard Drucker, the senior partner at H and D. Joyce asked her to meet her for a drink at the Corn Exchange.

'There,' Joyce said, presenting her with a large glass of wine. Heather thought it was bad news coming, but Joyce said, without preamble, 'No hesitation. He looks forward to seeing you carry on with H and D.'

'That's a relief,' Heather said and let news of her reprieve sink in. 'But what about promotion?'

Joyce said she thought there was every chance that, as she had been allowed to withdraw her notice, she should be considered for long-term promotion. 'But it could have been catastrophic if Tom Curzon had withdrawn his account,' Joyce added. 'I think you've come through it all okay.'

Heather nodded, then, 'Did Tom use his influence at all with Howard? To keep me on, I mean?'

'I wouldn't bother asking. I don't know,' Joyce said.

But Heather felt Joyce wasn't getting her point. 'The main reason I didn't want Tom was because he robbed me of my independence. If this was just one more little thing he'd fixed for me, then . . .'

'I think you're still confused, Heather,' Joyce said kindly. 'You worry Tom has lost you a good job, then you worry he might have saved it.'

'I know,' Heather said, turning to Joyce. 'Thanks. I'm just grateful the job's still there.'

Joyce came round to Heather's for supper that evening and as they sat over coffee in the living room, the doorbell chimed. It was Nicholas Black, the man with whom Heather had the accident with a few weeks before.

What followed was a bumbling conversation about Nicholas's opinion that Heather should go through her insurance company rather than pay for the repair herself. The cost was likely to be higher than he first thought.

Joyce watched, amused, as Nicholas, fiddling with his spectacles, offered to give Heather advice on handling accident claims, perhaps over lunch? Heather politely declined. Both women were intrigued as to why Nicholas should call round rather than telephone. He explained that his line was currently disconnected, then made pains to explain that it was for non-payment, but not by deliberate default or poverty. He simply hadn't transferred sufficient funds from his deposit account to his cheque account.

When Heather had seen Nicholas out and returned to the living room, Joyce was laughing. 'I hope you noticed that glint in his eye!'

'Don't be so silly,' Heather said.

'Well, hasn't he ever heard of telephone boxes?'

Heather hadn't thought of that. Joyce went on quickly, 'For heaven's sake he almost told you he's available.'

'What?'

'How many married men go to the corner shop to buy something for their tea?'

'But he is married,' Heather insisted. 'I remember him telling me.'

'But perhaps he isn't now, eh?' Joyce grinned again. 'And all your talk about not going on honeymoon and not getting married yourself ... Well he knows you're not married either. ...'

'Oh, shut up,' Heather said. It was the first time in a couple of weeks she had laughed.

'You be careful, my girl,' Joyce continued. 'I think you could be vulnerable.'

When Julia came back from the shops to find Doreen sitting counting the bottle full of twenty-piece pieces, the look on her face was pure guilt. She went red and moved to the chair.

'Anything the matter, Mam?' Doreen asked, quietly.

It did not take long to get Julia to admit that she had taken money from the bottle. But she denied taking eight pounds for the bingo and said she and Rod had planned to get the borrowed money back before Christmas.

Doreen demanded to know where Rod came into it and Julia explained about the football bet and how she had suggested borrowing from the turkey fund bottle.

'You encouraged one of my kids to steal!' she started to tear into Julia. Then the thought hit her. Today she had promised to get Julia back home. She decided to escalate the amount of outrage she felt at this grandmother and grandson crime syndicate.

'It's not the money that matters, it's the principle!' she stormed.

Julia hadn't expected such an attitude. Then she got on her high horse. 'Trying to treat your own mother like dirt. Well I'm not having it, I'm not – not anymore!'

Ten minutes later, Julia had her case packed and was standing in the hallway threatening to write Doreen and her family off for evermore. Doreen warned her that if she left now they wouldn't come chasing after her. But Julia wasn't bluffing. She turned her back on Doreen and slammed out.

Doreen sat down in the armchair. She'd done what she promised, but it was a rotten way to have gone about it. She knew her mother would have put the money back before Christmas.

When she tackled Rod about the missing money later, he backed up Julia. After the black eye incident, he was fearful of a lot more flack. But none came. Doreen had been hard enough on a member of the family for one day.

Billy was delighted to come home and find that his mother-in-law had departed. He laughed to hear how she had been evicted. But Doreen was worried about a permanent rift.

'No problem, love,' Billy said. 'We'll have her round for Christmas. It'll all be forgotten once she's settled back in at home.'

'Yeah,' Doreen said, brightening a little. 'Our Tracy's away, but we'll have a smashing Christmas. Get me mam round and really have a good time.'

Billy didn't go along with her enthusiasm. 'There's something I've got to tell you, love.'

Doreen looked at him, puzzled. 'Yeah?'

'I'm working over Chrissie,' he said.

'Oh, Billy!'

'I know it's a bind and that, love, but I got called aside today –'

'You're supposed to be having a fortnight off!' She'd been looking forward to their first Christmas together in the new house. Tracy going abroad was bad enough, but Billy working...

'Look they want a crew of maintenance sparks in to put in some new gear they've invested in –'

'Can't they ask someone else?'

'I was asked special,' Billy said. 'We're up to our eyes in flamin' debt and I'll be getting triple time! Triple time for easy work! Think of it love.' Doreen wasn't happy, but the money would come in useful. 'Just think of the cash, Doe,' Billy said, taking her arms. 'There'll be some of it left over for you to have a good spend an' all. The sales after Chrissie, remember?'

She smiled. 'I really wanted a good Christmas, though.'

'I won't be on twenty-four-hour shifts, love. You will see something of me.'

Billy didn't tell Doreen that the foreman had asked him to keep his mouth shut about the triple-time Christmas offer. Billy knew something was going on at the factory, but he couldn't guess what. He let such matters drift out of his mind and concentrated on what he might bring home after Christmas.

Chapter Thirteen

Karen Grant discovered that she liked going out with Guy. On his last night in Liverpool they had gone for a drink at the Swan, then gone into Liverpool for a Greek meal.

He was different than other lads she had been out with. For a start, he made her laugh. She remembered Andrew with his long silences and his outbursts of jealousy prompted by the slightest thing. Then David Hargreaves who always seemed so serious and just didn't take advantage of all university had to offer. No, Guy Willis was different. She could relax with him.

That night, as they parted, Karen made a point of saying that she hoped they'd see more of each other next term. She hoped he'd have a good trip back to Leicester. She was delighted when he said he'd postponed going home for one more day and promptly produced two tickets for the Everyman Christmas Show. 'Will you come?' he asked.

'Yeah, I'd love to,' Karen replied. 'When did you get those?'

'Yesterday.'

'But you were going to go home.'

'Well . . .' Guy said, putting his arm round her, 'if you'd been given two free tickets would you go home and waste them?'

'What if I'd not been able to go?'

He laughed. 'Don't worry,' he said. 'I already had a buyer lined up!'

Holcroft's office party was held on two floors. On the top floor the management held court, with small groups of underlings going upstairs for their statutory single drink and a handshake from the managing director. On the floor below, those who were fit to go upstairs were weeded out from the less promotion-conscious revellers.

James was top floor and Lucy was definitely bottom. Only when most of the bosses had drifted off home did the remainder of the management wander downstairs to drink with their subordinates. Lucy had to wait two hours before she saw James. She made a beeline for him as soon as he came in. But James was wary not to get too close to her and not to be alone with her for more than a few minutes. Consequently, Lucy was party to some boring conversations with various members of staff. James gave Christmas kisses to some of the other women, but not her.

All in all it was a dismal affair. Lucy said as much when she and James quietly made their way downstairs to leave. James told her that Penny had arranged to collect him after Christmas shopping in Liverpool, so as to allow him to have a few drinks at the party. Lucy had hoped they might go out after the party, but James said he couldn't change the arrangement now.

They were discussing that point when James' eldest daughter Rebecca came running in through the front door of the building. 'Daddy!' she shouted. 'Look what I've got!' She was holding a toy dog. Penny came in behind her, carrying little Emily. 'She's absolutely worn out,' Penny said.

'Come here, darling,' James said to Emily, and took her from Penny.

Lucy, meanwhile, had slipped out of the front door. Penny didn't even notice her. She stood in a doorway forty yards down the street and watched James, Penny and the two girls emerge from Holcroft's. The perfect family.

There were tears in her eyes as Lucy went to catch her bus.

Barry Grant hitch-hiked up the M6 and M62 from Wolverhampton and managed to get home to his parents' house by teatime. Earlier in the day as he scoffed a hotdog at Knutsford services, the coach carrying Tracy Corkhill, Peter Montague and twenty-five other pupils and staff from Brookside Comprehensive pulled out en route to Victoria Station, London.

Sheila had been on pins all day. Every car which came into the Close had her rushing to the windows and she was first to take any of the telephone calls. She dreaded getting a call to say that Barry had decided to spend Christmas elsewhere. It was important to Sheila to have the family together for Christmas.

When Barry knocked on the door, Sheila, of course, was first there. All day she had been wondering aloud when he would turn up. So much so that Bobby, Damon and Karen were tired of hearing her.

Barry dropped his holdall on the floor and threw his arms round his mother. The rest of the family clapped and cheered as though he was appearing on *This is Your Life*. Bobby came over and pumped his hand. 'All right, son, good to have you home.'

Barry went straight to Claire, who was playing on the carpet, surrounded by toys. He picked her up and hugged her. Sheila, with tears in his eyes, looked at them together. Her first baby and, no doubt now, her last child. It was true absence made the heart grow fonder, but there was no doubt she loved Barry. It was wrong to think it, but she believed she loved him more than any of the others. She put such thoughts behind her and started offering tea, soup, anything she could think of.

'Tea? Soup? What do you think this is?' Bobby laughed, 'the Band of Hope Christmas Party? Damon, get that bottle of Irish Whiskey I've been saving.'

Damon brought the bottle from the sideboard and they drank to Barry's homecoming. Then the phone rang.

Damon, mimicking his mother, said, 'I hope that's not our Barry ringing to say he can't come!' Sheila swiped him across the head as she went to the telephone. Everyone laughed.

'Been panicking, has she?' Barry asked. 'Don't worry, I'm glad to be here. It's been a tough year.'

Bobby was just about to ask why when Sheila called, 'Bob, it's for you.'

Bobby pulled a face and went to the phone. Sheila came over to Barry and pinched his cheek. 'Well what have you been doing with yourself, then?'

'Working hard and ... well working hard mainly,' Barry said. 'I could do with a rest.'

Sheila thought so too. Barry looked a little pale. And she thought he'd lost weight too. Probably not eating properly. Well, she'd soon put that right. There'd be no skipped dinners for her eldest son while he was in her house.

Bobby put the phone down and went back to his drink. His earlier ebullience had gone. 'Anything important, love?' Sheila asked.

Bobby sighed. 'Yeah. There's trouble at Pollocks. Some of our members are getting the bullet.'

'Trouble?'

'It won't be today, love,' Bobby said, sipping his whiskey. 'It'll be bang over Christmas.'

'Oh, Bobby,' Sheila said. 'Do you ever have a Christmas without problems?'

'Never seem to, do I?'

Sheila silently reprimanded herself for being selfish. She was worried about her husband having to work during the Christmas holidays, while other wives would soon hear that their husbands no longer had work. She was one of the lucky ones. She kissed Barry and asked him what he wanted for his tea.

Twenty-five members of the ETWU at Pollocks food processing got notices of their redundancy tucked into their Christmas wage packets. News spread like a forest fire around the plant.

Billy earwigged the gossip about the redundancies. He had kept quiet about the Christmas overtime. He didn't even know which others of his mates had been selected, but he could imagine, as he looked round the canteen and saw certain men staying silent or reading their newspapers.

It seemed that new equipment was to be shipped into the plant over the Christmas holiday and installed ready for action in the New Year. The Convenor was talking of an occupation, or perhaps a picket line to turn back the trucks bringing in the new electronic gear.

'That could get nasty,' Doreen said, when he told her later. 'Are you going to be all right?'

'Yeah,' Billy said. 'I'm not bothered. The fellas who're going ... the writing was on the wall ages ago. They knew it was coming.'

'But at Christmas,' Doreen said. 'That's a lousy thing to do.'

She was slightly alarmed when Billy told her it was the new equipment which he and others would install that was the nail in the coffins of the redundant men. 'You don't think there'll be anything, you know, violent, do you?'

'It's not the flamin' miners' strike, love,' Billy said. 'I'll be all right.'

'Don't you feel guilty?'

'Guilty? No way,' Billy said, starting to eat his tea. 'I never feel guilty about earning money and keeping my family properly. I need that cash, love. I'm more concerned about you lot than a gang of old fellers getting the bullet, especially when it was on the cards.'

She felt proud of his attitude. He did put the family first, always. But she still felt worried about his accepting the overtime. Some people wouldn't look on it kindly, that was for sure.

The first night of Barry Grant's homecoming, Sheila answered the phone to hear the scarcely audible voice of a young woman. She asked to speak to Barry. Sheila called Barry and told him the call was for him. He was puzzled, but took the phone. It was Jane. She was stoned. She wanted to see him. She said she missed him.

Sheila was amazed with the vehemence at which he told her to get lost. She asked who it was, but Barry was vague. 'Just something that didn't work out, Mam, that's all.'

Sheila let the matter go. But next night there was a knock on the door. This time, Barry answered. It was Jane. He didn't let her in, but stepped outside, closing the door behind him. Sheila moved to the window and peeked out. It was obvious Barry and the girl were arguing.

Barry was furious that Jane had followed him. He tried to tell her to leave, but she refused. 'You told me if ever I wanted to talk.'

'Yeah, well I've done enough talking to you,' he replied, 'I could talk to you for evermore and you'd never change. Get off that stuff for good and I might talk to you.'

'But I've nowhere to go, Barry,' she whined. 'Can't I stay?'

'No you bloody well can't.' As far as Barry was concerned, their relationship was over. And he certainly didn't want her in contact with his family. He frog-marched her across to Terry's. Terry was surprised, but pleased to see an old friend. Mind you, he thought, his bird's a bit rough.

The minute Terry let them inside, Jane went straight to the toilet. Barry knew what she was probably doing up there, but didn't mention it to Terry.

Terry made coffee while Barry and Jane argued in the living room. Jane had been kicked out of the flat they formerly shared in Wolverhampton and her parents in Kent had disowned her long ago. 'I've nowhere to go,' she pleaded.

But Barry was tough. 'I don't care where you go just as long as it's nowhere near me!'

At that point Terry got a phone call. His father Jack and his girlfriend, Eileen were in the city centre and, by the sound of it, drunk. He left Barry and Jane.

When he came back with Jack, who was dressed as Father Christmas from his temporary job in one of the big stores, Terry was in a merry mood. He'd expected to spend Christmas alone and here he was with a houseful. When Jane spotted her chance and asked for a room for the night, Terry said, 'Why not? Kate's old room's free.'

'Are you soft, or what?!' Barry protested.

'Oh, come on, Barry. It's Christmas.'

Jane excused herself for a bath. Jack and Eileen tottered out for some impromptu carol singing on the Close.

'What did you say she could stay for?' Barry said.

'Look, mate,' Terry replied. 'It's obvious you've dumped her, but I'm not seeing a girl just chucked out on the street on Christmas Eve.'

'You'd chuck her out if you knew her like I do,' Barry said. 'She's a frigging junkie.'

'What?' Terry said.

'She's a heroin addict,' Barry said.

'Jesus,' Terry said. Barry always managed to drop you in it. This time he'd excelled himself.

That night Terry played host to a junkie and two inebriates. Jack and Eileen were too drunk to go home.

Sheila was convinced the mystery girl was pregnant. When she tackled Barry he laughed and denied it. He explained she was a girl he had attempted to get rid of without success. As she'd been thrown out of her flat, she'd followed him to Liverpool.

Sheila suggested Barry invite her round. 'No way,' Barry said. 'She can stay at Terry's as long as he'll have her, but she's not coming here.'

Terry hadn't seen any signs of Jane taking drugs, but she more than made up for it with her consumption of cigarettes. She chain smoked all day long. Terry was disgusted, but there was nothing he could say that would make her stop smoking. Terry spent most of the time watching TV and Jane sat staring into space. One evening, he went for a drink with Vicki, but otherwise he never left the house.

He began to get uneasy. Junkies were supposed to start getting sick if they didn't have any heroin. Jane showed no signs of sickness. She must have some stuff in the house.

After dumping him with Jane, Barry hadn't come near. Terry, worried that he could be in trouble if anyone found a junkie staying with him, called over at the Grants and persuaded Barry to come over.

Barry treated Jane with contempt, despite her pleas to carry on their relationship. He cruelly branded her as frigid in Terry's presence.

'Keep her down here,' Barry said suddenly. Jane knew what was happening. She tried to follow Barry up the stairs, but Terry held her. She started screaming and sobbing. Minutes later, Barry came down with three paper packets of brown heroin.

'I haven't been taking it,' Jane was shouting. 'I just need it. It's just in case.'

Barry shouted back – everything he'd repeated time after time in an attempt to make her give up drugs.

'Barry, Barry!' Jane screamed. 'Don't take it away!'

But Barry stuck the packets of heroin in his pocket and walked out.

Sheila still kept asking questions about Jane, but Barry evaded them. It was Karen who approached him when they were alone and asked if Jane was a junkie. It seemed she had overheard him and Terry talking when Terry called over. Barry filled her in on the sort of life he and Jane had been living and warned her off dabbling in drug-taking herself.

It was about the same time that Sheila found the little packets of heroin in Barry's bedroom. All through the holiday she had been watching Barry. He seemed to be acting strangely. And she had noticed his gaunt look the day he came home. She broke down. Her son a heroin addict. Please, God, no.

*

Heather Haversham decided that the best way to get Tom Curzon out of her head was to keep busy. As the office had closed for Christmas, she had to find something other than accountancy to pass her time. So she decided to redecorate the house. On Christmas Eve she bought rolls of wallpaper, pots of paint and Polyfilla. It took days to strip walls and fill in cracks, but it kept her occupied.

When Joyce arrived during Christmas week it was a welcome break. She apologized for the mess and laughed about her new image as the single woman again. The complete redecoration was part of that image.

Joyce laughed and announced that she was now a single woman too. 'You've left him?' Heather asked.

'I should have done it years ago,' Joyce said. 'You can only spend so much time with someone like Bill.' Joyce became serious. 'The thing is, Heather, I've nowhere to stay. I wondered if you could spare a room. It wouldn't be for long.'

Heather smiled. 'Of course.'

Joyce moved in. And because she was at a loose end, she started to help with the decorating.

Pickets had lined up at the gates of Pollocks processed foods factory, determined to keep the new equipment from being trucked in. Each day and night, Billy Corkhill and his friends had been greeted by cries of 'scab' and 'traitor'.

Billy didn't like it, but he had not felt intimidated. There had been no violence like the scenes he had sometimes seen on television. Doreen, however, was a little frightened. While Billy was out she felt anxious, dreading the telephone ringing to say he had been hurt.

But the only thing that hurt Billy was the day he marched up to the picket line to find Bobby Grant sharing the heat of a brazier with the men on the picket. At first Bobby thought he had come to show solidarity. But Billy had quickly put him straight. 'You what?' Billy said. 'I'm here to put the flamin' stuff in. This new equipment.'

Bobby tried to persuade Billy not to cross the line, but Billy sneered at the suggestion. 'I'm more concerned with the wife and kids,' he said, 'and keeping a house going on a mortgage. I'm not bothered about a handful of blokes I never even speak to.'

Bobby was annoyed. 'Don't you see you could be next?' he said. 'The more new gear they put in, the more jobs they can get rid of. Think about it, son.'

But Billy took no notice. As he pushed through the pickets there came again the cries of 'scab'. Billy was undaunted.

Bobby was full of Billy's stupidity when he got home. But before he could start on one of his favourite themes, Sheila revealed her discovery of the bags of heroin. Karen was in at the time and tried to calm down her parents.

'It might not be what you two suspect,' she said. 'Don't jump to conclusions, ask him.'

When Barry came back from a visit to friends, Bobby and Sheila took him aside. Barry was amazed that they thought he was an addict. He told them the whole, sordid story of Jane.

Bobby flushed the heroin down the kitchen sink. Sheila was more concerned that he keep away from Jane and, above all, not let her anywhere near Damon.

'Why the hell do you think I wouldn't let her in?' Barry said. 'I feel guilty dumping her on Terry, but I've got to get shut of her. I've tried my best and it's not good enough. Nothing's any good with her.'

Terry was thoroughly fed up with Jane's boring company. She was getting sick now without supplies and she had been pleading with Terry to give her cash. He knew why she wanted it and wouldn't give her any money. She even offered to go to bed with him, but he pushed her away in disgust.

Terry almost felt like giving her the money she wanted,

just to see the back of her. But he couldn't. He tried to speak to Jane to find out why she had started to take heroin, but got nowhere. All she was interested in was money for another score.

Pat and Sandra returned that night and thought at first that Terry was ill. It wasn't like him to live in an untidy house with unwashed dishes. And the stink of cigarettes was immediately apparent. Then Terry introduced them to Jane and told them how he had spent Christmas.

The unkempt and dirty Jane tried to get money from Pat and Sandra. But with their hospital experience they knew too much about addiction to fall for all her lies and excuses. They spent two days trying to talk her into a more positive attitude to her problem, but without success. Jane locked herself in the bathroom for long periods and continued to smoke.

On the second evening they had all had enough of her. Terry joined Pat and Sandra down at the Swan for a drink, just to get away from Jane. It was a fatal mistake. When they arrived back at the house, Jane had gone. She had left a thank-you note and a crumpled pound note – 'towards her keep'.

'The cheek!' Terry said.

They were all relieved that the house was back to normal. Terry eradicated every dirty ashtray and cigarette end. It wasn't until next morning they discovered Jane had taken with her Pat's watch and Sandra's expensive camera.

Barry too was relieved to hear that Jane had gone. He expected her to drift back to Wolverhampton if she hadn't found a better line of supplies in Liverpool.

He felt like leaving Brookside himself but with the lay-off he had nowhere to go and nothing to do. And he had to stay at least until after Claire's first birthday on 7 January. He offered to give Terry a break, partly out of guilt over Jane, by helping Pat on the van business. Pat welcomed the offer. He got on well with Barry.

*

Tracy Corkhill enjoyed her holiday. Skiing was exhilarating when you finally got the hang of it and the social activity at the end of the day on the slopes had been more grown up and enjoyable than anything she had known before.

Then there was Peter. It was marvellous spending Christmas with him, hundreds of miles away from home. They managed to find time to slip out alone together during their fortnight in a small skiing centre in the Alps. As long as they kept away from the rest of the party, they had no reason to fear being seen together.

But for Tracy the highlight of the holiday was on the second to last night in Switzerland. She and some of the girls had drunk from a bottle of schnapps. Tracy hadn't been reckless like some of the others and hadn't had enough to become drunk or ill. She felt warm and happy.

It was in that mood, later that night, that she crept to the small single room occupied by Peter Montague. It was close to the other staff rooms and Montague was alarmed by the quick knock at the door and Tracy's entry into his room. He tried to reason with her, but Tracy wouldn't listen. Tracy was ready for anything. Eventually, her persistence and affection had dissolved Peter's resistance. Tracy undressed and got into her teacher's bed. They made love for the first – and last – time.

Chapter Fourteen

'On your own?' Heather asked.

'Yes, and why not?' Joyce replied. 'I'm a single woman now. Why shouldn't I have my own practice?'

Joyce had just announced to Heather that she was quitting Hamilton Devereux. She had already rented offices in Chester. All she needed was an assistant. She offered the position to Heather.

Heather was flattered, but she felt she had to decline. 'I don't fancy walking into Drucker and telling him I'm leaving. It's only weeks since you had to go in and tell him I wasn't.'

'I think we'd work well together,' Joyce said. 'Think about it.'

But Heather insisted she would feel better with a little more stability in her life just now. She at least knew Hamilton Devereux. She would stay there for a few years yet.

'Well the least I can do is put a word in for you. Don't forget they'll need to fill my job. . . .'

'Would you?' Heather said. She was interested.

'Yes. I think you could manage it without any problems.'

Heather was pleased. She and Joyce continued with the decorating. It was a slow business, but the next stage was the living room. It had already been stripped and the paintwork sanded smooth.

They were discussing the likely opposition if Heather were to apply for Joyce's job when they were interrupted by the arrival of Nicholas Black. He'd come to discuss the car accident again.

Heather had decided not to jeopardize her no claims bonus, despite Nicholas's earlier suggestion to conduct everything via their insurance companies. Instead she had posted him a cheque just two days earlier. Nicholas had brought it back because she'd dated it 1985 instead of 1986.

'Oh, no problem, I'll change it and initial it,' Heather said. But Nicholas wasn't too keen. He asked if she could manage cash. Heather was curious. 'I'm afraid I don't keep that kind of cash on me,' she said.

Nicholas explained that he had lost his cash card. He explained that he was always losing things. 'It's a bit of a habit, I'm afraid,' he said. 'It would save me going to the bank tomorrow and I've a few bills to pay.'

With Joyce's help Heather managed to raise fifty-five

pounds, which she gave to Nicholas with a cheque for the balance. 'I see you're choosing wallpaper,' he said, flicking open one of the pattern books stacked on the settee.

'I was trying to,' Heather said. 'I can't decide.'

Nicholas walked round, examining the room. 'It would have to be a small pattern in this room, otherwise it'll look cluttered.'

'You aren't an interior decorator by any remote chance?' Joyce asked.

'Lord, no,' Nicholas replied, 'just an architect. But decoration comes into it of course.'

Joyce and Heather looked at each other. They had both thought the same thing. Here was a bit of welcome help. Joyce nodded to Heather to take the initiative.

'Perhaps we could ask for some free advice?' Heather asked.

Nicholas agreed straight away. 'Mind if I look through there in the kitchen?' he asked.

Heather shrugged. 'Please do. . . .'

As Nicholas went into the kitchen, Joyce stifled a giggle. Heather poked her and whispered, 'Shut up!'

James Fleming came to dinner at the Collins' house one evening after New Year. What Lucy stupidly thought might be a giggle was a disaster and James was extremely nervous.

She had to prompt him that his parents lived in Leeds. They didn't. That the mortgage he had started to talk about was in joint names with his sister. He hadn't got a sister.

Paul and Annabelle thought he was a rather odd character, as well as being older than they had imagined. Annabelle felt let down after her initial excitement at meeting Lucy's 'young man'.

What capped their disappointment – and started Annabelle's suspicions over James – was when he announced before ten o'clock that he had to leave. He explained his early departure with a remark that he had an early start the following day.

When Lucy had gone to bed, relieved her ordeal was over, Annabelle and Paul sat up late over a cup of tea. Annabelle expressed her disappointment, first at James' age, then at his unsociable manner.

'He didn't seem quite right, I agree,' Paul said. 'Very unforthcoming over his work. As though he had something he wanted to keep quiet.'

'Like a wife, possibly?' Anna asked.

Paul considered his wife's suspicion. 'Good God, Anna, that would explain quite a few things. A mortgage and going home early. But I can't see Lucy starting any sort of relationship with a man who –'

Annabelle cut him short. 'Unless, he's hiding it from Lucy. She wouldn't be the first girl to be told that sort of lie.'

They decided they would have to voice their suspicions as soon as possible. Lucy could get hurt.

The following evening, as Lucy prepared to go out, Anna asked if she was seeing James.

'Yes,' Lucy said. She detected a tension between her mother and father.

Tentatively, they questioned Lucy about his age. Then even more carefully they suggested that it might be wiser if Lucy did not get too involved with James Fleming.

Lucy said, evenly, 'Why?'

Paul and Annabelle looked at each other. Paul said, 'Well . . . has it occurred to you? I mean, have you ever thought that James might be married?'

Lucy looked from one parent to the other. 'As a matter of fact he is married.'

There hadn't been a row like it in the Collins' household since Lucy had lied to her parents about attending an all-night vigil with the Campaign for Nuclear Disarmament when she was supposed to be revising for O Levels. Paul demanded she give up the relationship immediately. Anna sided with James' wife and daughters.

'How would you feel if it was your husband involved with young girl?'

'I have feelings as well!' Lucy shouted back. '*I* don't like the fact he has kids. I wish he *was* single!'

Paul said he realized it wouldn't be easy, but she had to end it with James immediately. It was a hopeless romance. It had to stop.

Lucy screamed at them. 'I love him. I love him! I won't give him up!'

For days the tension in the air at the Collins' house was thick enough to cut with a knife. Lucy came and went, hardly speaking to her parents. Paul and Annabelle tried to talk to her, but she wouldn't listen. She merely left the room.

Pat and Terry had spent the days after Christmas ferrying round Mike Henty's gaming machines. The Christmas and New Year club and pubgoers had taken their toll on the expensive equipment and many clubs were screaming for replacements.

Terry was glad of a day off when Barry turned up one morning and offered to take his place. When the lads had driven off, Terry decided to phone Vicki Cleary and ask her round for the day. He was confident now that the aggression from the Clearys' was just hot air. Keeping cool had paid off. And on the one or two nights out he had had with Vicki recently, she felt sure her brothers had forgotten the matter. They were pretty busy with other work.

Unbeknown to all of them – Pat, Terry, Vicki and Barry – Joe and Eddie Cleary had followed Hancock and Sullivan's van as it left the Close that morning.

Joe and Eddie Cleary certainly weren't archetypal tough guys. But they felt a genuine resentment at the way Hancock and Sullivan had undercut them. It was that bastard Henty's fault, but they couldn't attack him without big trouble. No, the best way was to force these new boys out of business. They had a few ideas just how to do that.

The Clearys' shadowed the green van driven by Pat with Barry in the passenger seat all over North Liverpool. Not till Pat and Barry ducked into Mary's Café, near Goodison Park football ground, for a bacon buttie, did they make a move.

Joe opened the back door of their van and carried out a stack of breeze blocks. Eddie was already jacking up the back of Pat's van. They mounted the van on breeze blocks at both sides and Joe set about wrenching off the back wheel nuts with a brace.

Unfortunately for them, Pat and Barry were quick eaters. Barry was first out of the café. Immediately, his adrenalin started to pump. He hit Eddie Cleary like a ton of bricks.

'What do you think you're on?' He laid into Eddie viciously.

Pat was on the scene a second or two later. Joe Cleary was just putting a wheel in the back of their van when Pat grabbed him round the neck. The fight only lasted moments, but Eddie and Joe Cleary were bruised and battered. Eddie's nose ran with blood from a butt in the face. Joe was panting and holding his chest.

Barry spat at them. 'Don't try that again! Do you hear me!' He pushed Eddie viciously in the chest. 'Next time you'll be in the blood wagon! Right?!' Barry pointed at Joe. 'And that goes for him an' all!'

The wounded brothers dragged themselves to their van and left. Barry went to pick up the loose wheels. He was grinning to himself. He liked a bit of lumber now and then, if he was on the winning side. He still remembered his beating from Tommy McArdle's heavies.

Pat, however, was worried. Barry said to him, 'Cheeky gets! We were only gone five minutes. But they picked the wrong blokes, eh?'

'No, I think they got the right ones. . . .' He told Barry about the van war.

'Are you two daft?' Barry said. 'You let two pricks like that walk all over you for weeks!'

Pat looked apologetic. He wasn't as handy as Barry when it came to fighting.

Barry shook his head. 'It's Terry, this,' he said. 'I leave him for a few months and he goes soft!'

Doreen was still worried that Billy might be the target for revenge at Pollocks after crossing the picket line for the Christmas installation work. But the vote at the factory after Christmas had been overwhelmingly against a strike. Billy said he had been proved right. Nobody cared about the twenty-five redundancies.

'I don't want you to do it again, love,' Doreen said.

'Ah,' Billy said, scornfully. 'Never mind that. Think about the money!'

Billy had picked up a big pay packet after the triple-time payments. It was the best he'd ever had, more than £600. He'd promised Doreen she could go out and buy something for the house. 'What are you getting?' he asked, smiling.

'You'll see when I get it,' she said. 'It's practical, like, not something stupid.'

Billy was off work, a day in lieu of Christmas, one of the other perks of the installation job. He decided to wash his car while Doreen went into town to shop.

Bobby Grant had been spoiling to have another talk to Billy after seeing him cross the picket lines. He saw his chance when he nipped home for something to eat and spotted Billy in the Close.

They discussed the failed strike call at Pollocks. Billy was scornful and repeated his earlier statement that the twenty-five redundancies weren't worth bothering about.

'They didn't vote for a strike because it's January, everyone's skint,' Bobby said. 'Don't think the management didn't know that.'

'I could've told you that,' Billy said.

'Yeah, but what about the next holiday? The Easter shutdown – the summer holidays? There'll be another twenty-five blokes on the list then. Maybe fifty next time.'

Billy said he'd do the same again. He repeated his familiar theme, that his family was more important than anything else. 'Yeah,' said Bobby, 'but if you don't look out you'll be working overtime to put yourself out of a job!'

'Scare tactics, eh?' Billy sneered.

'Just common sense, lad. You think about it next time you turn your back on your mates!'

'And if I don't, I suppose I'll get bricks through the windows, eh? Or have the house set on fire!'

Bobby forced down his anger.

Billy pressed on. 'If one union can do it, why not another?'

Bobby pointed at him. 'I'll forget you said that!'

Bobby drove his car up the driveway of his house and went in. Billy sneered after him. 'Bloody unions!'

Sheila was inside, making Bobby a snack. She got the brunt of his frustration over Billy's attitude. But Sheila was sympathetic to the Corkhills' position. 'They have only just moved in, Bob. Money must be tight.'

Bobby could not see money being more important than principles.

When Pat and Barry drove back to the house, Vicki was lying on the settee talking to Terry and listening to the stereo. They felt easy with each other and there was a definite attraction between them which Terry, for one, was anxious to cultivate.

Terry hadn't been expecting Barry and Pat so soon. He checked out of the window.

'I don't want Pat to see me here,' Vicki said. She kissed Terry quickly and went out the back door.

Barry told him what had happened. 'Oh, Christ,' Terry exclaimed to Pat. 'You've told him about the Clearys?'

'What else could I do?' Pat said, 'He beat seven colours out of them!'

Terry was horrified. Barry beating up Vicki's brothers. Terrific. That would really make the romance blossom.

Barry lectured Terry on letting people like the Clearys' try to force them out of business. Pat found himself siding with Barry's aggressive attitude to the threat. 'I'll leave you to talk some sense into him,' Barry said, as he left.

Next morning, Pat wanted Barry to go out with him. But Terry wanted Barry kept out of the Cleary business. He felt depressed that the Clearys' hadn't backed off from confrontation. He felt even worse when Vicki came round and angrily accused him of acting like some Godfather, entertaining the victims' sister while his heavies beat up Joe and Eddie. Vicki's brothers were not seriously hurt, but they had been X-rayed and treated in hospital before being discharged.

Terry protested his innocence and pointed out that Joe and Eddie had been the aggressors, trying to steal their wheels. 'Pat just lost his temper,' Terry said.

'It was just Pat?' Vicki said. 'Our Eddie said there were two of them.'

'Oh, that was a mate of Pat's. He thought they were just robbers.'

'From what I heard he should be in a straitjacket. He was a right vicious get!'

Terry despaired. He and Vicki had to get this stopped. Before they knew it there would be real violence, even police involvement. He eventually persuaded Vicki that he had nothing to do with her brothers' beating. She apologized. Things were all right between them, fortunately, but what about between him and Pat? Under Barry's influence, Pat was spoiling for trouble.

Heather decided to take Nicholas Black's advice on her interior decorating and bought the paper and paint colours he recommended. She rather liked Nicholas with his self-effacing manner and his rather eccentric ways.

She'd taken a lot of ribbing off Joyce who kept hinting that Nicholas was a dark horse, gradually trying to win Heather's affection with his advice and his apparent chaotic domestic life, in which he was forever letting the phone get cut off, or losing his cash card. 'An invitation to mother,' Joyce said, with a smile.

'He's a genuine guy,' Heather had said. 'He wants to help.'

But Heather hadn't anticipated the lengths to which Nicholas Black would go to help her. He arrived one night – unannounced as usual – and started to help with wallpapering the living room. Joyce was a little tired of decorating by now and she jumped at the chance to do some packing. She had found a flat at West Kirby in the Wirral and was due to leave the next day.

Heather and Nicholas worked until almost midnight. Joyce came down and announced she was turning in for the night. Heather had yawned. 'God is that the time?'

She offered Nicholas a coffee before he left. 'Oh, I'm not finished yet,' he replied.

Heather had pulled a face at Joyce. Nicholas continued, 'You two go up. I'll let myself out when I've finished.'

Joyce teased Heather about Nicholas's intentions. 'The lengths some men will go to. . . .' she said with a twinkle in her eye.

Heather had gone down after midnight to see if Nicholas wanted anything to eat or drink. She really did like him. He was certainly different. But Nicholas was intent on his work, he didn't want anything.

Heather went back to bed, amused at her late-night decorator. Next morning, she couldn't believe it. Joyce was up first and called her down. What had been chaos the night before was now immaculate, just as she hoped it would turn out. The wallpapering was finished, the furniture and carpet were back in place. Even prints had been rehung. Heather was speechless. 'He must have been at it all night,' she said.

It was Joyce who found the little cartoon propped up on the window ledge. The caption read, 'Hope you like it!' Above that was a caricature of Heather, the career woman, with briefcase, waving an arm around her newly decorated living room. A balloon from her mouth said, 'My architect advised me!'

'It's good, isn't it?' Heather said of the cartoon.

'Yes,' Joyce said, with yet another twinkle, 'he's a genuine guy. . . .'

Heather dumped the cartoon on Joyce. 'Do you want coffee or fruit juice?' she said, stiffly.

'Did I say anything?' Joyce said, with mock innocence.

Sheila felt a little guilty about Bobby arguing with Billy in the street. On the way to the clinic she spotted Doreen hurrying up the Close towards her own home. She stopped her and apologized on Bobby's behalf.

'Oh, that,' Doreen said.

Sheila tried to explain that Bobby sometimes got carried away. The conversation only moved up a gear when Doreen referred to the strike as 'daft'.

Sheila questioned her description and Doreen, following Billy's line, had let rip. Sheila hadn't wanted a row in the street between wives so she tried to quieten things down by switching tack.

'I can understand how it happened, love,' she said. 'I know how much it costs to run a house and that, especially if you're desperate for money.'

At that point a delivery van and two men arrived. They were bringing Doreen's new acquisition, for which she'd nipped home from work to pay cash on delivery. Doreen moved to the front door and opened up. 'Stick it in there,' she told the men.

Doreen continued her attack, blaming Bobby and the unions for what was happening in the country. Sheila was now angry. She was even angrier when she saw Doreen pay cash on delivery with a large wad of banknotes.

'You've got a nerve to say that after your husband broke that picket line!'

Doreen came back at her, 'Never mind flamin' picket lines! He was making sure his family gets what they need!'

'Like a flaming bedroom carpet! Cash on delivery!' Sheila said, angrily.

'I don't see what's wrong! I don't!' Doreen retaliated.

Sheila left her. Over her shoulder, she said, 'You just spend the money, eh? Forget about your feller's workmates – the ones he used to have!'

Doreen went in. The carpet was blocking the hallway. She kicked it. She was upset. Upset about falling foul of her new neighbours yet again. 'Flaming money,' she said to herself.

The bad feeling between the two women might have continued, but for Barry Grant. Doreen thought he was Karen's boyfriend and as he was passing she asked if he'd help her carry the carpet upstairs. He was pleased to oblige. When he told her he was Sheila's son, Doreen was horrified. She told him about the row.

Barry was just leaving the Corkhills' when Sheila passed, on her way home. Sheila glared at him, but he got the two women together. They apologized, and later were glad Barry had been around that day.

Lucy Collins was still uncommunicative. Her parents could get no further information from her. She was obviously still seeing James.

'If I knew where to find him, I'd have a damn good talk to him,' Paul said. But they knew nothing about him other than his name. Annabelle was worried that James's wife might find out about the affair and Lucy would be accused of wrecking a marriage. They knew now that James had two children.

It was Annabelle who remembered that James was involved in the export or import of reproduction furniture. She spent a whole morning ringing likely furniture firms from the Yellow Pages, asking each firm if they employed a James Fleming. But she had no luck. By the time she had finished it was early evening. Lucy hadn't arrived, so she decided to phone her to see if she intended to be home for dinner. She looked up the number where

Lucy had written it in the desk diary and dialled Holcroft's. The switchboard had closed down, but a security man answered.

'Is that Holcroft's?' Annabelle asked.

'That's right, love. Holcroft International, Import and Export,' he said, giving the firm's full name and business. Just on a hunch, Annabelle asked if they had a James Fleming on the staff.

'You're in luck,' said the security man. 'He's still in his office. I'll try and put you through.'

Annabelle just managed to hang up in time.

By now, both Annabelle and Paul realized Lucy had returned from France not to be with them, but to continue her affair with a married man. For Paul it was even more devastating to discover that Lucy and James worked for the same company.

'Yes, it all fits into place, doesn't it?' he said to Anna that evening. 'Getting a job so soon and so easily. He must have arranged it all. Well the job isn't worth a carrot, not if it was obtained like that.'

With Annabelle's agreement, he decided to contact James Fleming and talk man to man.

If Barry had been able to get hold of the Clearys that morning in the Close he would have torn them apart with his bare hands. Nobody threatened his sister – or anyone in his family – and escaped.

It was Karen, sitting up late the previous night pondering how to end an essay, who heard noises in the Close. She went to the window to see a man rush from a battered old car and start to slash at the front tyres of Pat and Terry's van with a knife. Eddie Cleary froze when he heard someone shout 'Ey!' But he continued when he saw it was only a young girl. Karen moved towards him, demanding to know what was going on. She reached him and dragged his arm away from the wheel.

Eddie snatched it back and threatened Karen with the upraised knife. 'Just leave it!' he said. 'Get back to bed!'

Karen shouted. 'Barry!' at the top of her voice.

'Get out of it!' Eddie Cleary warned. He didn't like this. It was messy. Joe gunned the engine of their parked car.

He set about the tyre again as Karen retreated to the house. She called Barry again, but there was no need. Barry was out of the front door and moving fast. Eddie Cleary only just got to his car in time.

'Did he hurt you?' Barry asked Karen.

'No, no. He just threatened me,' Karen said, beginning to shake.

'I'll bloody murder them,' Barry said. 'Come on, get back inside.'

Later that morning, Terry inspected the damage. Barry insisted they wreck the Clearys' van in retaliation, but Terry said he wouldn't take part in any venture of that kind.

'What's your way of sorting them, then?' Barry asked.

'I don't know, but I don't want this kind of thing. It doesn't solve anything.'

Barry looked disgusted with Terry's docile attitude.

Terry warned him. 'And I don't want you involved either. It's not your van and it's not your business!'

'It's my business when our Karen gets threatened by some toerag with a weapon,' Barry said. 'Be warned.'

Terry tried to discuss the matter with Pat. But Pat was on Barry's side. He accused Terry of giving the Clearys what they wanted when Terry had suggested splitting the contract with Henty between them. Then Pat sneered at Terry, accusing him of being influenced and used by Vicki so her brothers could get back the contract. Terry denied it, but Pat insisted that he wouldn't sit back and let his share of the business go down the tubes. Terry realized Pat was bent on a drastic act of revenge. Immediately, he phoned Vicki and asked her to arrange a meeting between him and Joe and Eddie.

Later that day, Barry loaded a sledgehammer into the van. Pat watched him. When Barry suggested he and

Terry fix up an alibi for that afternoon, Pat's face fell. 'What!' he said.

'Well if the bizzies start nosing around you'll be number one suspects, won't you?'

Pat was worried. He went into the house to try to find Terry, but he'd gone.

Down at the yard where the Clearys and other small businesses kept their vehicles and equipment, Terry had been introduced to the sullen brothers.

Terry had explained that after the tyre-slashing he thought the feud between them had gone far enough. Vicki tried to push her brothers into a more enthusiastic response, but they pointedly treated Terry like he was dirt. They seemed more concerned with fixing the timing on a car.

'For Christ's sake,' Terry said, eventually, 'can't you get it into your thick –'

They both looked at Terry. Vicki smirked. Terry thought of a better way of putting it. 'Can't you see that I'm here offering a deal. I want a stop to what's been going on.'

Eddie and Joe regarded him blankly. Eddie looked to Joe, who nodded. 'Better talk then, hadn't we?' Eddie said.

'How about a pint?' Vicki said. 'I'll pay.'

The brothers nodded. They drove down to the Swan in the Clearys' van.

Joyce Harrington had been given dispensation to leave Hamilton Devereux early and when Heather walked into her office she found Joyce clearing her desk and collecting together personal belongings.

Joyce came straight to the point. 'Tench got it.'

'Why?' Heather asked. Keith Tench was a colleague of about the same age as Heather. They had never got on with each other, despite having similar qualifications and previous experience. Tench had even started with Hamilton Devereux at the same time as Heather.

'I can't believe it,' she said.

'Neither can I . . .' said Joyce. 'But that's their decision. What can I say?'

'Do you think he's up to it?' Heather asked.

'He's not up to your standard in anything, as far as I can see,' Joyce replied. 'You don't like him, do you?'

'That's an understatement. We hate each other's guts,' Heather said.

Joyce sat back in her chair. 'I'm sorry, Heather. I did put your name forward. I suppose you could ask Drucker why they didn't choose you.'

'And is he going to talk to me after . . . well, Tom?'

'Perhaps not. But you can always try. Personally, I think he might be prepared to give you an explanation.' Joyce stood up, collecting together a sheaf of papers. 'I think it's the least he can do.'

Heather was put in an awkward spot when Howard Drucker delegated the task of seeing Heather to Keith Tench.

Tench was twenty-nine years old and clean cut. Generally, he preferred the company of men rather than women. He was a keen squash player and already had his cups and other trophies installed in Joyce's old office.

Heather told him she'd prefer to wait to see Howard Drucker when he was less busy. She made to leave the office, but Tench asked her to sit down. He told her he knew she was disappointed, but he didn't want that to spoil their professional relationship. Heather gave an involuntary laugh. Tench didn't like it. They fenced with each other before Heather asked to get down to brass tacks and said, 'Why didn't I get the job?'

Tench sat back in his chair, 'Are you sure you want brass tacks?'

'That's what I'd have asked of Howard,' Heath replied.

'Okay,' Tench said. 'Our clients are entitled to our time in the office and what's up here,' he tapped his head. 'You gave the chairman of Curzon Communications a little more. . . .'

It hit hard. Heather had to control her voice as she complimented Tench on his delicacy. After she had recovered, she told him that Howard Drucker had sanctioned her relationship with Tom Curzon. But he would have none of it. It was his opinion – and Drucker's, he informed her – that the senior partner had been put in an embarrassing position.

Heather was shattered to think her relationship with Tom had been discussed between the two of them. She asked if this had happened, and Tench said that it had. She was in a weak position and she knew it. God knew whether she would ever get any promotion. She phoned Joyce that night and asked if she could take her up on the offer of working as her assistant. Joyce regretted she had appointed someone that afternoon.

Heather sat back in her newly decorated living room and realized that, for the moment at least, she would have to get along with Tench, whether she hated him or not.

Pat had been looking for Terry all afternoon. He had no van and Sandra had taken the car to work. If he and Terry couldn't fix up an alibi, they'd be in dead trouble.

He eventually found Terry in the Swan with Vicki and the Clearys.

'What's all this?' he asked.

'We've made a deal,' Terry said, grinning.

'With these two?' Pat asked.

Joe and Eddie Cleary raised their pints to Pat. Joe said, 'Though it breaks me heart not to get the chance of having a go at you and your mate. My ribs are still killing me!'

Terry started to tell Pat about the deal. It involved splitting the contract by taking alternative jobs with Henty. But Pat cut him short.

'Listen, I don't want to scupper the peace talks here, but there's something you lot should know. . . .' They all looked at him expectantly. He continued, 'Barry's gone down to your place looking for trouble.'

'Christ!' Terry said, jumping up. 'Let's get down there.'

Ten minutes later they arrived. Barry had destroyed the blue van in the yard. There were no windscreen or windows intact and the bodywork had been turned into scrap by the fourteen-pound sledgehammer. When Terry grabbed his arm, Barry was about to lay into the engine block.

'That's what you get for threatening my sister,' Barry snarled. 'And if you two come any closer you'll get the same.' He raised the hammer in self-defence.

'Look, we've worked out a deal for Christ's sake,' Terry said. 'Now who does this belong to?'

Barry's mouth dropped open. Vicki answered, 'It's not ours if that's what you mean!'

Barry gaped at the destroyed van. Joe and Eddie were laughing. 'I'd make yourself scarce if I were you, son. It's Lennie Sharrock's van that. He'll murder yeh!'

Paul Collins met James Fleming by the river Mersey. The conversation surprised him and he told Anna that evening. Paul had gone expecting to deal with a man who was using a young girl. Instead, he had found James tortured by his inability to end the affair.

Paul poured himself a drink. 'It seems it's Lucy that's set the pace. As far as Fleming was concerned it had ended in France. Lucy looked him up the minute she got back to Liverpool.'

'He isn't going to leave his family?'

'What do you think? Of course, he isn't. He told me he couldn't see either party hurt – his wife, or Lucy.'

'They have slept together?' Annabelle asked.

'I think that's obvious. He says he's tried to end it, but he can't for fear of hurting Lucy. He says it would crucify her.'

'Then what's he going to do?'

Paul sat back and sipped at his drink, pleased with the way he had handled the affair. 'Don't mention it to Lucy, of course, but I've given him a week to end it.'

Annabelle sighed. 'Does he love her?'

Paul snorted. 'The man doesn't know the meaning of the word. It's a sexual attraction, nothing more.'

Annabelle remembered Lucy as a child. It seemed hard to believe she was involved with a married man, with children of his own. 'Do you believe him? That he'll end it?'

'I think he realized I mean business.'

James tried to tell Lucy their affair was over. Instead he found himself telling her that he had met Paul to discuss the matter.

'You asked him to meet you?' Lucy demanded to know.

James glanced across the pub. He didn't want everyone in the world listening. 'He contacted me by phone. I had to go.'

'You should have told him to get lost,' Lucy said. 'What did he want?'

James was silent. Then he said, 'He's given me a week to finish it.'

'What!' Lucy was furious. When she got home she demanded to know why Paul had interfered.

'Because I had to!' Paul insisted. 'There's no way that this man is going to leave his wife and family for you! And you can't carry on as you are!'

'Think about his family,' Anna said. 'If they found out it could tear them apart. It's wicked for you to continue this!'

'You still have no right to interfere in my life,' Lucy said. 'If he didn't love me he would never have told me you gave him a week.' She was starting to cry. 'He does love me!'

It was that thought that convinced Lucy that James really felt for her. Next day she asked him to meet her and told him that, if they kept their affair totally secret, but told her parents it was over, they could get back to normal.

James tried to suggest it was deceitful. But the whole

affair was deceitful. And this way he had no need to hurt Lucy – *and* he would have kept his promise to Paul. He allowed himself to be carried along by Lucy, who seemed to be revelling in the extra spice this secrecy added to their relationship. He felt ashamed of himself, but it was an easy path. Or so it seemed, until Lucy announced that this was the time to consider telling Penny about his affair. 'It gives her time, James,' she said, 'time to prepare.'

'I'll have to wait until the time is right,' James said, as positively as he could. 'I can't just come straight out with it.'

That night, Lucy surprised her parents by announcing that she had changed her mind over James. The affair was over. She offered a few token tears and was consoled by her father. Annabelle, however, was sceptical about such a sudden change of heart. 'Did he tell you today?' she asked.

But Paul waved Anna's question aside. 'I think an early night might help, in the circumstances,' he said.

Chapter Fifteen

Carol Tidyman had been drunk on the second to last night of her holiday with the school in Switzerland. She had to get up in the night because she felt ill. But she was not so drunk and ill that she had lost her memory. She had seen Tracy Corkhill leave a room on the corridor below her own, the corridor with the toilets and bathrooms. It had been after three o'clock in the morning.

Tired, she had thought little of seeing Tracy on the corridor at that time of night. She had gone back to bed and slept late in the morning. She was only reminded of the fact when she was walking along the corridor the next day and saw Peter Montague coming out of the same room.

Had Tracy been in there with Monty? she wondered, and found that she had stopped in her tracks.

'What are you doing, Carol?' Montague asked.

'Nothing, sir,' Carol replied, snapping out of her thoughts.

'You should have been down at the ski lift by now. Where've you been?'

'I had . . . I was feeling sick, sir. I stayed in bed.'

'Are you better now?'

'Yeah.'

'Yes, sir,' Montague snapped.

'Yes, sir,' Carol replied.

'You'd better get moving then, hadn't you?'

Montague was paranoid about the night before. He'd taken an enormous risk. What if one of his male colleagues had knocked on his door as they had done earlier in the holiday, suggesting a late drink? God, he'd been foolish. But his mind kept going back to those few hours with Tracy. He hadn't been able to help himself.

When the new term started Carol Tidyman was quick to start rumours spreading round the school. It didn't take Montague long to find out about them. He saw them in black and white, or rather red on grey.

Montague was undertaking a spot check of the school toilets for illicit cigarette smokers when he went into the science block lavatories. They were empty, no one hiding in the cubicles, and Montague turned to leave. It was then he was confronted with the lurid graffiti in red felt-tip – 'Tracy Corkhill gave Monty a Swiss roll.'

His mouth dropped open. He moved quickly from the lavatories only to be confronted by Rod Corkhill on his way in.

'Out!' Montague said.

Rod stared at him. 'Get out. On your way!' Montague snapped.

'I only –' Rod began.

'Get out, do you hear?' Montague was panicking. He must have been coming over like a madman, but he couldn't let Rod go into the lavatories.

Montague's face was glowing red. Rod couldn't be bothered arguing so he did as he was told. Montague hurried off, trying to find the caretaker. Rod watched him leave and, as he still needed to use the lavatory, nipped round the corner and through the door.

Rod was just picking up his bag when he saw the graffiti. Frantically, he wet toilet paper, then paper towels, trying to scrub off the words. Montague was trying to hide this from him? That's why girls had been sniggering behind his back all day. Everyone must know about this. Tears of frustration came to his eyes as he realized the ink would have to be painted over.

Two other boys came in and spotted him. 'Aye, aye. Keeping his sister's good name, eh?'

'If the coppers find out about Monty he'll get it chopped off!'

'Piss off!' Rod spat at them and charged out of the lavatories. The bell had just gone for the start of afternoon lessons and the corridor was full. Rod barged his way through the groups of pupils, tears stinging his eyes.

The staffroom door had a notice saying 'Please Knock', but Rod merely barged in. Everyone looked up. Peter Montague was mopping his brow and pouring a cup of tea. Rod moved straight for him.

'Yes?' Montague asked.

A split second later, Rod's head collided with the bridge of the teacher's nose. Montague sank to his knees and Rod started to kick and punch him. It took two other teachers, including the games master, to get Rod away from Montague.

Tracy Corkhill was trembling with fear as she tried to concentrate on the maths lesson.

Elsewhere in the school, Doreen, Billy and Rod were being interviewed by the headmaster. Rod had been suspended on the day of the attack on Montague and summoned to the headmaster's office with his parents.

So far Rod had refused to talk about the attack to his parents, even when Billy had threatened him with a good hiding. Doreen was frantic that he would be expelled, that his chance of university would go down the drain. Billy was totally bewildered. It was the kind of thing his elder brother Frankie, now dead, had once done. People talked about 'bad blood'.

The headmaster had called in Montague, who was officially on sick leave. Doreen was appalled at the sight of his bruised nose and blackened eye.

The headmaster introduced them. The first thing he demanded of Rod was an apology, but his request was met by silence from Rod, who stared resolutely at the floor. The headmaster pressed him. Rod refused to apologize. Billy was all for belting Rod there and then, but Doreen touched his arm. She wanted to do things right.

'Perhaps we can leave the apology till later,' said the headmaster. 'Rodney, would you like to explain why you butted Mr Montague here?'

Rod again refused to speak.

'You speak, lad, or you'll be in more trouble. Off me!' Billy said.

The headmaster intervened. 'It seems some mindless person in the school scrawled an obscenity on the wall of the toilets which in some way suggested that your daughter . . . that there was some kind of . . . was involved in some way with Mr Montague.'

'Is that all?' Billy said. He looked at Rod. 'You pillock! If someone's saying stupid things about your sister you belt *them*, right!'

'Billy!' Doreen said, nudging him. 'Shut up, will you?'

The headmaster, sensing he was winning, continued. 'I can understand the reaction, if Rodney's sister's good name was somehow brought into question. . . . But – let's get to the point, shall we? – an attack like this would normally have meant expulsion, but I've decided the suspension Rod had suffered so far . . . well we'll take it no further.'

Doreen sighed with relief. 'He can stay here?' Doreen said.

'I'd still like the apology though, Mrs Corkhill,' said the headmaster, 'and a promise that he won't discuss this business with any other pupil.'

Rod continued to refuse to apologize. Next morning he refused to go to school. Doreen and Billy renewed the hostility against him. 'If you don't apologize, lad, you'll be out on your ear!'

Up till now neither Billy nor Doreen had asked what the offending graffiti said. Doreen asked.

Billy said, 'I don't want to hear any filth, especially about our Tracy.'

'Well I do,' said Doreen. 'Come on, Rod, what did it say?'

Rod eventually said, flatly, 'Tracy Corkhill gave Monty a Swiss roll.'

The dreadful possibility sank into their minds. Billy sent Rod upstairs and called Tracy down. 'Don't go screaming and shouting at her, will you?' Billy said.

'Maybe she's not the baby you think she is, Billy.'

'Just keep it down,' he replied.

When Tracy appeared, Billy asked if Montague had gone to Switzerland with the school party. Tracy flippantly said, 'So what?'

Billy and Doreen swapped looks. Tracy was beginning to become nervous. There was a silence. 'If you're gonna ... if you're gonna believe them lies then ...' She rushed upstairs.

Billy and Doreen looked at each other. Bewildered.

Later, Tracy crept into Rod's room, carefully, so her parents wouldn't hear. She asked if he would apologize.

'You're joking, aren't you?' Rod said. 'I should've killed him.'

'You hurt him. You shouldn't have done that.'

'Leave me alone,' Rod said.

'If you don't you're gonna get expelled, everyone'll know about me, me mum and dad'll find out....' Rod remained silent. Tracy continued, 'You don't want that, do you?'

Rod shook his head. Next day he went into school and sullenly apologized to Montague in the headmaster's presence.

Billy and Doreen continued to mull over the matter for a day or two more. Billy was uneasy about the whole incident, but he thought it impossible his little girl would be involved with a man of that age – and a teacher. Doreen wasn't so sure. For months, Tracy hadn't mentioned boyfriends – she always had earlier. And she was so keen to go to Switzerland. The matter might have been forgotten in time, but for a telephone call to Julia's – the Corkhills' former address – by Reg Kane, the owner of Kane's Mini-Mart. Julia came round to pass on the message personally.

'Oh, that's our Tracy's boss at the Saturday job,' Doreen said. 'What did he want?'

'He says does she want her job back,' Julia said, going to put the kettle on. 'Do you want tea, Billy?'

Billy had pricked his ears up. 'No, no ta,' he said.

'What's he on about? She's worked there over a year.'

'Oh,' Julia said, she hesitated, then, 'well, he said she hadn't worked there since September. . . .'

Billy and Doreen were looking at each other.

'He wanted to know what if . . .'

'The holiday?' Billy said.

'Yeah, the flaming holiday.'

Doreen and Billy were obliged to tell Julia what had happened and the comment written on the wall at school. Their minds were racing. Julia remembered the conversation with Tracy before Christmas. She had promised not to mention Tracy's boyfriend, but – she felt she should let the confidence be broken now. She told Doreen and Billy about the letter to 'Peter'.

The minute Tracy walked in from school she was confronted with questions. What's Mr Montague's first name? Why haven't you been to your Saturday job since September? Where did the money come from for Switzerland?

Tracy couldn't stand any more. There was more gossip at school, now this at home. And Peter was too scared to see her these days. Months of deceit were weighing heavily and she broke down.

Billy was shattered. He stood, open-mouthed, as Doreen relentlessly questioned Tracy and finally got her to confess that she had had sex with Peter – just once – in Switzerland.

'Did he force you into this?' Billy shouted. But Tracy was sobbing. Billy turned to Doreen, 'Giving her money to get her over there then . . . Jesus!'

He snatched up his jacket. Before Doreen could make a move to stop him he was out of the house.

It took him half the usual time to drive to Brookside Comprehensive, even in the old Renault. There was nobody in the staffroom. But there were noises in the hall. Montague was involved in a rehearsal for *A Midsummer Night's Dream*. He had his back to the door where Billy entered.

Billy started to run as he recognized Montague. The boy on stage stopped in mid-speech.

'Montague!' Billy said. And Peter Montague turned.

Billy butted him in his still bruised face. Then laid into his ribs with a flurry of vicious punches. As Montague fell, he started to kick him. Only the arrival of some sixth-form lads and two other teachers stopped the violence. A sixth-form girl sprinted off to call 999.

Ten minutes later, an hysterical Billy was in custody. Two hours later, he was released on bail to attend the magistrates' court on a charge of causing actual bodily harm.

Meanwhile, at home Tracy was sobbing in Doreen's arms. She had convinced Doreen that she hadn't been used by Peter Montague. It was she that had gone to his room; she who had persuaded him to give her the money.

*

Lenny Sharrock found Barry Grant in the public bar of the Swan.

'Come and sit in the corner, son,' Lenny said menacingly, taking Barry's arm and propelling him away from the bar. 'I want to talk to you about a van.'

The Clearys had got their revenge for the beating. It must have been them that tipped the wink to Lenny that Barry had destroyed his van. Barry's throat had gone dry. Lenny had convictions for just about everything, including violence.

'It's going to cost you £1,500,' Lenny was saying, 'or you can pay in easy instalments. Like a little slapping for now, then a bit bigger, then a bit bigger . . .'

'How am I going to find £1,500?' said Barry.

'How am I going to find a new van?' Lenny said. 'You've got a week to come up with it, right?' He moved away from Barry, pinching his cheek viciously, as he stood up. 'Oh,' he added, 'and don't be thinking of bunking back to Wolverhampton.'

Barry looked at him. How did he know about Wolverhampton?

'I've done a bit of homework on you, Granty. Harper's Shopfitting. Nice family at Brookside Close. Nice house.' He smiled, 'A week, eh? No more!'

Sharrock left. Barry had to get the money.

Sheila was still enjoying the Return and Learn course. Her project had finished and she had started another one with Sally Dinsdale, her classmate. She had tried to get together with Matty, but he had paired himself off with Mo Francis.

She was pleased when Alun Jones, their tutor, announced a weekend residential course – just one day and night – at a country-house college on Deeside. She put her name down to go and so did Matty.

Bobby, however, was not so pleased. 'I can pick you up from there in half an hour. What do you have to stay the night for?'

'The idea's to get students together socially, to get to

know each other better. It's like . . . like going to university for the night, I suppose.'

'You'll enjoy it, Mum,' Karen said.

'Oh, aye and who's going to look after our Claire, eh?' said Bobby.

'It's only one night. You can manage between you!' she said. 'And who was the one who was on about changes in the role of women, eh? After our Claire was born?'

'So I have to look after the baby while you go out boozing with the fellers on the course? Great.'

'Oh, grow up, Dad,' Karen said.

Sheila was indignant. 'That's why some women daren't go to night school and things like that, you know! Because of that attitude. When any woman wants to spend a bit of time away from home they automatically think it's to chase blokes.'

'Sorry I spoke,' Bobby said. He looked at Karen. 'But if I'm busy or anything, you and our Damon'll have to make sure you're here.'

Sheila looked at Karen and raised her eyes. Whatever Bobby thought, she was going.

Nicholas Black refused to take any payment for decorating Heather's living room. This embarrassed her as he'd made such a good job. She repeatedly tried to get him to come out for a meal, but dates were always inconvenient for him. Finally, he fixed a date and they went to an Italian restaurant, which Tom Curzon would not have been seen dead in.

Heather found him interesting company. During the veal piccatina, he apologized for being so difficult over the dates, but Heather always seemed to pick an evening when he was spending time with his children. He told Heather he was divorced, but he and Barbara were still on good terms. She had custody of the three children.

Heather found his openness refreshing and it wasn't long before she found herself discussing Tom Curzon.

'I don't suppose many women would turn down a chance like that. Travel, big house, plenty of money,' Nicholas said.

'I was in danger of being a possession though,' Heather said. 'Just something on a list for the insurance company.'

They got on well together and Heather laughed when Nicholas asked her out for a meal in return for the one she had just bought him. Nevertheless, she accepted. Nicholas took her to a Chinese restaurant. Over the meal he told her about his work. He was an architect in the offices of a local council. In the Swinging Sixties when he'd started training, the sky seemed the limit for architects. These days, with spending cuts, you only got to design mundane, strictly economical buildings.

'Somehow I don't think I'm ever going to get the chance of a cathedral,' he laughed. 'Even a block of public loos costs scores of thousands these days!'

Heather felt no threat at all from Nicholas. Unlike some men, he never made any attempt to be invited back for a drink. Nor did he try to push the relationship along in any way. She took the plunge and asked him to dinner at her own home.

'I'd love to,' Nicholas said.

Heather went to town on the meal. When she was with Tom Curzon it was always restaurants. She'd rarely made anything more than a snack for him. She quite enjoyed making a special meal, if not the drudgery of everyday cooking.

Nicholas arrived at the due time, but in a state of panic. He apologized for causing any trouble, but explained he'd been left to look after his son, Adam. The boy was outside in the car. Nicholas assumed the dinner was off, but Heather was pleased to split the dinner three ways and invited Adam to stay.

With conversation on such subjects as robots and motor racing, pop music and sport, Heather realized just how out of touch she was with younger people. How the people she knew well never seemed to have children.

When he left, Adam got a kiss. His father was only kissed second.

Billy and Doreen were frantic. Tracy had left home. There was no note or anything to indicate where she might have gone.

They didn't know that the previous evening, Tracy had sat on the landing with tears in her eyes while Billy told Doreen how he planned to clear himself by exposing Montague in court for using his child. 'That's why I haven't told the coppers,' he said. 'I want it to come out in the court, then the bizzies can have a field day on Montague. He'll get three years easy.'

When they discovered Tracy's disappearance, they imagined all sorts. Had she run away with Montague? Was she pregnant?

Billy was so worried he phoned the police.

But Tracy phoned after two worrying days. She was at Julia's, where she had asked her nan not to tell her parents her whereabouts. Julia had finally persuaded Tracy to phone home. 'Your mum and dad have got enough trouble, love,' she said, 'without worrying about you going missing.'

Billy and Doreen were relieved to hear Tracy was safe and well. At Tracy's request, Doreen met her in a café near the shops on the estate. Billy was asked to stay away. In the café, Tracy poured out her heart to her mother. 'I'm sorry, Mum, but I'm scared of what's going to happen. If me dad starts telling everyone why he did it, me and Peter are gonna be ... our names are gonna be mud. Don't let him tell anyone, will you?' She told Doreen again that Billy had got it all wrong. It was she who had seduced him. It was she who had persuaded him to pay towards Switzerland. 'I don't want either of them to go to jail, honest I don't, Mum.'

Tracy was allowed to stay a few days longer at Julia's. That night Billy and Doreen wondered how they could protect their daughter. The answer came next day when the headmaster visited their home.

Montague had confessed to having sex with Tracy and the headmaster had dismissed him. He put it to Billy that the matter should be forgotten.

'Like hell it should!' Billy said. 'I want him jailed!'

The headmaster said he understood Billy's feelings, but what was the point? 'He might get a suspended sentence, or a short prison sentence,' he said. 'As it is he's been well punished. Your attack and the fact that he'll never get a teaching job again.'

The headmaster also announced that he had arranged transfers to Hollowcroft Comprehensive School for both Rod and Tracy, to spare them any gossip or embarrassment. Doreen was grateful for that. Tracy had not been back to school since Billy was arrested.

'The other point is that young Tracy has had a lot of strain just lately,' the headmaster said. 'I don't think it would be helpful for her to be called to give evidence at any trial of Peter Montague.'

That hadn't occurred to Billy or Doreen. They were beginning to see the headmaster's point of view, though they didn't realize that his main concern was his school's reputation among parents, not to mention the governors. He had managed to keep it from them.

'I don't know what to do,' Billy said aloud.

The headmaster saw his chance. 'I know a little about the legal system,' he said. 'Montague tells me he's trying to get the police to drop the charge of assault – for his own sake as well as young Tracy's. . . . If you *did* have to go to court, you could plead guilty and decline to tell them why you assaulted the teacher. . . .'

Billy thought about it.

'You're not forced to give the reason why and a respectable family man like yourself wouldn't expect to get a harsh sentence. A fine, perhaps. Or at worst a suspended sentence.' The headmaster thought he might have gone over the top a little with talk of 'respectable'. Respectable family men didn't usually beat up members of his staff. But he felt he was persuading Billy. 'I'll leave you to consider my suggestion,' the headmaster said.

After he'd gone, Billy sat for a while, thinking. 'He's right you know, Doe,' he said. 'If I keep my gob shut, then . . .'

'I think so, love,' she said, 'for Tracy's sake.'

Billy decided that if it came to court he would stay silent on why he attacked Peter Montague.

Barry had a problem. He'd worked out how to get the money, but he needed the house to himself for a few hours.

His opportunity came on the evening before Sheila was due to attend her residential course. Bobby announced that he was working and couldn't mind Claire next evening. Karen said she couldn't as she had a date with Guy.

'Isn't it always the way,' Sheila said, 'I fix something for myself and suddenly everything goes wrong.'

'Ask our Damon,' Bobby said. 'He's got nothing to do.'

But Damon produced two tickets for a discotheque. 'Ar, Mum, I've paid three quid for these!'

'I can't help it if I'm working,' Bobby protested. 'It's the Branch tomorrow. The date's been changed because there's a retirement do after.'

Barry walked in on the discussion. Sheila hadn't even thought of asking him. But Karen suggested it.

'All right,' Barry said. 'I don't mind.'

Sheila kissed him. 'Thanks, love.'

When Lambert, a representative of Fast Credit, arrived at the house the next evening the only occupants were Barry and Claire. Barry had removed the picture of his mum and dad from the sideboard and replaced it with the framed picture of Karen and Claire taken by Damon's mate Neil.

From the sideboard drawer he'd taken Bobby's carefully stored payslips from work. All the other documents were available too, like the mortgage repayment card and past, completed HP agreements.

Lambert admired the picture of Karen and Claire and tried to get Claire to play with his pen. It was one of the easiest stunts Barry had ever pulled. Lambert glanced through the payslips.

'I see you're with the union then?' he said. He mentioned a recent dispute concerning the ETWU. Barry didn't know anything about it and had to struggle to answer Lambert's question, 'Oh ... it was one of my assistants that handled that one,' Barry said. 'I'd been on holiday when it started, like.'

But that was the only real hurdle, other than when it came to asking if he could collect the cheque at the Fast Credit office. Lambert said that was a little unusual, but Barry explained he was due to go away. In the end, Lambert agreed. Barry collected the cheque two days later and got a fast clearance on it through the moribund bank account he'd held for years.

Chapter Sixteen

Karen and Guy were watching a German film by Wim Wenders called *Kings of the Road*. Karen had been asked by the student newspaper to review it at a local film-society showing. The film was due to do the rounds of the film societies that summer.

The tickets were perks of the job and though Guy had often teased her about her journalism, he had been keen enough to accompany Karen. That afternoon he had commiserated with Karen because she hadn't been able to persuade the editor, Richard, that she should be picked to interview *Tube* presenter, Paula Yates. Karen expressed her determination to be a maverick and do her own interview with Paula to sell to the teenage magazines. Guy had wished her good luck.

Karen now knew Guy well enough to spend a lot of time in his study-bedroom at the Hall of Residence. The relationship, so far, had been platonic, but that afternoon Guy had obliquely suggested that he wouldn't mind sleeping with Karen. She said she wouldn't mind either. They had kissed properly for the first time, but Guy hadn't pushed her at all.

Karen was a virgin. She presumed that her friends in turn presumed she wasn't. But she had never felt enough for anyone to go as far as making love. Now, she knew she was closer than she had ever been. But she was worried. Her mind wandered from the film showing before her. Guy put his arm round her shoulders. With Guy, she really wanted to experience sex. But the thought still frightened her.

Willaston Court was a rambling old country house looking out over the Dee Estuary towards the hills of North Wales. Not that Sheila had much time to admire the view. The whole day, apart from lunch in the canteen, had been session after session with speakers on all aspects of Merseyside's history and economy.

She had enjoyed the group sessions, too, and played her part in stimulating conversation among students from similar backgrounds to her own. The sessions continued after evening dinner, then the students were turned loose on the bar.

Sheila joined Alun Jones, Sally Dinsdale, Matty and Mo Francis. Other people they had met wandered in and out of their group. Sheila brought the conversation on to the attitudes of men to these kind of courses. Alun Jones cited a number of examples of how his sessions had been upset by jealous husbands. 'Not to mention wives, I might add,' he laughed.

Sally confided in Sheila about her home life. Her husband, despite being a member of senior management in a construction company, was a wife batterer. The residential course was a welcome break away from perhaps another bout of unexpected, drink-inspired violence. Her children had been left with a friend's. She hadn't revealed their whereabouts to her husband. 'Just in case,' Sally said.

'You mean he'd hit the children?' Sheila said, horrified.

'Yes,' Sally said, 'if they happen to get in the line of fire.'

Sally told Sheila how she had suffered the violent attacks for more than eight years. Sheila asked if she had sought help, or perhaps gone to a refuge. Sally shook her head. 'It's not every day,' she said. 'Other times it's marvellous. I didn't come here to talk about all this. . . .'

Sheila suggested another drink, but Sally was ready for bed. 'Me too,' Sheila said. 'Anyone else?'

But Matty and Mo were staying for another drink. Sheila noticed them giggling between themselves. 'I'll have another Martini before I'm ready for bed,' Mo told Matty.

Sheila also noticed she gave him the money to buy the drink. Matty seemed to be really thick with Maureen Francis these days. She bet he hadn't mentioned her to his wife, Teresa. She used to be really jealous when they were all younger. Still, they'd been a devoted couple for years. Sheila privately reprimanded herself for thinking that a man like Matty would have his head turned by someone like Mo Francis.

Life with Lucy had been easy since she had renounced her affair with James. She hadn't been out quite so much, but she seemed to be looking up more old friends. Generally, she was quiet. Annabelle decided she deserved a treat. She planned to arrive at the Holcroft's office and surprise her with an invitation to lunch at a hotel.

Unfortunately, she was delayed by traffic and it was five past one before she reached the street where Lucy worked. Anna was waiting for the green light to come on at the pedestrian crossing when she spotted Lucy leaving the office and turning up a side street. She called but the traffic noise drowned her voice.

Anna crossed and hurried round to the side street. She was just in time to see Lucy enter a pub. As Anna arrived at the pub she turned up her nose involuntarily. It was a dump. Fancy Lucy frequenting a place like this. Still, it had a plaque on the wall which read 'bar lunches served', so Anna went in. It was smoky and mainly full of businessmen. Annabelle felt a little out of place.

She moved through the groups of beer-drinking men, checking the cubicles.

James saw her a split second before Annabelle saw him. He was sitting holding hands with Lucy at a table in the far alcove of the pub. Lucy stopped speaking and followed James' gaze.

'Mum!' Lucy was on her feet, ushering Annabelle to join her.

James had coloured up. He rose politely. God, why did she have to come here?

'I thought . . .' Annabelle began. She was shocked.

'It's all right, Mum,' Lucy said, holding James' hand. 'James and I are getting married.'

'What?' Annabelle said.

James tried to control his shock. Lucy continued, 'He's told his wife about us and we're going to be married. Isn't that marvellous?'

'Well I . . . Well this is a great surprise,' Annabelle said. 'How long ago was this decided?'

She looked at James, but Lucy answered, 'Oh, a couple of days ago. . . .'

'I see,' Annabelle said.

Lucy was full of enthusiasm. She asked James to get Annabelle a drink. 'Time to celebrate, mm?' she said.

Annabelle tried to question James further, but Lucy kept chipping in. She even talked about a wedding next year. Annabelle left earlier than she had anticipated – and in a state of shock.

Paul was furious when he confronted Lucy that

evening. He ranted to her about the complications and difficulties of dissolving a marriage, particularly where there were children involved. 'Then there's the division of property. We know he has a house. He just won't want to go through with it, for God's sake!'

Lucy remained calm and cheerful, 'I realize all this Dad. But I'm prepared to wait, for as long as it takes. We love each other.'

In private, Paul told Annabelle he was going to see James again.

They met by the river again. James had not been surprised to get Paul's telephone call. The pressure for James to tell Penny had been getting greater every day. For Lucy to tell her mother that they were going to marry – and in front of him – it was all too much. He felt Lucy was unbalanced by the whole affair. She seemed to be playing a crazy game for her own benefit.

He told Paul that he had no intention of leaving his wife, that the pressure from Lucy was getting too much to bear. Paul extracted from him a promise that he would end the affair as soon as possible. 'There's absolutely no question of you telling your wife?' Paul asked.

'None,' James said.

That evening, Paul and Annabelle told Lucy that James had discussed the affair with Paul.

Again, they tried to impress upon her the messiness of divorce. She wouldn't listen. 'I know all this. I realize,' she said. 'Can't you see I'm prepared to wait?'

When Paul played his trump card and said he had a categorical assurance from James that he had no intention of marrying her, it was as if he was talking to her in a foreign language.

Lucy merely said, 'We're only going to live together to begin with.'

Annabelle said, after Lucy had gone to bed, 'She can't seem to get it into her head.'

'Fleming has had enough now. I'm pretty sure that'll be the end of it.'

Annabelle hoped that the *coup de grâce* by Fleming would not hurt Lucy too much.

Sheila Grant was walking back from the shops when she saw Lennie Sharrock walk out of the Swan. Following him was Barry Grant. They sat down on a low wall outside and Barry handed over a bundle.

Sheila had stopped. She hoped Barry wouldn't spot her spying on him, but she was curious. Lennie Sharrock started riffling through the bundle. Sheila's curiosity turned to worry as she saw that the other man was counting a wad of banknotes.

Sharrock nodded and Barry gave him the thumbs up. Barry went inside and the other man left in a car. Nothing had changed hands. Barry didn't seem to have bought anything. What was he doing?

Her thoughts went immediately back to Jane Smith, the drug addict. She had had an assurance from Barry he was not involved in drugs. Before she got a chance to approach Barry about the matter, he had gone. He left a note saying he was going back to Wolverhampton.

Day after day, Lucy waited in the company car park at Holcroft's for James to appear. She had found out he was in London, but not how long for. There had been no phone calls for her, not even a letter.

When James arrived, Lucy went straight to his car. 'Where've you been?'

'London,' he said, flatly.

'Why didn't you let me know?'

'I was called away suddenly.'

'You could have phoned, or written,' Lucy said. 'Why did you tell my father you weren't going to marry me?'

'Lucy, I have to get into work,' James replied. He was conscious of other people in the car park. This was unbearable.

'You were just telling him a lie, was that it?' Lucy said.

'We can carry on like before, mm? When you leave Penny we'll tell him then, shall we?'

'I have to go into work!' James was brusque.

'Meet me at lunchtime. I want you to tell me you were telling Dad lies, James.'

'I have an appointment for lunch,' James said, walking off.

Lucy sank back against his car. She wanted to see him at lunchtime and he didn't want to see her. How could he?

Next morning, James didn't turn up at all. Lucy waited in the car park for over an hour. He must be at home, she thought. Ten minutes later, she was riding the train out to the suburbs.

When Penny opened the door to her, James was in the garden, playing with their youngest daughter, Emily. Lucy announced herself by name, but it didn't register.

'James never told you?'

Penny was curious. She called for James to come in, but he was busy pushing the little girl on the swing and didn't hear. A sickening thought began to creep into Penny's mind and she invited Lucy in. After a few more questions, which Lucy was eager to answer, Penny had the truth.

'You have to be told,' Lucy said. There was a pleasant smile playing about her lips.

James came in. 'What the hell are –'

'She has to be told, James.'

Penny fled from the room in tears leaving little Emily staring at Lucy.

James followed her out. In the kitchen she was hysterical with rage and hurt. James was desperately trying to calm her, trying to explain. It wasn't his fault, Lucy had followed him from France. But Penny wouldn't listen. 'Don't come near me, don't come near me!'

James came back into the room. 'Get out. Get out and stay away!'

Lucy was shocked. 'I only wanted her to know, James.'

Penny came back into the room. Her face was twisted

with hate, her eyes red. She screamed at Lucy and called her a whore. Lucy sat calmly as Penny vented her anger on the girl who had slept with her husband; for whom her husband had told lies. James tried to push her out of the room, but she was shouting almost incoherently about the times she must have been lied to so he could go to bed with Lucy.

When Penny went upstairs James followed her, throwing a look of pure hatred at Lucy. But Lucy merely stood up and walked round the room, looking at the photographs and childish drawings done by the children. Emily played on the carpet apparently unconcerned.

James came back in.

'How did she take it?' Lucy asked.

James was incredulous. 'Christ Almighty!' He could hold his fury back no longer and laid into Lucy, calling her a tart and a stupid bitch for following him home. How he regretted ever meeting her.

Lucy tried to go to him, put her arms round him, but he pushed her away. 'Christ, if I hadn't been so weak, so bloody weak, I'd have told you then. Before I came home. I didn't want to hurt you. Now look what you've done. To me, to her!'

Lucy couldn't believe this was James.

'Get out!' he said. 'Come on.' He dragged her by the arm and threw her out of the front door. 'I never want to see you again, do you hear? Ever!'

Lucy went home in a daze. Everything had crumbled. When she arrived home early, Annabelle was concerned. 'What is it? Is it something to do with James?'

Lucy nodded. Then went upstairs. Lying on her bed, drained, she kept hearing Penny refer to James as 'Jim'. All those months he had let her call him James. It had all been false. Every single day they had been together.

Lucy didn't go back to work for over a week. In the afternoon of her first day she was called into the transport manager's office and sacked. For bad timekeeping. She knew James had arranged it.

After that Lucy blamed her parents for everything going wrong. They were full of concern for her, but each time they tried to reach out to her, she was rude, or insulting. She always brought the conversation back to the same theme. 'Are you happy now? Are you happy with what you've done to me?'

She started spending more time going out. She went to clubs and picked up men, having sex with them in their cars or flats. She stole, too. Once she was caught trying to take a skirt. The shop assistant stopped her as she left the store. Lucy turned on the shop assistant with an unwavering stare. 'James likes me in red,' she said. The shop assistant, rattled, had taken the skirt off her and not bothered asking her to return to the boss's office.

Then she stole shampoo. It smelt of apples. James had liked her hair when it smelt of apples. She bought it time and again and when she had no money she walked from store to store, stealing the same brand. But she never used it now. She hid it under her bed.

Doreen and her brother-in-law Jimmy had tried to persuade Billy to get a solicitor. But he refused. 'I'm not saying a word in that court so I don't need anyone to speak for me, do I?' he said.

The three magistrates on the Bench at North Liverpool Magistrates' Court had asked him twice if he was represented. They seemed concerned that he should not have someone to represent him. After listening to the evidence from the prosecuting solicitor, they asked Billy a third time if he wished to be represented.

Billy shook his head.

'Is there anything you'd like to say on your own behalf?'

'No thanks,' Billy said. 'I'm sorry, that's all.'

Doreen was sitting at the back of the court with Jimmy. It sounded so bad, what the prosecuting solicitor had said. It seemed like Billy was a wild man who made unprovoked attacks on teachers. As the case started, Tracy, in her school uniform, had slipped in through the double panelled doors and sat near Doreen.

Doreen whispered, 'What are you doing here?'

'I wanted to be here. He is me dad!'

'And he wouldn't be here if it wasn't for you!' Doreen, in her fears for their future if Billy was jailed, had become aggressive towards Tracy. Billy was confident, though, that he would get a suspended sentence. He was only concerned for Tracy, it seemed, and he had told Doreen not to pick on her.

Billy was standing, waiting anxiously, for the court sentence. But he was dismayed when the magistrates announced that they wanted a verbal report prepared so as to find out a little more of Billy's circumstances.

'I wanted to get it over with,' Billy protested. But to no avail.

In the interview room at the court, Billy and Doreen were confronted by Spencer, a probation officer. He sensed from long experience that there was more to this case than met the eye. But Billy would not co-operate. When Spencer asked about the presence of his daughter, Billy clammed up completely.

Back in court, the probation officer confessed failure to glean any useful information.

After a preamble on the severe penalties to be incurred by those who make violent attacks, Billy was jailed for three months. The shock was enormous. Billy felt his legs shaking.

But Doreen, who had listened to enough against her husband, rose to her feet and ran towards the Bench. 'This is all wrong! You can't do it!' she screamed. The court reporter started to scribble. 'That teacher was carrying on with my daughter!'

'Shut up, Doreen!' Billy shouted. A policeman tried to shut him up.

But Doreen persisted. Jimmy was trying to restrain her, but she shouted at the Bench, 'Montague slept with my daughter! He used her!'

Billy was beside himself. He had planned all this so nobody knew anything. 'Doreen. Be quiet!' He was taken down the steps. 'Say nothing!' he shouted up. 'Say nothing!'

Tracy fled from the court, pushing through the waiting defendants. She ran till she ran out of wind. Her dad had been jailed and it was all because of her and Peter. And her mum had told everyone!

Doreen sobbed on Jimmy's shoulder. Urgently, the chairman of the Bench called for the duty solicitor.

Billy had no appetite for his lunch of pie and peas from the police canteen, and neither had Doreen. They were sitting in the cells beneath the court waiting for an interview with Mr McGinn, the duty solicitor. 'Why did you shout out?' Billy asked.

'I couldn't help it, after what was said. It should be Montague in jail, not you!'

'It's going to be in the papers now,' Billy said. 'Everyone'll know.'

McGinn the solicitor arrived. He said he realized there might be extra evidence to be used in mitigation of Billy's offence, but he was more concerned with getting Billy out on bail.

Billy and Doreen jumped at the chance of bail pending an appeal. Their hearing before the Bench, at which McGinn presented the notice seeking leave for appeal, lasted five minutes. Billy walked out of court a free man – for the time being.

Doreen, her head full of worries about Billy's job and the house, was relieved. Billy seemed more concerned about Tracy. His concern mounted at home when Tracy was late home from school.

When she finally walked in her face broke into a smile. 'I thought you'd . . .'

'I'm all right, love,' Billy hugged her. 'I'm all right.'

'What's your game, coming to the court like that, then running away? You had me and your dad worried sick!'

'I ran off because of you. Shouting about Peter like that!'

'Your dad nearly got sent to jail because of him. The dirty get!'

Tracy pushed her mother in the chest. 'Eh!' Billy said.

Doreen pushed Tracy in return. 'Don't you do that! If it wasn't for you we wouldn't be in this mess!'

Tracy replied, 'You shouldn't have done it!'

But Doreen was getting hysterical. 'Tell her Billy! Tell her why we're in this mess. You don't realize what you've done!' She slapped Tracy across the face. Then tried to hit her repeatedly.

As Tracy fled upstairs crying, Billy said, 'It might have been better if I'd just gone to jail. What the hell did you have to yell out for?'

'I'm sorry,' Doreen sobbed. 'I am, love.'

'It's our Tracy's name that'll be dragged in the muck for evermore, not mine!' He subsided into a chair. 'I just wanted to keep it quiet. The whole bloody world's going to know now....'

Chapter Seventeen

The only female company Ralph and Harry had enjoyed in months was the previous New Year's Eve at the Commonwealth and Empire Club. Julia Brogan had been escorted there by Harry and Ralph in the Fiesta, but the night had been a let down because Ralph, the driver, had to stay sober and Harry would have preferred the Railway Club.

Harry pondered the lonely hearts ads in the free-sheet newspaper and decided to have a go himself. Ralph was equally enthusiastic. Harry kept slipping into periods of depression. He could always tell because his requests to be driven to the cemetery increased. And he'd been every week this month.

'Why not?' Ralph said. 'I'll help you with it.'

'Hey,' Harry said, 'just remember, I'm paying for it.

So it's my companion.'

They worked together to prepare the ad. Harry asked for the replies to be sent to a box number. Two weeks later, a large envelope arrived from the paper. In the meantime, Harry went through feelings of disloyalty to Edna, but Ralph had told him Edna wouldn't have wanted him to be lonely. Harry was delighted to get eighteen replies.

One was from a man and another was from Julia Brogan. 'They can go in the bin for starters,' Harry said, then he organized a points system to see which of the remaining sixteen letters was going to be the lucky woman.

Ralph was keen to read the replies and together they sifted through them. Finally, both men were convinced that Madge Richmond was the best prospect. She scored nine out of ten.

'It's Madge, then!' Ralph said. He rather liked the sound of her. 'Are you going to write?'

'Too right, I am,' Harry replied, rereading Madge Richmond's letter. 'She sounds well set up. No chance of her being a gold digger.' He paused. 'Shall I ask her here?'

'Oh, I wouldn't do that,' Ralph said. 'It might be misconstrued, you know.'

Harry posted a reply to Madge suggesting a meeting outside St George's Hall in Lime Street. After posting it he began to get cold feet. 'What if she's not suitable?' he asked Ralph. 'If I don't like the look of her I think I'll do a bunk!'

'No you won't, not with a decent type like Madge,' Ralph replied. 'I tell you what. I'll go with you. If you need to be rescued I'll see to it, but with a bit of respect for the woman.'

Madge phoned two days later to confirm the appointment and said she'd be wearing a green coat.

Unfortunately for Harry, green coats seemed to be popular in Lime Street that afternoon. He spied a middle-aged woman in a green coat standing by one of the big stone lions opposite the railway station.

The conversation was disastrous. She thought Harry was a dirty old man trying to pick her up. A passing policeman eyed him suspiciously. Harry had the embarrassment of explaining his behaviour to the copper and a very unamused lady, who only wanted to catch a bus.

Meanwhile, Ralph had introduced himself to another lady in a green coat. By the time Harry joined him, Ralph had invited her back to the bungalow.

Harry felt even more out of things when Madge Richmond had settled into the armchair at the bungalow with tea and cakes. Ralph was making all the running in the conversation. When Madge started to talk about her hobby of exploring Britain by train, Harry saw his chance to get involved in the conversation. But Ralph beat him to it.

'Ah,' Ralph said, 'you can't beat a good train journey. Do you know, Madge, I can still remember every signal, bridge and water tank from Lime Street to Euston.'

'Really?' said Madge.

'That's not the only journey either. I might be getting on a bit, but I could do the same for any amount of the other runs I used to do. If I put me mind to it.'

Harry tried to push in. 'I was at King's Cross, you know,' he said. 'They were the real long runs. I was up to Edinburgh and back a couple of times a week at one time.'

Madge merely smiled at him and turned back to Ralph, who was continuing with a description of driving trains in and out of the city in the dark days of the May Blitz. Madge was most impressed. Her brother had been on the railways in Liverpool at the same time.

As Harry had been serving king and country abroad at the time, he felt unable to join in the reminiscences. He finished his tea and cakes behind that morning's *Daily Post*.

When Ralph returned from running Madge to the

station for her train back to Prenton, just across the Mersey from Liverpool, he breezed back into the bungalow. 'Nice person, isn't she, Harry?'

'Yeah. She's nice and she's mine!'

Ralph had a problem.

Work had not been very pleasant for Heather since Joyce was replaced by Keith Tench. Increasingly, she found him picking holes in her work, or putting her on jobs which could have been tackled by people like Greg, a younger, less experienced colleague.

Increasingly, she looked forward to outings with Nicholas and his daft habit of drawing impromptu cartoons. Some of them were really good. He did one of Harold Cross – whom he nicknamed 'saggy chops' – peering over the roof of his bungalow, spying on diminutive figures in the Close.

Nicholas was kind and gentle, not always having to prove himself. Heather admired the genuine interest he took in his children, despite the fact that Barbara still had custody of them.

Once or twice, Nicholas had surprised Heather by meeting her on the doorstep when she returned from work with a hot meal already prepared at his flat. His job was boring and he was on flexitime. He often started early in the morning, so he could leave the office early.

Heather had never met Barbara and she did so by accident. Tench had asked her into the office one morning and said, 'I've something that's right up your street, Heather.' That was annoying because she was already half-way through the audit of a company. When she pointed it out, Tench said he'd put Greg on that for the time being. 'No, this is something that needs doing in a hurry.'

He wanted her to visit a silk-screening co-operative run by a group of women. They were applying for a local authority and Arts Society grant and the local authority had requested an independent audit. Heather arrived to find a group of women basically antagonistic to Heather's role as a woman in a man's world, dressed in a two-piece suit and carrying a briefcase.

The audit was simple, but coping with the snide remarks of one or two of the women was not. Heather didn't agree with their views and told them she'd sooner be making her mark in a field dominated by men than joining other women, banding together merely to show some sort of solidarity.

While at the co-op, Heather spotted a print of a stone archway with a jungle scene beyond. She asked how much it was. It was only twelve pounds, so, as she thought it might make a present for Nicholas, she bought it. That rather changed the attitude of the co-op women. Heather had seen the books. Their cashflow was desperate.

She was just leaving the shop when a small boy came in. He rushed past Heather and straight over to a woman with lanky, blonde hair and a long cheesecloth dress. She had been one of the most cutting critics of Heather's job.

The boy ran up to the woman. 'Ginny, what's for tea?'

'Haven't got it yet, love. What do you want?'

Heather didn't stay. She didn't want the boy to recognize her. It was Nicholas's son, Adam.

That evening Nicholas called round, and, over coffee, Heather presented him with his print. She had wrapped it up and as he tore off the paper, Heather said, 'I got it in a small studio in town.'

Nicholas opened up the print. 'Style-screen Women's Co-Op.'

'That's right.'

'I know their work,' Nicholas said.

Heather paused a moment as Nicholas examined the print critically. 'I saw Adam there actually.'

'Did he speak?'

'He came in as I was leaving. He didn't really get a chance to see me.'

Nicholas laughed. 'He'd be there to meet Barbara from

work. She's one of the gang at Style-screen, eking out a pittance.'

'I know. I had to audit their books. What does Barbara look like?' Nicholas described her. 'That was the girl who went through the books with me. I quite liked her,' Heather said.

Nicholas tapped the print. 'This is her work. See.' He pointed out the initialled BB in the bottom corner of the print. 'Barbara Black.'

'She still keeps your name then?' Heather said. 'I changed mine back . . . after the divorce.'

'I don't know why Barbara didn't. Laziness probably. Didn't want the bother of changing all the official things.'

Nicholas declined to accept the print as a gift. Now that Heather knew it was the work of his ex-wife, she quite understood.

'It'd look good in here,' Nicholas said. 'And there's a companion print to this one, I remember her doing it. You should have a matching pair.'

'You wouldn't mind being confronted by your ex-wife's work every time you came here?' Heather asked.

Nicholas smiled and shook his head. He really was an easy-going man.

'I'll buy the other one then,' Heather said. 'I have to go back there soon anyway.'

Bobby Grant was puzzled, then furious when the letter arrived from Fast Credit telling him that he had not paid his first instalment on a loan for £1,500.

'This is computers gone flaming mad,' he said.

But it was Sheila who reminded him of her seeing Barry hand over a large sum of money to a man outside the Swan. The penny dropped. Barry had used Bobby's status to take out the loan. 'What's he want £1,500 for?' Bobby said. 'Can you imagine the interest on that?'

Neither of them knew where Barry was and nor did Damon or Karen. Bobby was furious that he should lumber the family with a bill of that size. God knew how many instalments had to be paid. 'I'll tear him to bits when I get him!'

But Sheila was more concerned about what Barry was involved in. Bobby thought her drugs theory was a little unlikely. Hadn't he assured them he would have nothing to do with heroin? Bobby was going to contact the loan company, but Sheila stopped him.

'He could be done for fraud or something. I don't want that!'

'And I don't want this, either,' Bobby said. 'It'll do him good. If he's prosecuted for this perhaps he'll think twice about being dishonest again!'

But their main problem was paying the instalment. Sheila persuaded Bobby they should pay and wait to see if Barry got in touch. Bobby was not happy. It was a drain on his monthly salary he couldn't afford.

Relief only came a week later when a large envelope dropped through the Grants' letter box. The note with it was signed by Barry and had a flippant message, 'Had you worried there, didn't I?' With it was £1,500 in grubby tenners and fivers.

'Good God,' Bobby said, flicking through the money.

There was no apology, no explanation for his behaviour and deliberately risking his parents' livelihood. 'Not a bloody word of explanation,' Bobby said. 'Well he's gone too far this time.'

That day, Bobby paid off £1,500 at the Fast Credit office. But he was annoyed to discover that the annual interest rate was 29 per cent, which meant he still owed £435, which had to be paid off in monthly instalments for twelve months, and as the loan had been agreed for a year, the company refused to waive the interest.

'If he comes back here, he's out,' Bob told Sheila later. 'His feet won't touch!'

The only good news for the Grants that week was that Damon had been talking to his foreman, Ted Cook. Cook had given a reference on Damon to the boss, Derek

Halligan, who would have to interview Damon at the end of his twelve months with the YTS. His first year was nearly up. Damon was confident that as Ted Cook was pleased with him, he might be taken on full-time.

Vicki was now spending more and more time round at Terry's. Now that the van war was over there was no animosity from Pat. But sometimes he was jealous of the closeness between Vicki and Terry.

Sandra was often out in the evenings working nights. Some weeks they hardly saw each other. So he could spend evenings playing gooseberry to Vicki and Terry, only to see them disappear upstairs at bedtime, leaving him fed up and often lonely.

Vicki was also full of ideas for the van business. She put them on to a number of contacts and the work load grew. It was another aspect of his life that Pat felt alienated from. Terry had come into the house as a lodger and now Pat sometimes felt he was the visitor.

Increasingly, Sandra seemed more concerned with her working life than her home life, never more so than the morning she received a message asking her to report to the senior nursing officer. Sandra wasn't known for keeping her mouth shut when she disagreed with something at work, so she went to see the SNO feeling slightly wary. What had she protested about recently?

What the SNO told her was firstly a relief – then a surprise. She suggested Sandra should apply for a Number Seven job, the equivalent of the old rank of sister. Sandra was interested, until she learnt that the post was on the hospital's private ward.

'You know my attitude to private medicine,' she told the SNO. 'I don't think I could apply.'

'Don't dismiss it out of hand, Sandra,' Mrs Mason said. 'You're a good nurse. You deserve promotion and you've a very good chance of this one.'

Sandra wasn't at all sure. She wanted a Number Seven, but on a private ward? The times she'd sounded off about private medicine; all those privileged brigadiers' wives getting better treatment than anyone else just because they had the cash.

But the SNO pointed out that Sandra could always move sideways back on to a National Health Service ward. 'It's easier to go sideways than upwards,' the SNO said. 'Another job like this'll be a long time coming. Why don't you apply?'

'Let me think about it,' Sandra said.

'Don't think too long,' Mrs Mason replied. 'There'll be no shortage of applicants, I can tell you.'

Sandra raised the subject at home that night. Vicki said she should forget about agonizing and apply as quickly as possible. 'What have you got to lose? See if you're good enough, for your own sake. I mean, you might not get the job. Use the system.'

Terry agreed with Vicki. 'It's a sort of means to an end, isn't it?'

But Sandra really wanted to know what Pat thought. He'd worked in the hospital. He knew the private ward as well as the public wards. 'I don't know,' he said.

'You don't know?' Sandra flared.

'It's your job, isn't it, eh, Sand?' he replied. 'I can't make your mind up for you.'

She was exasperated with him. When he worked at the hospital he had opinions. He even had opinions of private medicine, but now ... 'I will make my own mind up then,' she told him.

She decided to apply and a week later heard she'd got the Number Seven job. She was pleased, but afraid she wouldn't like the people she would be nursing.

Doreen Corkhill had hardly dared show her face in the Close since the court case. As well as the worry of Billy going to jail if his appeal was unsuccessful, she worried about the neighbours' attitude. It seemed everything had gone wrong since they moved to Brookside.

'I don't know whether we should move,' she said to

Billy one night. 'Somewhere people won't know us.'

'You've got to be joking!' Billy said. 'Move? After what it's cost us coming here? We've done nothing wrong, so we're staying.' It was his last word on the subject.

But Doreen still continued to worry about their relationship with the neighbours. They must all have seen her outburst reported in the newspaper. She kept an eagle eye on Tracy, not letting her go out. And Rod was continally warned to stay out of trouble, especially at his new school.

There was still no date fixed for the appeal, but she and Billy were glad to hear they would get Legal Aid. It was one less expense to worry about. They still hadn't paid Julia's solicitor's bill or the fine for the meter fiddle.

Keith Tench had now developed a policy of keeping Heather on the smaller, less important jobs, so it was a surprise when he called her in one day and announced he had an important job for her. It seemed that Hamilton Devereux had decided to mount a public relations exercise in Aberdeen, the centre of the North Sea Oil industry. The object was to boost the image of the firm among the oil companies and the other offshore back-up concerns in the Aberdeen area, with a view to winning some good accounts.

'It'll be you and me going up,' Keith said. 'Just for three-weeks.'

'Three weeks?' Heather said. 'And why me?'

'There'll be a lot of entertaining to do,' Keith said.

Heather realized. It was all right for her to play a clothes horse in Aberdeen on some PR exercise, but giving more than brains to someone like Tom Curzon, that was wrong. Hadn't Tench told her once that Heather distracted men with her looks?

'I don't want to be there as an office girl – or a glorified H and D hostess,' she said.

'You're so touchy,' Tench replied.

'If I have to go, I'll go,' Heather said, 'but I won't

pretend to enjoy it.'

'Howard wants you there. So do I . . .' Tench smiled. He came round the desk to her. 'It's not going to be all work, you know. There's going to be plenty of spare time to fill. . . .' He paused. 'Perhaps we might learn to get along better . . . the two of us?'

Heather made no reply. The prospect of his company for three weeks appalled her.

'So Bonny Scotland in the morning?' Heather was boiling at his patronizing manner. But Tench continued, 'And as you'll need to pack you might as well take the rest of today off. . . .'

Heather moved to the door. Tench stopped her. 'Er, Heather . . . Don't forget your best dresses. That dark blue one you wore for Howard's last drinks do – I liked that. . . .' He smiled. Heather walked out fuming.

She was still in a rage when Nicholas knocked on her door at three o'clock that afternoon. 'I rang the office and as you had the afternoon off . . .'

She let him in. Immediately, he noticed something was wrong. 'Don't tell me – Tench.'

He started to ridicule Tench's name. He made a joke about the fish of the same name which spent its time lying in mud. Heather giggled, but moments later she was in tears. She tried to stop. 'I'm sorry.' She put her head on Nicholas's shoulder.

'Don't hold it back,' he said. 'Let it all come out.'

She cried for fifteen minutes. 'I'm sorry. It's ridiculous letting him get at me like that,' she said.

'Do you feel better now?' he asked.

She nodded and smiled. 'It does help . . . you know . . . having someone to talk to. Thanks.'

Nicholas lightened her mood. He made another joke about Heather murdering Tench and dumping him over the sea wall at Aberdeen. Heather laughed. Then, pulling herself together, she told him she'd been back to the women's co-operative earlier that day. She showed him the second of Barbara's prints which she had taken his advice over and bought to match the other. Nicholas examined the print and suggested a place to hang it, close to the first.

'Did you talk?' Nicholas asked.

'We did actually.... She mentioned the children, that's how I know for sure. It was the girl who showed me the books.'

Nicholas was looking at the floor.

Heather added, 'I like her.'

Nicholas looked at Heather and said, 'I think it's time I told you something.' Heather waited. 'You seem to tell me everything, cry on my shoulder even! When I said Barbara left me for someone else ... It wasn't a bloke it was a woman.'

There was a silence. Heather said quietly, 'Ginny?'

Nicholas looked at her and said with no edge whatsoever. 'Aren't you clever?'

'It was seeing Adam go to her and ask what was for his tea,' Heather said. 'It sort of crossed my mind.'

'You're not shocked?'

'Why should I be?'

They ended up laughing at it all, but Nicholas said he had had some nasty reactions from people he had told.

Later, while Heather packed, Nicholas noticed a copy of *Accounting* magazine open in the kitchen. There was a photo and short article about Keith Tench's promotion.

Nicholas got out his felt-tip pen and a piece of card and sketched a cartoon of Keith Tench wearing a highland evening dress. He was mincing up a slope, marked 'To Scotland'. A balloon from his mouth said, 'Heather, don't forget to pack your best dresses, too!'

When Heather came down to cook them something for supper, he showed it her. She laughed, 'If he saw that I'd get the sack!'

'Put it in his room at Aberdeen!'

'You're joking!' The cartoon really was good.

When Nicholas was leaving that evening, he warned Heather not to let Tench upset her in Aberdeen.

'I'll try, but nasty is his second name.'

'Are you sure he doesn't fancy you?'

Heather was sceptical. 'But it's nice to know you're concerned,' she smiled at him, then she kissed him lightly.

Privately, Nicholas was worried Tench might upset Heather, or make a pass at her. 'If you need to talk to me, you know where I am,' he said.

'Do I *need* to talk to you? Can't I ring anyway?'

He kissed her again and left.

Chapter Eighteen

Sandra found that she was enjoying herself on the private ward. True, there were some awkward, supercilious patients, including a dreadful army officer's wife having her varicose veins treated, but she was interested to find other ordinary people who had opted to go private. A trade union official with a heavy workload and even a doctor specializing in transplants who couldn't risk waiting in case his call for treatment came at a critical time.

Sandra was also pleased to meet up with the garrulous Jackie O'Shaughnessy. Jackie had worked for Pat when he ran his abortive kissogram service. She had dressed up in exotic lingerie as a 'Naughty Night Nurse'.

Jackie was definitely there for the money. 'It's easier too,' Jackie told Sandra. 'You've got the equipment, you've got the time and there's no nights either.'

Sandra soon discovered Jackie was right. There was more time to actually talk to people. In days she knew more people on the ward on a personal basis than she'd ever been able to manage elsewhere.

Jackie was quick to point out Dr Hurrell, a registrar, who was a young attractive man, not long in the job. 'I keep coming into his line of vision, but he doesn't seem to notice,' Jackie winked at Sandra. 'Why don't you have a go?'

Jackie was interested to know about Pat. At one time Sandra thought Jackie fancied Pat, but it was just a case of mutual benefit. Jackie was one of his 'leg-men' on some of the rackets he and the other porters ran.

Sandra was more relaxed at home now she was enjoying the job. And she was pleased not to be working nights. She told the others about some of the patients. They noticed she was changing some of her opinions about the private ward. But not about the consultants. She was told some of them picked up £50,000 a year from just minor operations.

'Not quite a Tory yet, then?' Terry teased her.

Bobby Grant wasn't too happy when he arrived home late from work to find Sally Dinsdale and her two children staying the night. He followed Sheila into the kitchen.

'What's going on here, Shei?' he said. 'It's like a refugee camp.'

'I had to take her in,' Sheila said. 'She's the one . . .' She lowered her voice. 'Her husband knocks her about. She's on the course.'

'Do you have to bring all the waifs and strays home? I mean, it's all right knowing them, but this lot!'

Sally was watching television. Her children were ready for bed. They were running round the living room, where Bobby usually had his tea when he was late back from work. That night Claire was in her parents' room and kept waking up. Sally's children seemed to be in and out of the bathroom all night.

'How long are they staying?' Bobby asked, irritated.

'It's only one night,' Sheila said. 'I've got the address of one of those refuges for battered wives. I'm going to try to get her to go there in the morning.'

But in the morning, Sally wasn't at all keen on the idea. 'I don't need you to give me the address, Sheila. I know them all and I wouldn't set foot in any of them.'

Bobby was listening in the kitchen, having breakfast.

Sally said, 'It'll be all right this morning. He'll be sorry for what he did last night . . . until the next time.'

Sally left soon after. Sheila was a little upset that giving her a refuge for the night had been thrown back in her face.

'Don't get involved with it,' Bobby said. 'It might be helping to you but some people might call it interfering.'

The next night Bobby arrived home to find a tutorial for the Return and Learn going on in his living room. One had already been held there and Bobby hadn't liked that. He was off-hand with the people attending – Matty, Mo, Sally and Alun Jones.

Sheila went upstairs after him, excusing herself to the others. 'What's up with you?'

'Every time I come home there's something going on here. I hope that Dinsdale woman's going home!'

'We were going to have it at Sally's, but her husband objected. You know what he's like.'

'He's obviously not a mug like me. When are they leaving?'

When he was calmer, Bobby came down. He still made a few sarcastic remarks, but his anger had dissolved. He remembered Sheila annoying him when she complained of him having meetings on union business at home.

When the tutorial was over, Sheila saw them out. Matty was laughing and joking with Mo. Sheila noticed he put his arm round her from time to time, usually when he cracked a joke. Sheila again felt a twinge of concern about his relationship with Maureen Francis.

She mentioned it to Bobby when she came back in. 'She's not a bad-looking girl, is she?' Bobby said.

'I'm being serious Bob. I know they spend quite a lot of time together at the library.'

'They're doing a project together, aren't they?' Bobby was more interested in settling down in front of the television. 'Anyway,' he said, 'you want to watch that tutor. Good-looking feller. He might have his eye on you!'

'Don't be stupid!' she snapped.

'I'm only joking, love.'

Sheila did like Alun Jones. She found him interested and sympathetic. And always patient. She did have a better relationship with him than some others on the course.

Bobby had settled down in front of *News at Ten*. She looked at him. She wondered whether his joke had a purpose; whether it was the start of some sort of emotional blackmail. If he made remarks like that often enough would she feel guilty and leave the course? She didn't want that. It was Matty that Bobby should worry about.

It was a bit much, Harry thought to himself, Ralph taking *his* car and going off to meet *his* woman. He was sitting alone at home. Ralph was visiting the Maritime Museum with Madge.

Ralph had been open from the start. He'd had two 'dates' with Madge after their first meeting when Ralph had stolen Harry's thunder.

Harry had done his best not to appear envious, but he had got used to Ralph's company. Even if he slipped off for a few hours, he missed him. Why had he sent in that flaming lonely hearts advertisement?

But he was determined not to let Ralph see it had got to him.

Bobby's forty-ninth birthday was due the following day and Sheila had taken Claire into town by bus to buy a book on the history of the Liverpool Trade Union Movement.

The book had been recommended by Alun Jones who thought Bobby may find it of interest. On the way home she had seen Matty out jogging. He was well away from his own home and she was surprised to see him turn into a house on the street and go round the side, rather than to the front door.

When she got home, she looked up Mo Francis' address in the phone book. Matty had been going into Mo

Francis' house. It could be innocent, but the suspicions were piling up. It wasn't as if Matty was carrying any books. Why go round when he was out jogging?

Next morning she gave Bobby his birthday present. At first he was pleased with the book, but when it slipped out that Alun Jones had recommended it he was put out. Sheila had to remind him that Bobby's former colleagues Janet Hanson had once bought him a book for his birthday. He hadn't liked it when she made snide remarks about the relationship between them. She repeated that he should be more concerned if Matty was carrying on with someone, like Maureen Francis. 'Not that again!' Bobby said.

'There's something funny going on, I'm sure of it.' She told Bobby about seeing him calling at Mo's house.

'They're working together, aren't they?' he said. 'So what? He can call round if he likes.'

'In his jogging gear and not carrying any books?'

But Bobby was dismissive. 'I know Matty better than that. He's devoted to Teresa. They're a great couple, always have been.'

'I think I should mention it to him, sound him out,' Sheila said.

'Jeeze, Sheila, don't do that!' he said. 'Talk about interfering. It's getting a disease with you!'

Sheila said she thought she should as it was becoming more and more obvious to everyone on the course how close Matty and Mo had become.

'He's got enough problems not having a job,' Bobby said. 'And don't forget you talked him into this course.'

'That's what worries me,' Sheila said.

Damon Grant had gone out to work with a spring in his step. Today was the day Derek Halligan was to see him, as he had finished his twelve months with YTS. Now he was sitting smiling as Derek complimented him on the last job Damon and some of his colleagues had completed – an old swimming pool which had been renovated.

Derek picked up a sheet of paper and said, 'This is your reference off Ted. It's a good'un. I don't think I've seen one better.'

He read out the reference. Damon couldn't believe his ears. It was brilliant. Nothing like his old school reports. His confidence was growing. Derek congratulated him on the reference.

'That'll come in handy. Keep hold of it,' he said, getting up and coming round the desk. He shoved the reference in Damon's hand. 'Well, Damon, it's been nice to know you. You did us proud.'

Damon was thunderstruck again. 'Aren't you taking me on?'

Derek laughed. 'It's just a year with you YTS lads, you know that.'

All Damon's hopes were disappearing fast. He'd told his parents, Karen, everyone that he was almost certain to be kept on full-time.

Dazed, he was shaking hands with Halligan. 'Well, there's work to do, people to see.'

Damon didn't say another word. With tears in his eyes he stormed out of Derek's office. Only to collide with a shy looking lad.

'Sorry,' the lad said. He wondered whether Damon was the Mr Halligan he'd come to see. Damon stopped and looked at the lad.

'YTS?' Damon asked.

'Yeah,' said the lad.

'Well if they tell you you might get kept on after, don't believe a . . .' But his voice started to crack. They'd sacked him and he couldn't believe it. That lad was walking into his job.

Sheila was as disappointed as her son when he arrived home, very upset. She tried to comfort him, but he insisted he had got the sack. She tried to boost his morale, telling him it wasn't the sack. Didn't the reference prove it?

But Damon was desolate. He had no chance of getting

an apprenticeship, he told his mother. She couldn't comfort him. He wasn't helped when Karen came in brandishing a teenage pop magazine with an article of hers published inside.

The magazine had used the interview she managed to get with Paula Yates when she came to Liverpool University to judge the Panto Week floats. Karen was over the moon, boasting about the job she'd get if she carried on getting published in the magazines. Then she noticed Damon was red-eyed and upset. When Damon had fled upstairs, Sheila broke the bad news.

Later when Bobby came in, he tried to talk to Damon and reassure him that he had not been sacked. But Damon was thoroughly depressed.

'I think I'll get him to write off for jobs,' Sheila said later.

'I've told him already,' Bobby said. 'I don't want to see him going down the nick like I did.' He banged his fist on the table. 'It makes you sick, doesn't it? That reference he's got. It's brilliant and he gets pushed out.'

The telephone rang. Sheila answered. It was Teresa, phoning to ask when Matty wanted his tea after going to the pub with Bobby for a birthday drink. Sheila didn't know what to say, so she played along with Teresa. She came back and told Bobby. 'There's got to be some explanation,' he said.

'Yeah,' Sheila said flatly. 'He's out with that Maureen Francis!'

Bobby tried to dissuade her from speculating about Matty and Mo. But she kept on worrying at it, remembering little things she'd noticed. Matty's clothes for instance – much smarter these days and he had his hair cut more regularly.

When Matty called at half-past nine with an armful of canned beer to celebrate Bobby's birthday she was cool. Matty picked up on it immediately. But before he could say anything, Sheila said, 'Where did you leave her?'

'What?' Matty said.

'Well you weren't out with Bob, even though Teresa thinks you were.'

Matty looked shocked.

'She phoned to see when you wanted your tea,' Sheila explained, then added, sarcastically, 'seeing as she thought you were boozing with Bobby.'

Matty knew he was caught red-handed. He started to tell them how he was worried about Teresa being jealous if she knew he was working with Mo. So he used excuses to cover their visits to the library. And sometimes her house.

'That's up to you, but I'm not having you using us to cover up what you do,' Sheila said, coldly. 'It's as bad as . . . a criminal looking for an alibi.'

Matty left ten minutes after he arrived, taking the beer with him. Next day he phoned Bobby and invited him for a drink. When they met, he told Bobby that he loved Mo Francis. Bobby didn't believe him, but Matty insisted, saying he didn't want to hurt Teresa.

'I feel alive now, Bobby,' he said, 'for the first time in years.'

But Bobby believed it would all blow over. Matty was just living out some stupid fantasy. He decided not to tell Sheila.

Sandra wouldn't tell Pat why she was in such a bad mood. He accused her of regretting going on the private ward, then of feeling guilty about the work she was doing. But Sandra denied that was the reason. Pat asked if he'd done anything to upset her, but she denied that too. 'We never talk to each other,' Pat grumbled. 'How can we be a couple if we don't confide?'

Sandra stared at her cup of coffee on the kitchen table.

'Even Terry and Vicki seem to talk together more than we do now.'

And he kept on at her. Eventually, she told him. 'I think I might be pregnant.'

Pat practically whooped. 'You don't.'

'I'm only two weeks late. It could be anything.'

But by now he had her in his arms. 'That's brilliant, Sand, brilliant!'

Sandra didn't think it was brilliant at all. She was enjoying her work. She'd been promoted. She had a future at last. The last thing she wanted was a child.

'Are you going to tell your mum?' Pat was saying.

'Pat! I'm two weeks late, that's all.'

'The later the better, eh?' he said. 'Come on, come and sit in the front and I'll get you some tea. Just think, eh? Me a dad!'

Next day, Sandra found Pat's attentions irritating. He was treating her like cut glass. 'This is ridiculous,' Sandra said. 'And don't go telling Terry and Vicki.'

'Not till it's official, eh?' He felt euphoric. He tried to talk seriously to Sandra about how it was time he settled down. Perhaps time to try for another job?

'You mean marriage?'

'Well, we don't want him or her to be a little whatsit, do we? Why not?'

Sandra explained she had not long ago got herself out of a disastrous marriage. She didn't feel inclined to rush into another one.

She handled him gently, but Pat was sad. He hoped that the pregnancy was confirmed. Sandra would change her mind then, surely?

In his euphoria next day he offered to babysit for Sheila Grant when she needed to go down to her day course. 'I always mind me sister's when I'm down in London,' he said. 'No problem.' He let his high spirits get the better of him and hinted to Sheila that he might have a child of his own soon. Sheila offered her congratulations. 'That's top secret, mind,' he told her. 'Sandra doesn't want anyone to know.'

That night when Sandra got into bed and gently told him that her period had started he felt cheated. The images of him and Sandra with their own child had been ballooning in his head all day. Now they were gone.

Guy Willis had decided not to go to his parents' home for the Easter holidays. It would have meant missing Karen and he preferred to stay in Liverpool and keep her company.

One morning she woke up determined that she would go to Guy's room at the Hall of Residence and go to bed with him. He was still in bed when she arrived. She couldn't have gone about it a worse way. She was tense. Guy was understanding, but it was a disaster.

Later, over a mug of coffee Guy said he didn't mind. But Karen did.

'It was good just being with you,' he said.

'It was terrible. I feel ashamed,' Karen said. Her back was turned towards him.

He said she was wrong for rushing into sex. And he was unable to be very helpful because he had only ever been with experienced girls.

'It takes time, Karen,' he said. 'And we've got plenty of that, haven't we?'

But Karen wouldn't be comforted. She went home earlier than she might otherwise have done, refusing to go out for the evening. When conversationally Damon stopped her on the landing at home and asked her how she'd enjoyed her day, she slammed the door in his face.

Aberdeen had been quite interesting for Heather and she had been pleasantly surprised to find that she had not fallen out with Keith Tench. He had not made a pass at her, and she had been careful to accept only those invitations where they would be in company with others.

Heather shared a taxi from the station with him after their long train journey and invited him in for coffee out of courtesy, forgetting she had asked Nicholas to call that afternoon with some milk and bread. Heather and Tench were making polite conversation when Nicholas arrived with a carrier bag and a bunch of flowers.

Heather let him in. 'Hi.'

They kissed each other briefly. Tench watched, interested to see Heather with a man she knew well. Tench thought that Nicholas seemed an unlikely partner for someone like Heather. Unlike himself.

Heather made more coffee for Nicholas and Tench delved into Nicholas' working life, responding with platitudes like 'How interesting'.

But Nicholas was not concentrating. He had spotted the cartoon of Tench he had drawn three weeks earlier. It was propped on the corner of the window-ledge. It was a miracle Tench hadn't spotted it. Awkwardly, Nicholas moved to place himself in front of it.

Heather noticed and wondered why he was behaving strangely. Then she realized.

Nicholas had to stay where he was for the rest of Tench's visit. Tench had him down as an eccentric as he shook hands and said goodbye. When Tench had got into the cab he had called and left the Close, Nicholas let out a long breath. 'That was close.'

'Thank God you came. I'd forgotten all about it.'

Nicholas examined the cartoon again. 'Hm. I got him right, I think.' He looked at Heather. 'How was it?'

'Not bad,' she replied. 'Hopefully, we'll get on a little better from now on.'

'Good,' Nicholas said. 'I've missed you.'

Damon had been ringing round and writing for decorating jobs for over a week, but without luck.

Terry and Pat sympathized. 'Why don't you go down south,' Terry said.

'Yeah,' Pat agreed. 'The season's coming up. You want to try the seaside places. Southend's always good for casual work. In the summer.'

'I don't fancy being a holiday camp Red Coat or anything soft like that,' Damon said. 'Or hiring out deck chairs.'

'I did that once,' Pat said. 'Good money. One for you, one for me.'

'There's nothing for decorators though, is there?'

'Painting the pier at Brighton, maybe,' Pat said.

'I'm being serious.'

'So am I, Damon, son,' Pat said. 'Go down the south coast. If I didn't have Sandra up here, that's where I'd be.'

Damon thought about the suggestion. It might be better than hanging round Liverpool on the dole all summer.

When Ralph told Harry he was planning to take Madge on a Golden Rail holiday to Torquay, Harry tried hard not to show his envy.

'Has she said yes?' he asked.

'As a matter of fact, she has,' Ralph said. Harry tried hard to hide his disappointment. But how could he manage to go too?

'She probably has the idea I'm coming too,' Harry said. 'I mean, it was my advert that brought us all together, wasn't it? You take it from me, Ralph, she'll expect a threesome.'

'I'm not so sure about that, Harry.'

'I can't let Madge down. She'd never forgive me,' Harry said. 'Have you got a brochure?'

Lucy Collins was still behaving strangely and Paul and Annabelle worried. Annabelle had noticed the stolen items in her room, but had kept it to herself. They didn't seem to be increasing, so perhaps her own private theory that Lucy was shoplifting was wrong. But the number of times she was coming home late, and sometimes drunk, continued. Paul had tackled her several times, but all he had got was abuse.

'I can't find another James,' she said drunkenly early one morning, 'but I'm looking.'

Paul was disgusted and told her so. But Lucy merely laughed, then she pointed at him and said, 'It's your fault. You went to James.'

Annabelle was disgusted, too, but gradually the late nights started to get fewer and fewer. Paul and Annabelle began to wonder if it would help her to go back to Gordon and the Dubois in France. Perhaps when she'd calmed down a little more.

Chapter Nineteen

Bobby couldn't believe his eyes when Dave Butler, an ETWU shop steward, showed him the wageslips of two workers at Bragg's Engineering and explained that the one for two hundred pounds was for a labourer and the one for a hundred and seventy pounds was for a skilled turner working in the same shop.

'We're on a fixed bonus, us turners,' Dave said. 'It's twenty per cent.'

'I know that,' said Bobby. 'But what the hell are the labourers on?'

'They negotiate locally don't they?' Dave said. 'And it's seventy per cent. There's no way we're standing for this!'

Bobby put the case to George Williams, the man above him at ETWU, the next day. They were driving along to a meeting in Manchester. George listened, then dismissed the argument. 'I've heard it all before, Bobby.'

'That's not the point,' Bobby insisted. 'The only way they can sell their labour for a fair price is by going to the union, our union. They pay our flamin' wages and we sit back while bloody labourers clock up thirty or forty quid a week more than fellers who've served their time!'

George was impassive.

Bobby continued, 'Christ, George we should be creating a God almighty stink about this!'

'How?' George asked, flatly.

'Oh, don't act stupid,' Bobby said. 'What I always used to do. Make it an official dispute. Back our members!'

George moved into the fast lane, staring at the road ahead. 'We can't do it, Bobby,' he said.

'You watch me, mate,' Bobby said.

George sighed. 'If you must know, Braggs is on the black list.'

'What?' Bobby said.

'Militants,' George said. 'They've too many militants on board for comfort there and head office wants them kept down.'

'Christ, we wouldn't have a union if it wasn't for militants,' Bobby said. 'And the fellers there trust me. They always have. They pay their subs and they look to us to help when they need it.'

George looked sideways at Bobby. He thought he'd knocked the rough edges off Bobby Grant a while ago. Apparently not.

'They've got a simple, bloody good case, George,' Bobby said.

'So, what are you going to do about it?'

'I'm going to represent the fellers I've lived and worked with all my life. To hell with head office. I'll go with the fellers at Braggs.'

George didn't like this at all. They drove the rest of the way in silence.

At breakfast the next day, Bobby tried to talk about the Braggs case to Sheila, but she was preoccupied. 'What?' she asked.

'Never mind,' Bobby said.

Sheila was brooding about Matty and Teresa. Only yesterday, Teresa had been round visiting. She'd gone on about how the course had put new life into Matty. She'd even hinted that their sex life had been rejuvenated.

Sheila had tried to sound pleased for her. But all the time she felt sick that she was keeping her suspicions away from her best friend. Teresa had helped her through lots of problems, not least her post-natal depression after Claire.

'I think I'll have a word with Mo Francis at the course today,' she said. 'If it is all just my suspicions then there's no harm done. Teresa doesn't need to know.'

'Sheila, you can't go messing around with other people's private lives like this,' Bobby said. 'If anything goes wrong people'll blame you. And haven't we got enough problems without going looking for them?'

He tried to talk her out of it, but she reminded him of the years they'd known Matty and Teresa. She had to do something.

Down at the centre she found Sally Dinsdale catching up on her project work and asked her advice on whether to tackle Mo or not. Sally's advice was simple and straightforward. 'Don't bother.'

Sheila came out with her argument with Bobby; that Teresa was a friend and needed to be protected. But Sally said the best way to be her friend was to leave well alone.

'But I'd be going behind her back then, in on the conspiracy, wouldn't I?' Sheila asked.

'If there is anything going on,' Sally said.

'What do you think?' Sheila asked.

'I think there is, but I couldn't prove it,' she said. 'Take my advice Sheila, keep out of it.'

Sheila left Sally to continue her work and drifted away. A few minutes later, Alun saw her and gave her back some work. 'I liked it,' he said. 'I thought the way you expressed it was really good.'

'Thanks,' Sheila said.

He handed her a leaflet. It was for a course for amateur historians, with sessions on research and presentation of material. 'You should consider attending this,' Alun said. 'I think you should come.'

Sheila saw it was a weekend residential course. 'I don't know whether Bobby would . . .'

'You mean, whether he'd let you?' Alun smiled.

'Yeah.'

'It'd be a shame to let him stand in your way, Sheila.'

He left to start the session. Sheila couldn't concentrate. She kept glancing at Matty and Mo Francis. Touching each other, acting like teenagers.

It wasn't until lunchtime that Sheila managed to get

Mo Francis on her own. She tackled her head on. Mo was determined not to be frightened off. Sheila grew progressively more upset, especially when Mo said she and Matty were in love.

'You don't know what it means!' Sheila spat at her.

Mo told her to mind her own business and Sheila called her a tart.

'Think what you like,' Mo Francis said. 'Matty and me are getting married.'

Sheila was speechless.

Matty was upset, not least over the fact that Bobby seemed to have forgotten to keep Matty's affair to himself. When he asked Sheila what Bobby had told her, Sheila was confused. Then it dawned on her. That's why Bobby had been so keen on her not interfering. He knew.

Matty repeated what he had told Bobby. That he loved Mo. 'It's a new start for me, Shei, another chance.'

'But don't you care about Teresa?'

'I love Teresa. I do. But I love Mo now, Sheila. It's true.'

Sheila had to turn away from him. Later, Sally came up to her. 'I can see you're upset. Wouldn't it have been better to say nothing?'

'But what about Teresa?'

'Don't tell her. Let this thing with Mo, let it burn itself out.'

'But he says he loves her. They're going to marry.'

'I'd take what Mo says with a pinch of salt, actually,' Sally said.

Sheila was left alone. Alun Jones approached her. He'd guessed what Sheila had done. He was warm and friendly, telling her not to worry. He put his arm around her. 'I'm sure it'll be all right.'

'Why didn't you tell me?' Sheila asked Bobby later.

'I promised him I wouldn't, that's why!' Bobby said.

'All the time you've been telling me to keep out of it you've known he's been carrying on with her. You knew! And here's me in agony wondering what to say to Teresa!'

'For God's sake, Sheila, it's nothing to do with us. He's big enough to run his own life.' Bobby was exasperated with her. 'You've got a lad thinking of going down south to look for work, another lad God knows where, a baby to look after and you're more concerned about something that's got nothing to do with you!' He stormed out of the kitchen and flopped in an armchair. 'You might even try taking a bit of interest in me. I've got problems too.'

Sandra found herself getting on well with Dr Hurrell. It seemed he held similar views about the abuses of the health service by some of the consultants. Jackie had winked at Sandra once or twice when she saw them talking together.

'What do you find to talk about?' Jackie said, with mock innocence.

'Oh, be serious,' Sandra said, 'I think he'll go far, our Dr Hurrell.'

'Who with?' Jackie giggled.

'Don't you think of anything else?' Sandra laughed. 'Go on, get some work done.'

A few days later, Sandra was having trouble starting her Citröen in the hospital car park when Hurrell pulled up alongside her. 'Problems?'

'It never starts when you want it to, this thing,' she said. 'I bought it off a neighbour and then discovered it had a list of previous convictions for failing to start even on summer mornings.'

Hurrell laughed. He offered her a lift home and on arrival she offered him a coffee. 'If it'll keep me awake a bit longer, I don't mind,' Hurrell said. 'Over a hundred hours this week and we've not finished yet.'

Sandra introduced him to Pat and Terry. After he'd gone Terry started winding up Pat about having a doctor as a rival. 'You'll have to get a white coat,' he taunted him. 'Or a bigger stethoscope!'

'Get lost!' Pat replied.

Terry went out to see Vicki, and Sandra told Pat to take no notice. 'He's only pulling your leg.'

Pat confessed that he felt a bit small when Sandra told Hurrell that he was an ex-porter. 'I mean you could have left that out. He didn't know me when I was still at the infirmary.'

'I'm sorry, but no matter what Terry says, he's just a colleague. You could say we're both on a private ward, but we're not on the same, you know, wavelength.'

Pat wasn't jealous of Hurrell. But he did feel overshadowed. His chance of settling down, the pregnancy that never was, had robbed him of a sudden feeling of having a purpose in life. At his age, he felt he should be doing something more than running a hire van.

Madge agreed to go to Torquay, but only if it was a foursome.

Harry was a little put out when Madge asked him, 'Who are you taking, Harry?'

'It depends on who the lucky lady is that I choose, doesn't it?'

Later, he said to Ralph, 'You've stolen my woman. So you'd better come up with some ideas. Who do I take?'

'Leave it with me, Harry,' Ralph said.

The following day when Damon payed in his football stake money, he noticed Harry reading a Golden Rail brochure for Torquay. 'Is that down south?' he asked.

'The English Riviera,' Harry replied. 'It's on the south coast. In Devon.'

Damon was interested to learn Harry and Ralph were going there for a holiday. He found out when. An idea had occurred to him. 'I'm thinking of going down that way myself,' he said.

'What do you want to go there for?' Harry said.

'Looking for a summer job.'

'Good idea,' Harry said. 'And you can carry the cases.'

*

Damon did carry the suitcases. It gave him the perfect cover to sneak on to the platform without having a ticket for Torquay. He didn't mind playing bellhop for Harry, Ralph and Madge.

Harry was still in suspense over who would be his travelling companion for the Golden Rail holiday. Ralph had kept him in the dark, saying he would be pleased when he saw her.

'I'm too old for blind dates,' Harry grumbled.

'Put a bit of spice in your life,' Ralph told him. 'Live dangerously.'

'You'll be living dangerously if I get some old bag,' Harry said.

When they left Brookside for Lime Street station by taxi, Harry had thought his luck was in when he saw Heather also crossing the Close to the cab with a suitcase. 'You've never fixed me up with her?' he asked Ralph.

'Sorry, mate – she's just sharing the taxi. She's going to London.'

Harry grumbled about his travelling companion to Heather on the way to the station.

'I'm sure Ralph will have found the right lady,' Heather said sweetly.

The train was four minutes from pulling out when Ralph, Madge and Harry turned at the sound of a loud 'Coo-ee!' Julia Brogan was tripping up the platform towards them with her suitcases on a trolley.

'Hello, Harry,' she said. 'Did you think I was going to miss the train?'

Ralph grinned.

'Live dangerously?' Harry said. 'I don't know whether or not I should commit suicide!'

Julia talked non-stop all the way down to Torquay. Meanwhile, Damon volunteered to fetch drinks and sandwiches from the buffet bar. Anything to keep moving and away from the ticket collector. He had a few narrow squeaks. When he was confident the danger was past, he rejoined the others.

Moments later, the ticket collector came back.

'Hey.' Harry said. The ticket collector turned. 'Haven't you forgotten something?' Harry asked him. The man was puzzled. 'Him sitting there. You haven't checked his ticket.'

Damon could have died. He had to confess he hadn't got a ticket. Harry wished he'd kept his mouth shut too. It cost him twenty-five quid to buy Damon a ticket.

'Listen son,' Harry said. 'Whether you get a job or not, I want that back when I get home.'

Damon nodded. No job and he was twenty-five quid down already.

While the older generation went to the Victoria Hotel on the front, Damon had to find less salubrious accommodation in the same area. That night he slept in one of the shelters on the promenade. But next morning he found himself a job. It was long hours and lousy pay, but it was a job.

He left Torquay that afternoon to hitch hike home.

Earlier that day, Sheila opened the letter. It was a local postmark, but the address was scrawled crudely across the envelope, as though it had been done by a child. Inside was a piece of folded paper. Similar handwriting read, 'I'm warning you. Keep your nose out you interfering bitch.'

Sheila gave an involuntary shiver. She felt frightened. She examined the envelope. It was totally anonymous. Who could have sent it? The obvious suspect was Mo Francis. But it could have been Sally Dinsdale's husband.

Sheila's immediate reaction was to tear it up. But she didn't. She folded it and put it in her bag. She didn't know what to do. She couldn't tell Bobby. Hadn't he warned her not to interfere in other people's private lives?

She sat chewing her fingernails. She decided to call Alun Jones and ask him to come round. She rooted out his number. He had been sympathetic the day she tackled Mo Francis. Yes, Alun would help her.

He didn't turn up until late afternoon. She showed him in and thanked him for coming. The strain of waiting was telling on her. She'd read and reread the letter several times.

She didn't produce the letter straight away. Alun asked her if she was feeling all right and she started sidetracking about her problems, with Matty and Mo, her friend Sally refusing to leave her violent husband, despite what she'd tried to do for her.

Alun said she needed to get away and reminded her of the amateur historians' course. In fact, he was attracted to Sheila and felt he could get closer to her on a weekend course. The main problem was her slob of a husband.

Sheila said it was impossible to get away for the weekend, but every reason for not going which she brought up was brushed aside by his persuasive voice.

Sheila asked who else was going from the course. She couldn't face Matty and Mo. 'Just yourself,' Alun said.

'Just me?' Sheila said, pulling a face.

'And me.' Alun smiled.

Sheila had forgotten the letter. God, here she was thinking about Matty and Teresa, and their course lecturer was suggesting they go away together for the weekend. She started to make frantic excuses. 'I'll have to see to the baby.'

Then Bobby came in. 'You're early, love,' she said in a strained voice.

'I can see that,' Bobby said.

There was an atmosphere. Alun got up. 'I'll have to go.'

Bobby didn't acknowledge him.

'Er . . . thanks, Alun.'

'Oh, about the letter,' Alun said.

'It doesn't matter,' Sheila said. 'Another time, eh?'

Sheila asked Bobby why he was home so early. He had to go to the turners' ballot meeting. They were voting on whether to strike over the differentials dispute. 'I'll put some tea on,' she said.

'What's all this about a letter? That's what he mentioned when he went out,' Bobby said.

'Oh, he wondered whether I'd seen it in the *Echo*. About the docks.'

Bobby didn't believe her, but he didn't pursue the matter. He didn't trust that Jones bloke. He was too smooth tongued by half.

Sheila had a sleepless night. Problems seemed to be piling in on her from all sides. But she hated lying to Bobby. Wasn't there enough deceit around at the moment with Matty? Finally she decided to show him the letter. 'This is the letter I was talking to Alun about,' she said the next morning.

'You showed him this before me?' Bobby asked.

'No. You came in. I didn't get a chance.'

'This is something that should have been shown to me, not some bloody school teacher,' Bobby said. 'What's wrong with showing it to me?'

'Because I thought you'd go spare, that's why!' Sheila said. 'You've been going on about me interfering. I didn't want to hear "I told you so".'

'Well I was right, wasn't I? You've got someone's back up.'

'It frightened me, Bob.'

'Take no notice,' Bobby said. He paused for a moment. 'The thing is, if I hadn't come in early last night, you'd have shown it to him and not me. Talk about deceit, eh?'

Sheila didn't reply.

'Why didn't you show him then, if he came round about this?'

'We just got talking about the course. Like I said, you came in and ...'

When Bobby went down to breakfast he found Damon waiting to talk to him. Damon announced that he was returning to Torquay to take up the job he was offered.

'You're a mug, son,' Bobby said. 'Stay up here. Look for a painting job.'

'I'll wait for ever, Dad,' Damon said. 'Look, I know it's not much of a job, working in a hotel kitchen, but – it's better than nothing. I have to try or no one'll touch me. They'll think I'm a dolite.'

Sheila joined in, 'I wouldn't mind you going away Damon if it was a good job. But it doesn't seem worth it.'

'I have to go,' Damon replied.

'Well I'll leave it up to you then, son,' Bobby said.

'Bob,' Sheila protested.

'Look, he's eighteen now. He can make some of his own decisions. I've got Braggs turners on an overtime ban and the big wigs in our union don't like it. As well as that I've got all that stuff you've thrown at me. I can't handle everything, Sheila.'

Bobby was on his way out to his car when a taxi dropped Barry off.

'All right, Dad,' he said.

'It's back is it?' Bobby said, nastily.

'What's up?' his son asked.

'What's up?' Sheila had by now come out to see what the noise was. Bobby continued. 'What's up? You go off to God knows where and leave me and your mother with a debt of £1,500. That's what's up.'

'I paid you back, didn't I?'

'Oh, aye and what about the interest? That's £435 on top and I've been paying it off for months.'

'I'll pay that. There's no need to go on about it!' Barry said.

'Haven't you ever heard of principles?' Bobby said.

'You wouldn't think so. If it hadn't been for your mother I'd have had you in court!'

Bobby went to his car and drove to work. At least he could understand the problems of shop stewards. Family was much more complicated.

Barry was upset that his father should be so nasty. 'I mean it, Mam, I'll pay it back.'

'I know you will, love.'

Sheila was more concerned that Barry was not in trouble. He assured her he wasn't. 'And I haven't been taking drugs or anything like that,' he said, grinning.

He certainly looked well, Sheila thought. She asked about Jane Smith. 'Haven't seen her since I was up here,' he said. 'And I don't want to either.'

Sheila was glad. Gently, she probed about how he managed to get the fifteen hundred pounds. Barry sighed, 'I did plenty of overtime and I borrowed off some mates. It's all square now.'

'Good,' Sheila said.

'I was going to apologize to you and me dad, you know. It's one of the reasons I'm up here.'

'Oh, aye, and what's the others?'

Barry laughed. 'It's a deal. It's all legal and everything, so don't worry.'

'What sort of deal?'

'Videos,' he said. 'And before you say it they're not video nasties!'

Sheila was glad to have him home. For one thing, she felt safer with Barry around. But she wouldn't tell him about the poison-pen letter. He was like Billy Corkhill across the Close. He'd probably attack the first name that came into his head.

Chapter Twenty

Lucy Collins had become friendly with Sandra. Sandra had learned about her affair with James and how Lucy blamed her parents for the breakup. She was concerned about Lucy's attitude with her one-night stands and her shoplifting.

Gradually, Lucy had become calmer. Sandra had noticed. She noticed her brighten up when Barry called over to borrow the van. Sandra didn't like Barry very much and she was surprised to see he and Lucy knew each other.

'Go back a long way, don't we,' Barry laughed. 'Since the day I fixed your bog — your first day in Brookside.'

Lucy laughed too. She remembered the incident. And her father's outrage. Barry told her what he had been doing and asked her where she'd been. She told him about France and coming back for James. 'Didn't work out, eh?' Barry asked.

'Unfortunately, no,' Lucy said.

Barry was curious about France. He had vague thoughts about going abroad to look for work. Lucy told him she had found it easy to get a job, but her hosts over there had pulled a few strings. 'And it helps if you speak the language.'

'Do you?'

'Fluently,' Lucy said.

He told the girls about his deal with videos. Sandra was unimpressed. 'I suppose it's crooked,' she said.

'Well perhaps a bit bent, that's all,' Barry said. Lucy laughed. 'Can you tell Terry he'll have a customer soon, then?'

Barry left. Lucy said she thought he was an interesting character. 'If you're looking for trouble,' Sandra said.

Even Annabelle and Paul noticed how much brighter

Lucy seemed that evening. At last she seemed to be getting over James.

Keith Tench might have been pleasant in Aberdeen, but it was different when Heather was back working with him in Liverpool. All he did was criticize and pick holes in her work.

After her business trip to London she was called in and reprimanded on minor points. Tench took the job off her and replaced her with Greg. Heather felt sure that the fact she had made it quite clear she did not find him attractive was the cause of his nastiness. She tried to protest, but he slapped her down. 'I'm in this chair, Heather, not you,' he said. 'I want this section run on certain lines and I don't want any interference.'

Heather went home upset. Fortunately, Nicholas met her as she arrived and she was able to forget her troubles with Tench.

Nicholas made her supper and promised to take her out the following night. 'I'll meet you at the office,' he told her.

Barry showed Lucy the video tape from the cases containing over a thousand he had bought through a contact in Liverpool.

Lucy confirmed his worst fears. They were recorded on the SECAM system, not the sort of television system used in Britain. 'Looks like you'll have to cross the Channel to get rid of them,' she said. 'It might be an idea.'

'If I had a van I might do that,' Barry said. 'How would you fancy being a native guide?'

Lucy laughed. 'Well there's not much happening at home right now.'

Barry liked the way Lucy had grown up. He was amazed that in three or four years someone could change so much. She wasn't like the schoolgirl he remembered.

*

Karen picked up the phone, expecting Guy.

The voice was quick and to the point. 'Keep your nose out, you interfering bitch!'

'Charming!' Karen said and slammed down the phone.

'What's up?' Sheila asked.

'Some crank call,' Karen replied, repeating what the voice had said.

'Was it a man's voice —' Sheila asked.

'There's no need to get nervous, Mum,' Karen said. 'It's just some loony.'

Sheila sat down. Karen noticed she looked worried. Sheila told her about the letter and showed it to her. 'The same message,' Karen said.

Sheila explained she was worried it was Sally Dinsdale's husband. 'I shouldn't have had her to stay that night. I bet she told him I said she should go to a refuge.'

Karen said, 'If he's not man enough to complain to your face, I shouldn't be worried about it.'

'I don't know whether I should pack this Course in. Your dad doesn't seem too keen and . . .'

'Don't be soft!' Karen said. 'You've worked hard.'

'Yeah, but look what it's landed me in.'

'Just a crank phone call and a stupid letter. Forget it.'

'It's not just that.'

'What then?'

'Oh, nothing, love. I'm just a bit tired, that's all.'

George Williams swept into Bobby's office. 'Right, Bobby, what's going on?'

'What?'

'Don't play the daft lad with me,' George said. 'I've had head office on. They want to know who's rocking the boat with this differentials business at Braggs.'

'They've voted for an overtime ban, that's all.'

'And you're backing them?'

'Yeah.'

'Bobby you can't,' George said. 'You know the attitude at head office to that lot.'

'I've told you my thoughts on head office,' Bobby said. 'They're more interested in what's going on down there than what they're paid for. Anyway, we never see them.'

George sat down. 'You could be a lot closer to head office than you realize.'

He told Bobby that he was in line for a job on the national executive. 'Oh, that's the reason, is it?' Bobby said angrily. 'You're in line for a job so to hell with Braggs.'

George kept his cool. 'Listen, Bobby. If I'm in line for London, then you're in line for my job.'

'Is that a bribe?'

'No, it's not a bribe. But let me remind you of something. I got you elected to that chair you're sitting in now. You owe me one for that.'

Bobby sat back in his seat. 'When will I ever stop owing you for that, George?'

'It's not just a matter of owing me one,' George continued. 'You're short sighted. Forget the heroics. Think about your own job, your family. If you don't stop making waves, Bobby, you won't have a job. It won't be anything to do with me. It'll be our friends in head office.'

'I'm talking about principles,' Bobby said. 'I don't want to know about this. Those lads should be on strike, never mind an overtime ban!'

George looked at him. 'Bobby, Braggs couldn't stand a strike. They'd go under. Then what would you do, eh? With a couple of hundred blokes' jobs on your conscience?'

Bobby exhaled. George stood up. 'I just wanted you to know the full picture, that's all.'

'I've never felt so embarrassed in all my life,' Sandra said.

Pat rubbed his face. What a mess. She had been talking to Sheila and Sheila had asked, in a roundabout way, how she was feeling. Sandra had been mystified. Sheila had to prompt her. 'The baby,' she said.

'I had to stand there and tell her I wasn't having a baby. I was just two weeks late. What did you tell her for?'

'I couldn't help it,' Pat said. 'I'm sorry.'

'You made me look a right wally.'

'And me now, I suppose.'

'You didn't get asked!' Sandra said.

'I suppose I was just happy,' Pat said. 'I wanted to tell someone.'

'You're not a kid, you're supposed to be an adult. Why don't you start behaving like one?'

Pat knew it was no use arguing when she was in a mood like this. 'I'm sorry, Sand . . .' he began.

'Oh, forget it,' she said. 'I'm going to work.'

'Hello again.'

Keith Tench had spotted Nicholas Black waiting in the car park at Hamilton Devereux to pick up Heather for their dinner out.

'Oh, hello,' Nicholas said.

'Waiting for Heather, are you?'

'Yes, we're eating out.'

'Special occasion, is it?' Keith asked.

'No, we often do.'

'Well I don't think she'll be long.'

'Is she all right?' Nicholas didn't quite know why he said it.

'All right?' Tench queried. 'Why shouldn't she be?'

'Oh, nothing,' Nicholas said.

'It seems an odd thing to say?'

Nicholas came out with it. 'Well it seems that she often comes home upset. You don't seem to be the most encouraging superior.'

Tench stared at him. 'Are you telling me you have the cheek to find fault with the way I work?'

'No, I didn't mean it like that,' Nicholas said, frantically. 'I really just meant that Heather was upset last night. I . . .'

But Keith Tench turned away and walked to his car. Nicholas followed him. He grabbed his arm. 'Keith, listen –'

He tugged at Tench's sleeve. Tench was embarrassed. 'Leave me alone,' he said, trying to put his key in the car door and opening it. He tried to get inside.

'I want to explain my remark,' Nicholas said, pulling at Tench in his panic to right the wrong.

Tench's temper snapped. He stood up straight and punched Nicholas in the face. Nicholas fell over and Tench drove off. Nursing his face, Nicholas went to his own car and drove away himself.

Five minutes later when Heather came out she wondered where he had gone. She drove home and phoned the flat. No answer. Half an hour later Nicholas arrived.

'My God, what's happened? Were you robbed?'

Heather couldn't believe it when he told her. 'How could you?'

'It was a misunderstanding.'

'A misunderstanding! You act like that man next door, assaulting someone in their place of work and you say it's a misunderstanding!' Heather shook her head. What sort of a reception would she get at the office tomorrow? Drucker would probably sack her. She'd been nothing but trouble, it seemed. She continued, 'Don't you think I might like to lose my temper with Keith Tench? But I can't. I have to bottle it up!'

'I just wanted to try to get through to him,' Nicholas said, 'to make it easier for you. You've had a rough time with him.'

But Heather wouldn't listen. 'Tomorrow I'll probably get the sack. Then how do I stand? Where will I go? I'm amazed, Nicholas, I really am!'

Nicholas tried to reason with her, but she refused to listen. She dreaded tomorrow.

Nicholas apologized and left and Heather broke down and cried.

Tench was worried that he might get into trouble for hitting Nicholas Black. But fortunately there were no witnesses. Heather came straight to him the next morning and apologized.

'I'm sorry, Keith,' she said. 'But he was only trying to stick up for me. You see, I was upset the night before, after we'd spoken.'

'I really don't see what it had to do with him.'

'He should never have mentioned my being upset. And I assure you he wasn't trying to hurt you.'

'Just insult me.'

'Or that, I know him. Attacking people just isn't Nicholas.'

A smirk crossed Tench's face. 'That's pretty obvious!'

'Pardon?'

'Well, if you want middle-aged friends of yours to fight your battles, play knights in shining armour, pick one who isn't so out of condition.'

Tench thought of the satisfaction he'd experienced at hitting Nicholas. He hadn't liked him the day they'd met at Heather's. Little weakling.

'He didn't set out to fight any battles for me,' Heather said, controlling her anger.

'Wets never do,' Tench said. 'Do they?'

'I object to that remark,' she said.

'I object to being accosted and manhandled in the staff car park. I don't know what Howard would say about it.'

Heather couldn't go any further. She might lose her temper completely.

Keith showed her the door. 'Tell him to take up

squash,' Tench said, as she left. 'I find it just the job for keeping fit.'

Nicholas would never treat a subordinate like Tench had just treated her, she thought. He was worth a hundred like Keith Tench.

Billy Corkhill's appeal lasted only half an hour.

Earlier, he had said goodbye to the children and he and Doreen had gone to the Crown Court alone. Doreen was worried sick, but Billy tried to reassure her. The solicitor was confident, he told her. Nevertheless, Billy had misgivings. Hadn't the last two court cases gone dreadfully wrong?

But he needn't have worried. He gave evidence of what had provoked the assault and the barrister had spoken for him. The judge finally announced that the three-month prison sentence would be suspended, conditional on his good behaviour.

Doreen practically danced into the house where Rod and Tracy were waiting. Billy hugged them and Rod shook his hand. 'Well done, Dad.'

'Put your feet up, love,' Doreen said. 'No need to go in this afternoon.'

'No, back to normal for me,' Billy said. 'That's what I want. Anyway, I've got to see Percival the personnel feller. The works outing. I can get cracking on that now, eh?'

He changed and went off to work. Doreen sat down and Tracy made her a cup of tea. 'I'm sorry, Mam,' Tracy said. 'It was all my fault.'

Doreen ruffled her hair. 'I know love, but what's done's done, eh?'

'I'm glad he got off with it,' Rod said.

'He didn't get off with it. He's got a suspended sentence. It still doesn't mean he did right.'

'He did as far as I'm concerned,' Rod said.

Doreen allowed herself a little grin. 'Just you think on next time you feel like raising your fists, eh?'

'All right, Mum.'

Doreen was happy. For the first time in months.

Lucy sat in the garden and thought about France. This time last year she'd been on holiday with the Dubois in Nice. She wished she was there now. She wondered if Barry Grant would go to France.

She found him in the Grant's garage checking through his crates of French-system videos. 'Hi.'

'Hi,' Barry said.

'Just wondered if you'd thought any more about your big export order?'

'Taking them to France, you mean?'

'That's right. Well?'

'Well they're not much use here I suppose. I was thinking of trying to find another mug to buy the lot of them.'

'Which wouldn't be as interesting as you and me taking them across the Channel.'

'No,' Barry admitted. 'But what's in it for you?'

'A lift, what else?' she said. 'Come on Barry, my parents don't mind me going back over there. Why don't we go?'

Barry thought. He looked at Lucy. She was definitely not bluffing. 'I'll handle all the language problems. . . .' she offered again.

'Okay,' he said. 'Try anything once.'

She flung her arms round him and kissed him on the cheek.

'Both sides isn't it for frogs?'

She laughed. She was on her way back to France. She felt marvellous.

Paul too was pleased to hear that Lucy was planning to return to France. Annabelle said she would phone the Dubois right away and book a flight. But Lucy insisted she wanted to surprise them. 'They'll only make a fuss, booking an air ticket and everything,' she said. 'I'll make my own way.'

*

There was a slight shadow across the Collins' day later when Annabelle pointed out a press item in the *Echo* about Petrochem. It seemed that American Consolidated Industries were going for a takeover bid.

'First I've heard of it,' Paul said. 'Let me see.' He scanned the report. 'Nothing confirmed. Probably rumour.' Annabelle was concerned about it nevertheless. 'It seems to me that takeovers mean redundancies,' she said. 'Do you think you'll be all right?'

'I'm not prepared to let it worry me,' Paul replied. 'I've doubled the production in the past year and the external orders are building up month by month. I think I'm safe enough.'

Annabelle hoped so. The past five months had been almost unbearable. She couldn't stand any more bad luck.

Billy's interview with personnel had not concerned the works outing. He had been sacked. A conviction for violence was a breach of contract, he was told, and in addition he had a poor record for timekeeping and absenteeism.

Billy was shocked. He expected to get sacked only if he went to jail.

'I'd have mentioned it before, Billy,' said Bill Percival, 'but I was convinced you'd be jailed. I'm glad you haven't been.'

'I might as well have been, mightn't I?' Billy said, ruefully. The full shock had not yet hit him.

'I'm sorry to have to do it, but we've no choice,' said Percival.

Billy wondered about the installation at Christmas. 'Has this new gear got anything to do with it? The stuff we put in at Christmas?' he asked.

Percival smiled. 'I thought you might think that. All I can say is it would only have been a matter of time.'

Billy left the office and drove to the playing fields near the factory. Then he went for a drink. He didn't get home till the early hours of the morning.

*

Damon badly needed the money to return to Torquay. He planned to hitch hike, but he needed some money for food and moving around. He checked his pockets and found he had less than ten pounds and that was supposed to last him more than another week. Then he remembered the soccer bet with Rod and, more importantly, all that money being held by Harry Cross. If he could just win the bet everything would be fine. He went round to the bungalow and consulted Harry. He found that he and Rod were level-pegging.

'Only one League match each before the season ends,' Harry told him, going through his fixture list. 'Everton versus Southampton and your lot versus Chelsea.'

Flaming Chelsea! Slap bang in the middle of London! Just his luck to have to go more than two hundred miles to win the bet. All Rod had to do was catch one bus down to Goodison Park for the 'Saints' game and he'd win!

Later, as Damon sat staring blankly at the telly, Barry put down his newspaper and said, 'How do you think they'll do against Chelsea, Dame?'

'I don't know,' Damon replied.

'What? Aren't you bothering going?' Barry said. 'Don't tell me you've packed in going to the match?'

'Skint, aren't I?'

'Can you afford the ticket?' Barry asked. Damon suddenly took an interest. Barry was a lot tighter with the pocket money these days. Once, he'd have paid his fare to London for him on the footy special, the lot.

Damon plucked up some courage. 'Could you lend us –'

'No, I can't lend you money,' Barry butted in, 'but I can give you a lift!'

'What?' said Damon.

Barry told him about the French trip planned for the following day and that he had to get to Dover. Damon was overjoyed. He could hitch hike back and he had enough money for a ticket and a programme. It could still be a draw. He would get his hands on half of Harry's £84 kitty.

He was still grinning when he met Rod outside the chip shop later that evening. The conversation went immediately to the subject of the next day's games.

'Are you going?' Damon asked.

Rod pulled a face and then made a fatal mistake. 'Don't know whether I can afford it or not,' he said. 'This is costing me a bomb. I've already had to borrow off me dad for the last few away games.'

Damon's mind raced. 'Don't know if I can either,' he said. 'It costs a packet getting down to Chelsea.' He was finding it hard not to grin. If he attended the Chelsea game and Rod couldn't afford even to go to Goodison Park, he'd be laughing. What a mug! Fancy showing your hand like that!

'Are you going then?' Rod asked. He was worried.

'I don't know yet,' Damon said airily.

Rod made up his mind to keep an eye on the Grants' house early the next morning. If Damon did go, he would have to find the cash to get to the Southampton game. He didn't mind a draw, but he wasn't going to let Damon win the bet.

Karen and Guy were working together in Guy's room at the Hall of Residence.

'Are you cold?' Karen asked.

'Sorry, it's the window,' Guy said, pointing out half a missing pane at the top. 'Vandals.'

Karen felt the radiator. 'This is off too.' She shivered. 'Do you want to go to the library?'

'No, I'll fall asleep in that place. It's too hot there.'

Guy pondered. 'You could always get into the bed. Put my coat on top, if you like.'

'To work?' Karen giggled. 'Tell you what. We'll both get in.'

She climbed into the bed. 'Come on, it's cold in here too.'

Guy got in beside her. 'It's a bit cramped.'

'Better though,' Karen said. 'Much comfier.'

She tried to continue with her article for the student paper. Guy found it uncomfortable trying to read a large textbook. They moved closer. But they soon forgot their work. Half an hour later Karen, with no prompting, no pressure, was no longer a virgin.

She kissed Guy. 'Thanks.'

'I said it was only a matter of time,' he said and kissed her in return.

The birds had only just started singing when Damon Grant crept downstairs on the Saturday morning. Late the night before, Barry – now in on the soccer bet – had obligingly reversed the van right up on to the Grants' driveway. It was easy for Damon to open the rear door of the van and slip inside with a flask of coffee, a packet of corned beef sandwiches and a sleeping bag.

Rod Corkhill didn't wake up until a hour later. He'd checked the times of the London trains and was determined to keep watch on the Grants' house for signs of Damon leaving. He spotted Barry up and about early, but there was no sign of Damon. And his rival's bedroom curtains were still drawn.

Rod hung about the living room window until the rest of the household surfaced. Damon's curtains were still drawn. Rod didn't know that Damon's last request to Sheila before going to bed was to leave his curtains drawn all the following day.

Paul and Annabelle got up early on the Saturday morning to say goodbye to Lucy. By van with Barry Grant was not the way they expected her to travel, but they were glad to see her happy.

'Give our love to Gerard and Monique,' Paul said.

But Lucy wasn't too sure she'd be seeing the Dubois.

Annabelle kissed her daughter. 'Take care. Don't forget to ring.'

Barry pipped the horn. In the back of the van, Damon was lying snug in his sleeping bag after breakfasting on his corned beef sandwiches.

'Any sign of him?' he asked Barry. Barry peered out of the van towards the Corkhills' house.

'Yeah, he's sitting on the window ledge.'

'Dozy sod,' Damon said. He laughed. 'He hasn't got much imagination, has he?'

Barry pipped the horn again. Lucy ran out to join them, waving to Paul and Annabelle. She climbed in the van and they swung out of the Close. Rod Corkhill watched. He thought Damon was still in the house.

As Paul and Annabelle went back inside, the phone rang. It was confirmation that American Consolidated Industries had taken over Petrochem. There was no news of jobs.

'Come on,' said Paul 'There's was no point in needless worrying. Let's go out for the day, shall we?'

Later that morning, Matty Nolan called at the Grants' house to find Sheila in the house alone. The atmosphere was awkward. Matty hadn't wanted to come, but Sheila had left a pair of Claire's shoes at their house and Teresa insisted he take them round.

'I didn't want to come, not after what's happened,' Matty said.

'I'm not surprised,' Sheila replied. 'I still don't know whether to tell her.'

'For God's sake, Sheila, don't do that. Haven't you caused enough trouble already?'

'Me?' she said. 'Me?'

'Yes, you! Why didn't you keep your nose out. Everyone down at the centre's talking about me and Mo. I can feel it. And all because of you!'

'I didn't tell you to go carrying on behind your wife's back, did I?' Sheila said. 'I haven't been sneaking round to her house, committing adultery!'

'It's not like that. You know how I feel about Maureen. We want to get married.'

'You're already married, for God's sake. It's adultery. I don't suppose you've been near a confession box in months!'

'Oh, don't start with that,' Matty said, moving to the door. 'You cause me trouble. You cause all sorts of gossip –'

'You caused it. You caused it yourself!'

'Then you have to start shouting about flaming adultery. Face it Sheila. You're a busybody. An interfering busybody!'

'Bitch! Don't you mean bitch?!'

'I don't call women names like that, Sheila. I leave that to you. You upset Mo with the name you called her!'

Matty left. Sheila's stomach turned. Interfering busybody, interfering bitch? God no, surely Matty couldn't have sent that letter, made that call? Suddenly, she felt sick.

Billy Corkhill felt sick. Sick with drink from the night before and churning inside thinking how he could tell Doreen. She was still as happy as she had been yesterday after the appeal hearing. For Billy, that was now all history. He toyed with the large cooked breakfast Doreen had set down before him.

'What's up, love? A hangover?' She said it with an indulgent smile. Hangovers were usually treated with a lecture. But Doreen was in a good mood. Billy had been through a nightmare. Why shouldn't he let off steam by having too much to drink? She decided not to question him about where he had been until the early hours of the morning.

Billy apologized to Doreen for his inability to eat and offered the breakfast to Rod, who was hanging around the living room, occasionally going to look out of the window.

'No, thanks,' Rod said.

'Are you sick, or something?' Doreen said. Rod didn't usually turn his nose up at food.

'I'm just not hungry, that's all.'

Billy left the table and moved through to the living room. He sat down and picked up the paper. He tried to read the front-page story, but he wasn't taking it in. The tangle of worries which last night he'd tried to suppress with pint after pint were back stronger than ever. He tried to make conversation with Rod. 'Are you going to the Southampton match?'

'Can't afford it,' Rod said, flatly.

'Oh,' Billy said.

That hadn't been the reaction Rod had hoped for. Usually, it didn't take much prompting to get the offer of a loan from Billy.

'You're not going, then?' Doreen chipped in. Rod shook his head. Perhaps he should explain everything about the bet, plead for a loan and offer to pay his father back from the winnings. But to his surprise, his mother pressed a ten pound note into his hand.

Rod looked at her dumbly.

'Go on, go to the match,' Doreen said. 'Mind you, you can do something for me before you go.'

Rod stood up. 'Yeah, sure, Mam. What?'

Doreen asked him to take some washing she'd done for Julia round to the estate. 'With a bit of luck she'll give you your dinner,' Doreen added.

'Great,' Rod said. 'Where's the stuff? I think I'll go now.' Five minutes later he left the house with his blue and white Everton scarf and his thoughts firmly on the £84 stake money.

Doreen leaned over the back of the settee and kissed Billy on the cheek. 'What about us? What are we doing today?'

Billy went cold. He knew Doreen would like a run in the car, or perhaps an afternoon looking round the shops. But how could he act carefree with his secret ticking away inside him like a bomb?

The result of the game didn't really matter to Rod. The main thing was that he'd been there. He was now one match ahead of Damon, he had the programme in his pocket and he was the winner of the season-long bet. When he arrived back at the Close, his mother and father were still out. As he helped himself to coffee, the telephone rang. It was a gloating call from Damon in London. 'I bet you were sick today, not going, eh?' Damon sneered down the line. 'I went though. Surprise, surprise, eh? I'm in London.'

Damn! Had he gone? How had he managed to get past the early morning spying? 'Did you see that green van with our Barry driving?' Damon asked. He didn't need to say any more.

Rod might have guessed. He'd wondered about the van, what Barry was doing with Terry's van and that Collins girl. 'I hope you've got a programme to prove it,' he said.

'Too right, I have,' Damon replied. He laughed. 'See you tomorrow!'

'Just a minute,' Rod said. 'I went as well.'

There was a silence on the line. 'I thought you were skint.'

'Never mind that,' Rod said. 'It's still a draw.'

When Damon returned the next day, he was furious. All that effort. Now it was just a straight draw. They took their programmes to Harold Cross and asked to settle up.

Harry checked the programmes. 'I declare a draw,' he said.

'That's half each,' Damon said.

'No that's half for Rod and half minus twenty-five quid for you!'

'What!?' Damon said.

'Twenty-five quid. The fare to Torquay, remember.'

Damon exhaled. 'Okay, let's have what's left then.'

'It's Sunday, lad,' he said.

'So what?'

'And it's Bank Holiday tomorrow. It's in a building society. Anyway I have to give twenty-eight days' notice or I'll lose interest.'

Damon looked at his pile of programmes. All that for nothing.

'What are we going to tell the kids?' That was Doreen's first reaction when Billy finally told her he'd been sacked.

Billy shook his head.

'They think you're in the clear. Oh, God.'

'I'm sorry, love.'

But Doreen wasn't listening. She was thinking about the house. The shame of possibly having to move if they couldn't pay the mortgage. Her whole life seemed to be crumbling.

By contrast, Paul and Annabelle were looking at the rumours pouring out of Petrochem in a philosophical way. Paul pointed out that their standard of living would not drop any lower than last time. At least they wouldn't have to move house this time if the worse came to the worst.

'We've had worse problems to contend with these past few years,' Paul said.

'I suppose you're right.'

Heather had not seen Nicholas Black since that night after he was hit by Keith Tench.

So when an envelope arrived at the weekend containing a cartoon by him which showed a repentant Mr Black with a message of apology for ruining her career, she decided to swallow her pride.

She wrote a letter. It took most of the weekend and explained her feelings for him. She redrafted it several times to get it right. Then she realized there was no post over the May Day holiday weekend. On the Monday morning she drove round to Nicholas' flat in Liverpool and climbed the stairs. He wasn't in. She posted the letter through his box and went home.

When she got back she found that Nicholas had been

to her house. Through the door he'd pushed a cartoon, this time of a lonely Mr Black with a note of his whereabouts, the Swan pub.

Heather drove round to find him sipping a glass of lager. She refused a drink and drove him back to the house.

That night Nicholas told Heather he loved her. She told him she loved him.

They decided to get married.

Meanwhile, Terry and Pat were hairless. Barry hadn't returned with the van. 'Every time he shows his face, it's trouble,' Terry said. 'Why did we agree?'

Pat turned on Sandra. 'Why didn't you tell us he was taking Lucy to France?'

'You didn't ask,' Sandra said.

It was typical of her attitude these days. She seemed to have no interest in the business, in him even.

'You know what he's like, you must have realized he was up to something,' Pat said.

'Oh, stop it, will you?' Terry shouted at them. 'This isn't getting the bloody van back!'

Then came the phone call, reverse-charge from Dover. It was Barry. He'd left the van parked near the docks with money under the seat to cover petrol and inconvenience. He said something about problems with Customs.

Terry put the phone down. 'Do you know, he'd have taken our bloody van to France if he could have got away with it.'

After a very definite refusal from Sandra to allow them to borrow her car, they decided the only thing to do was for Pat to hitch down to collect the van. He set off for Dover straightaway.

Confirmation of his redundancy reached Paul early in the morning. He was asked to report the following day to clear his desk. It hadn't come as a great shock, but Paul appreciated the irony that the men on the shop floor were being offered employment elsewhere or being kept on by arrangement with the unions.

Half an hour later Paul told Annabelle that now he was sixty-two he would not be seeking another job.

Bobby Grant was under pressure from Butler the shop steward at Braggs as well as George Williams and head office.

He had been obliged to sit in a pub with Dave Butler and tell him that head office didn't want any trouble at Braggs. He knew it sounded pathetic to a man like Butler, someone who had the same background as himself. But what could he say? He tried to tell Butler that a strike could perhaps close Braggs, but Dave Butler scoffed at the idea.

'You've got me behind you on the overtime ban,' Bobby said. 'You can count on that.'

'Big deal,' Butler said. 'That could take years to have an effect. And my fellers are losing money long-term carrying on with that kind of performance.'

Bobby said, 'I know.'

Butler finished his drink. 'Sometimes, I don't know why we have union officials, do you know?'

He left the pub. Bobby sat back. Suddenly, he had an urge to be like Dave Butler again. Not to be crushed from above and below. Just to be fighting for the things he believed in.

When Teresa called to see Sheila she pretended it was just a social visit. But Sheila could see she was worried. She regretted asking her if there was anything wrong. For Teresa spilled it all out. Matty was a different person. Yes, he'd been like a spring lamb until a few weeks ago. Now he was morose and moody.

'This course you're on, Shei,' Teresa said. 'Is there .... well ... you don't think he's carrying on with anyone, do you?'

'Who Matty?' Sheila said.

'I'm really worried.'

Sheila laughed and said, 'You sound like Bobby. I think he thinks I'm carrying on with the tutor. Soft beggar!'

Teresa smiled and didn't pursue the matter. But Sheila didn't sleep at all that night, or the next. She felt she had betrayed her best friend.

Two days later, Barry Grant and Lucy Collins arrived in Aix-en-Provence. He jumped down off the back of a truck and helped Lucy down.

'So this is the South of France, eh?'

'This is it,' said Lucy. 'Where's the nearest post office, I wonder?'

'What for?'

She held up a postcard. 'For my mum and dad. You've got to sign it!'

Barry grinned. He could imagine the reaction in the Collins' household.

While Pat was away in Dover, Dr Hurrell picked up Sandra from home and ran her home from work. That night he asked her out for dinner and Sandra accepted.

He told her he was concerned about a young patient admitted by one of the consultants for a hysterectomy. In his opinion, the operation was totally unnecessary. He asked if Sandra would like to know a little more about the activities of the consultants in the private ward.

'Yes, I think I would,' Sandra said. 'As long as it's a professional evening out, eh?'

Pat found the van where Barry said it would be. When he opened the back doors he found the crates of video-tapes.

Oh, yeah. This'll do nicely. Pat thought to himself. A bit of compensation from Granty. He mustn't have been able to get them through Customs. Silly sod. Well they'll do us.

On the way back, Pat worked out they could make maybe £500 from the tapes. Sandra had mentioned something about them only being French-system. But that was crazy. All they needed was a bit of sellotape over the hole in the back. Then they could flog them as blanks. He laughed at Barry's stupidity. What did he want to go to France for? Unless he fancied that Lucy Collins.

Good luck to him.

Paul Collins had cleared his desk. Now he was walking down the central roadway of Petrochem. Hard-hatted engineers turned to watch him go. He didn't look at them or wave. He could detect the smirks of satisfaction they must feel seeing him walk out of the gate for good. But Paul didn't care. He and Annabelle would be all right.

He walked into the car park and was about to put the key in the door of his car when a uniformed security man took the key from his hand.

'Sorry, Mr Collins. I've got orders to take in all the company vehicles.'

'Oh, of course,' Paul said.

So what, Paul thought, I'll get the bus. He hadn't been on the bus for years. He might start as from today. He might even be eligible for a bus pass.

He walked to the bus stop and chuckled to himself.

Billy Corkhill still hadn't told Rod and Tracy. He would do it today. But for the moment he was writing cards for shop windows. 'Qualified electrician seeks work. Anything considered.' He might be signing on, but he'd still need foreigners too – if they wanted to keep the house he bought for Doreen. Billy tried to forget the envelope lying on the kitchen table. Out of work a few days and he was already overdrawn. The bank had written to tell him.